Soviet Industrial Theory

American University Studies

Series X
Political Science

Vol. 3

PETER LANG
New York · Berne · Frankfort on the Main · Nancy

Voytek Zubek

Soviet Industrial Theory

PETER LANG
New York · Berne · Frankfort on the Main · Nancy

CIP-Kurztitelaufnahme der Deutschen Bibliothek

Zubek, Voytek:
Soviet industrial theory / Voytek Zubek. – New
York; Berne; Frankfort on the Main; Nancy:
Lang, 1984.
    (American University Studies: Ser. 10,
    Polit. science; Vol. 3)
    ISBN 0-8204-0085-8

NE: American University Studies / 10

Library of Congress Catalog Card Number:
83-49221
ISBN 0-8204-0085-8

© Peter Lang Publishing Inc., New York 1984

Printed by Lang Druck Inc., Liebefeld/Berne (Switzerland)

ACKNOWLEDGEMENTS

I would like to thank Professors Judith Gentleman, Frederic J. Fleron, Jr., Paul Diesing, Gary Hoskin and Georg Iggers for their help and advice in the completion of this project.

TABLE OF CONTENTS

Chapter I

Introduction

The goal of this study is to examine the development of Soviet industrial theory. The first problem that faces us is the need to determine a point of departure for the analysis. Specifically, the controversy here surrounds the meaning of the term Soviet. That is, in identifying that historical point at which to begin the analysis, we have to clearly define what we understand by "Soviet" industrial theory in the strictest sense.

Of course, the simplest solution would be to employ the broadest understanding of the word Soviet. Such a decision would push the beginning of our analysis well back in time, perhaps to the second half of the nineteenth century, when a number of Russian revolutionaries, influenced to some extent by Marx's philosophy, began to incubate their own theories of socialist transformation which were tailored to the conditions of their restive society. We would then move to even stormier waters, those of the twentieth century pre-revolutionary Russia where Lenin's philosophical system was actively competing with other revolutionary doctrines. Following the successful Bolshevik revolution, the subsequent emergence of the Soviet Republic transformed Lenin and other theoreticians into Soviet theoreticians by virtue of their relationship with the new regime. The decade of the nineteen-twenties was marked by an explosion in theoretical activity in the field of industrial theory which was preoccupied both with the more immediate problems of the N.E.P. as well as broader problems involving the future development of Soviet society, addressed during the famous Great Industrial Debate. Our analysis would then take us through the Stalinization of the Soviet Republic which, from the reforms of the Stalinist Second Revolution, would lead us to the emergence of the fully developed Stalinist system. Finally, the development of Soviet industrial theory throughout the post-Stalinist periods of Soviet social transformation brings us to the present juncture.

However, such a _sensu_ _largo_ understanding of Soviet industrial theory would pose a number of very difficult problems, which if not overcome, would leave us with a skewed vision of the development of Soviet industrial theory. The most fundamental danger would lie in that a _sensu_ _largo_ understanding of Soviet industrial theory would constitute, in our opinion, a very artificial combination of two different periods in Soviet social development: first, the pre-Stalinist period, and second, the Stalinist and the post-Stalinist periods. To put it somewhat differently, it could be argued that with the triumph of Stalinism, Soviet society, as well as Soviet theory in general and Soviet industrial theory in particular, entered a different phase of development which constituted _almost_ a complete separation from and rejection of previous Soviet traditions. It must be underscored, however, that this break _was_ _not_ _complete_. That is, one could observe a number of elements within the pre-Stalinist theory which were perpetuated to a greater or lesser extent during the later periods. Thus, some

continuity may be seen between these two periods in the
development of Soviet industrial theory, conferring upon it
the character of a general theory rather than suggesting
that these are two completely different theoretical creations connected in a merely superficial way.

However, beginning with the successful completion of
the Stalinist Second Revolution, i.e., the end of the
nineteen-thirties, and continuing to the present period, the
development of Soviet industrial theory has shown an amazing
degree of coherence, continuity and homogeneity. Therefore,
we consider this to be the period in which the term "Soviet"
took its fullest and strictest meaning for the industrial
theory.

Pre-Stalinist Soviet industrial theory ceased to exist
during the ten-year period which began with the ascendance
of the Stalinists to a position of political hegemony and
culminated in the completion of the Great Purge at the end
of the nineteen-thirties. During that period, anyone of a
non-Stalinist persuasion who happened to hold any prominence
in Soviet society could easily consider himself to be very
lucky if he had managed to survive. Virtually everybody who
represented non-Stalinistic views in the field of industrial
theory (as well as in every other academic or cultural field)
during the earlier period was either physically exterminated
or otherwise effectively silenced. Not only were those who
earlier had contributed to Soviet industrial theory in some
kind of independent, i.e., non-Stalinist fashion physically

removed from the Soviet academic stage, but their works published during the earlier period were censored and cast into oblivion.

On the other hand, the way in which the Stalinists dealt with the more prominent contributors to the revolutionary theory of the earlier period who were already deceased was very different. Marx, Engels and Lenin were declared geniuses and recognized as the superhuman founding fathers of socialist doctrine--those who truly had learned from the lessons of history and who had also mastered understanding of the future dynamics of human development. Consequently, these figures as well as their works were enshrined in an Olympus of socialist theory which was supposed to serve as the fount of wisdom for generations to come.

In view of the fact that Marx and Lenin were both exceedingly prolific writers and in light of the theoretical diversity of their works, one would have to regard the emergence of such a sanctified Olympus of socialist theory as merely having provided only very general theoretical guidance to its Soviet followers.

Thus, upon first sight, the creation of a socialist Olympus could scarcely be viewed as having created any particular kind of theoretical limitation. The emergence of Stalinism, however, provided a most ingenious means of reconciling the multiplicity of theoretical tendencies emanating from the socialist Olympus. Stalin himself became an

Olympic figure equal to the others. Not only was he now the
equal of Marx, Engels and Lenin; above all, he was alive.
As a consequence, Stalin became the paramount if not the only
source of valid interpretation of the works of the other
Olympic figures. Consequently, Stalin himself produced
several small works in this area, naturally viewed by his
contemporaries as immortal teachings which provided a selective interpretation of Marx's and Lenin's philosophies. These
interpretations, of course, met with little challenge. What
emerged from this context was the very specific and uniquely
Stalinist philosophy of Marxism-Leninism which, in turn,
became the fundamental philosophy of Soviet society. Thus,
at the end of the nineteen-thirties, interested Soviet
scholars began to create a new type of Soviet industrial
theory which was based upon very strict if not slavish adherence to the new Stalinist theory of Marxism-Leninism. It
is at this point that we begin our analysis of the development
of the theory which we now consider as Soviet industrial
theory sensu stricto. In examining the development of this
theory, we shall also analyze the parallel evolution of those
elements of Marxist-Leninist theory which determined the
eventual evolution of industrial theory.

Before we undertake the analysis of the development of
the theory, we must first stress the formidable character of
the challenge faced by Soviet industrial theoreticians who
not only were seeking to advance their discipline in accordance with Marxist-Leninist principles, but also, were

attempting to preserve the integrity and viability of Marxism-Leninism itself, in the face of the contradictions existing between Marx's and Lenin's theories of socialist industrialization. In order to explore this problem, we will begin by contrasting the respective views of Marx and Lenin on the subject of both the capitalist as well as the future socialist types of industrialization.

The respective views of Marx and Lenin on capitalist and socialist types of industrialization appear to contrast in their perspective and are even contradictory in many ways. Nevertheless, first Lenin himself, and subsequently, later Soviet theorists valiantly attempted to demonstrate the continuity between these two philosophical systems on this issue. The following chapters will examine how Marxist-Leninist theory and Soviet industrial theory sensu stricto have dealt with this theoretical problem throughout the last four decades.

The development of Soviet industrial theory may be seen as encompassing four distinct periods. The first chapter will examine the first two periods in the development of the theory: first, the Stalinist or early Soviet industrial theory which flourished from 1938 to 1953; second, the transformed theory which prevailed from 1953 to 1956. Chapters Two and Three will focus on what is conceptualized here as the "enthusiastic" period in the development of Soviet industrial theory which endured from 1957 to 1966. Chapter Two will examine the maturation of classical Soviet industrial theory during that period. Chapter Three will focus on the response formulated by Soviet industrial theore- ticians of the enthusiastic period to Western theories which elaborated the concept of the post-industrial society. Chapter Four will examine Soviet industrial theory from 1966 to 1973 in its quasi-pluralistic development. During this period, the theory was modified to reflect significantly moderated expectations in the wake of the collapse of enthu- siasm. Finally, Chapter Five will examine the latest period of theoretical development which began in 1974 and still continues.

Chapter II

The Early Industrial Theory (1938-1956)

For both Lenin and Stalin, the discrepancy between Soviet socialist reality and Marx's revolutionary social- ist theory existed because some fundamental premises of Marx's philosophy were, in their minds, outdated. Their conclusions on this subject were based not on a theoretical argument, but merely on the premise, that, since Marx's pre- dicted socialist revolution had not yet occurred, and Lenin's scenario for socialist revolution was likely to be fulfilled and eventually was fulfilled in the Soviet Union, Lenin's philosophy was therefore distinctly superior to that of Marx. Hence, merely on this basis Lenin felt free to take any kind of liberties with Marx's philosophy, i.e., accepting those parts which were suitable for him and rejecting or freely reinterpreting the rest. However, the theoretically free- wheeling Lenin left a very dubious inheritance for the Bolshevik leaders from the point of view of theoretical unity.

When the bedridden Lenin was awaiting his death, the Bolshevik leadership entered what is now called the Great Industrial Debate, during which the future industrial devel- opment of the society was discussed. However, one would look only in vain to this debate for answers to questions regarding the general character of Soviet industrialization. On the issue of whether to create some kind of unique, socialist industrial society, or instead to borrow wholesale the industrial design from advanced capitalist societies, the Bolshevik leadership followed Lenin's ideas, virtually without any discussion, relying as had Lenin, in the absence of any meaningful theory, upon their own common-sense approach to the issue. According to this reasoning, innovations would be limited mainly to the political and cultural spheres while industrial development would conform to the pattern effectively established by and proven by the advanced capitalist societies.

Many of the prominent Bolshevik leaders shared a similar intellectual background to that of Lenin's and were educated, well-traveled and literate. If men of such intellectual caliber and life experience eagerly accepted a common-sense approach towards the problem of socialist industrialization, what could be expected from those who in the late nineteen-twenties had begun to enter leadership positions? By far much less literate and more parochial than the old Bolsheviks, these new leaders were quite uninterested in, if not incapable of searching for new models and new horizons for Soviet industrialization. Such limitations notwithstanding, these leaders were very interested in and quite capable of the practical transformation of Soviet society along the path directed by their common sense.

Although their collective name, "the Stalinists" would suggest that Stalin somehow "created" them as a group, the argument here is closer to Trotsky's view that the opposite was really the case, that they had created Stalin, who in return provided them with both effective and symbolic leadership and finally lent them his name. As Trotsky ably puts it:

> Stalin represents a phenomenon utterly excep-
> tional. He is neither a thinker, nor a
> writer, nor an orator. He took possession
> of power not with the aid of personal qualities
> but with the aid of an impersonal machine. And
> it was not he who created the machine, but the
> machine that created him.   1

Regardless of how powerful a tool of transformation
this common-sense approach was, a body of theory had
to be developed to add intellectual legitimacy to the Stalinist position. Lenin's writings provided a more than ample
supply of the needed theory but in this blessing of plenty,
there was a hidden and formidable danger. Lenin's compul-
sive indulgence in theoretical speculation to contend with
the everyday problems of the revolutionary movement produced,
in the space of decades of such activity, a number of theoretical contradictions. After his death, during the "great
debates" of the twenties, basically every faction of the
Bolshevik leadership could find some support for its program in Lenin's writings. This embarrassing situation was
well illustrated by the discussion during the Fifteenth
Party Conference in 1927. There the already defeated
Trotsky still had an opportunity to present his case on the
floor of the conference. Trotsky's argument was heavily
supported by quotations from Lenin. At one point, he was
interrupted from the floor:

> INTERRUPTION: Do you think you are speaking
>   to children?

TROTSKY: I think I have the right to appeal
    from my words of 1917 to what Lenin said
    in 1921.

VOICE FROM THE FLOOR: And what did Lenin say
    afterwards?

TROTSKY: Afterward he said some other things.

GENERAL LAUGHTER

The problem faced by the Stalinists was not the
need to supplement Lenin's theories but instead to edit
Lenin's writings into a more compact and coherent form which
would provide clear theoretical support and would be well
synchronized with Soviet development policy. Clearly, this
body of work in no way sought to develop a theoretical model
for an original socialist mode of industrialization without
massive borrowing of industrial technology from the advanced
capitalist societies.

Sharing Lenin's attitude toward the problem, Stalin
conveniently dismissed ideological considerations, replacing
them with pure pragmatism and did not even bother to address
the problem. Stalin instead proved to be a supreme imple-
mentor and practitioner of the Leninist approach to Soviet
industrialization.

The most interesting and important feature of Stalin's
theoretical activity was his rather transparent lack of
interest in Marx's philosophy. Instead, he was an avid and
diligent student of Lenin and was primarily interested in
editing the writings of the Master into a clear, simple and
harmonious form. Without any doubt, it could be said that

Stalin truly abhorred the complexity of Marx's philosophy.
Aware of how the development of Soviet socialism contradicted Marx's theory of socialism, Stalin somehow found more
comfort in Engels' work. In fact, Stalin believed that if
Engels had seen the Soviet brand of socialism, he too would
have turned away from Marx (as had Stalin) and would have
declared: "To hell with those old formulas. Long live the
victorious revolution in the USSR."[3]

Moreover, it was obvious for Stalin that anyone with
good sense who was familiar with the Soviet brand of socialism would abandon any further general theoretical speculation
about socialism as this was now unnecessary. It was now time
to implement the general theory of socialism developed by
Lenin and shared by Stalin and the rest of the Bolshevik
leadership.[4]

For Stalin, anyone with good sense would have immediately understood that in view of the obvious underdevelopment
of Soviet society as compared to the advanced capitalist
societies, any activity other than the rapid implementation
of Lenin's blueprint for socialist industrialization would
have been plainly harmful and destructive. In light of the
fact that during the Great Industrial Debate, it became
apparent that every faction of the Bolshevik party was able
to find support in Lenin's writings for its position, the
eventually victorious faction--the Stalinists--undertook
a strong effort to finally close this theoretical "Pandora's
Box."

Unfortunately, this responsibility rested with the individual who was perhaps the least talented for such an endeavor amongst the Bolshevik leaders--Stalin himself. Despite the blatant crudeness and simplicity of Stalin's efforts in this field, they nevertheless provided the needed minimum; that is, they presented a picture of philosophical unity between Marx's and Lenin's theoretical systems. Stalin's "philosophical" creation was very appropriately termed the theory of Marxism-Leninism. Stalin dealt with the important differences between the two theorists in a manner similar to the way in which Lenin had solved this problem. Those parts of Marx's philosophy which blatantly contradicted Lenin's thought were rejected with the laconic explanation that they were just "too old" and thus, no longer fit changing realities. The abundance of Lenin's writings was reduced to a very limited set of conclusions, which unambiguously gave support to Soviet development. Considering the fact that Stalin's unifying effort was not supported by any kind of serious marshalling of a theoretical argument behind it, originally only Stalin's formidable political position accounted for its popularization. Stalin's political power undoubtedly deterred many Soviet Marxists from questioning his creation of a "Marxist-Leninist" doctrine. On the other hand, there were masses of Soviet scholars, academicians, political writers, ideologues and journalists for whom the creation of a unified socialist doctrine was a great intellectual relief and constituted an avenue of escape from the dilemmas inhering in the open debate on the application of Marx's and Lenin's theories to Soviet socio-economic development. Not only had the Stalinist Marxism-Leninism answered the needs of Soviet intellectual milieus which supported the system, but, most of all, this simplistic ideology was very well suited for reaching average Soviet citizens and party members, who, even if educated to some degree, possessed only a very practical type of education geared toward tackling the every day problems of the new society.[5]

As a result, the post-Great Purge period in the development of Soviet society was characterized by a conjunction between the social effort mounted to fulfill the blueprint for the industrial development of the new society and the official political doctrine--the doctrine of Marxism-Leninism that had been created by Stalin. Undoubtedly, such harmony was one of the reasons for the initial success of Soviet industrialization.

The very root of the Stalinist "Marxism-Leninism's" vulnerability lay in the existence and availability of Marx's and Lenin's writings in the Soviet Union. Although from the point of view of the Soviet masses this was only a minor problem as the Soviet masses demonstrated a low propensity to study the theoretical works of the prominent philosophers (as is the case in the West) there was, however, always a danger that relatively large numbers of intellectually active Soviet citizens could indulge in the unrestricted study of Marx's and Lenin's writings which might lead to an eventual reopening of the "Pandora's box" of intra-Marxist debate so abhorred by the Stalinists. What were the possible solutions to this problem? Efforts to further elaborate theoretically, to improve and make more credible Stalin's "Marxism-Leninism" held all the potential of walking in quicksand.

Given the situation, allowing even the most trusted Stalinist scholars to pursue independent efforts in advancing Marxism-Leninism would probably be the worst solution, because it could have eventually pushed the entire Soviet ideological structure into devastating chaos. Moreover, probably the only effective solution to the problem, i.e., making the writings of Marx and Lenin unavailable for popular reading, leaving the Stalinist Marxism-Leninism the only available source of popular knowledge on the subject was too preposterous to even consider. Finally, the traditional mechanism for maintaining a theoretically indefensible ideology, that is, the invocation of religious beliefs, of course, was impossible in such a militantly atheistic society.

The only remaining means of strengthening the Stalinist doctrine of Marxism-Leninism was to strengthen the position of Stalin himself. Considering the fact that he had already acquired the maximum political power, the only possible means of further strengthening his position was to resort to a cult of personality. Constant reference to

Stalin's genius served to strengthen the legitimacy of the new doctrine.

To accomplish this, an "Olympus" of socialist thought was created to which Marx, Engels, Lenin and Stalin were elevated. Only Stalin could interpret the others, as the only living member of the group and thus, he truly became the primus inter pares among them. The creation of the "Olympus" of the geniuses of socialist thought not only naturally dwarfed other contributions on the subject of socialist theory, but also practically made impossible any challenge to Marxism-Leninism without questioning Stalin's authority.

Following the Great Purge, at the end of the nineteen-thirties and in the beginning of the nineteen-forties, Soviet works on industrial theory appeared that exhibited the already fully developed pattern of argument typifying the Stalinist paradigm of industrial theory. The most striking characteristic of these works was the identical logic of their argument. Such unity was even further reinforced by their usage of common terminology and an almost identical style of writing that was very orderly and ritualistic.

Hence, each treatise from the period began with a declaration of Stalin's genius. The simplest, but still the most inventive means was the way in which Stalin was authoritatively included among the select group of Olympic geniuses. Rubinstein's work is emblematic of this style:

Marx's-Engels'-Lenin's-Stalin's teaching about
communism recognizes two phases of communist
society: the first or the lower phase--socialism
and second, the higher phase--communism.   6

After paying homage to Stalin's genius, a declaration of

the unity of socialist theory would usually follow. Some-

times this declaration would be stressed as strongly as in

Rubinstein's work where the contributions of the Olympic

geniuses were referred to as the teaching rather than the

teachings. However, the early industrial scholars did not

consider it sufficient to simply proclaim the unity of

socialist theory as they had done in the case of Stalin's

genius. Instead, they deemed it necessary to elaborate

upon this subject to a somewhat greater extent. Thus,

Kuznetsov viewed Lenin's and Stalin's theoretical efforts

as the brilliantly creative continuation of Marx's philoso-

phy:

The Lenin-Stalin theory of the construction of
socialism in one country constitutes a work of
genius, the enrichment and the development of
Marx's teachings.   7

On the other hand, Markus saw this process from an

historical perspective. According to him, Lenin's work

of genius continued Marx's work of genius and in turn,

Stalin's work of genius was a continuation of Lenin's work

of genius:

Lenin's teaching on the dictatorship of the
working class found its continuation in the
theoretical theses on the socialist state

which were developed by comrade Stalin's work
of genius during the XVIII Party Congress.   8

However, Markus too found that the strongest means of
stressing the unity of socialist theory was to hyphenate
the names of the Olympian figures. He too pointed out
that:

> The teaching of Lenin-Stalin on the socialist
> organization of labor is an inseparable part
> of the teaching on the dictatorship of pro-
> letariat.   9

When it came, however, to the more complex issue of
explaining the obvious differences between Marx's and Lenin's
philosophies, the safest way was to simply repeat Stalin's
own argument on this subject. Here, Kuznetsov maintained
that:

> Lenin's and Stalin's solution to these problems
> was made on the basis of the new facts and on
> the basis of the further development of science
> and technology. These new technological ten-
> dencies developed after Marx's death and are
> interrelated with the development of mono-
> polistic capitalism.   10

This new theoretical effort based on the emerging new
reality was originally initiated by Lenin, who was:

> the first amongst the Marxists who exposed to a
> comprehensive scientific examination the new step
> in the development of the capitalist system--
> imperialism. In his works he devoted much
> attention to the analysis of the newest achieve-
> ments in the development of the material and
> technological basis of social production.   11

Pointing out the shortcomings of Marx's philosophy

did not diminish the recognition of Marx's genius, but <u>vice</u> <u>versa</u>, his genius was stressed as strongly and frequently as the genius of the other three men of the socialist "Olympus". Marx was typically characterized in the following way: "In a genial way, Marx foresaw the fundamental directions of the further development of the technology of the socialist society."[12] Criticism of what the Stalinist industrial theoreticians viewed as the outdated parts of Marx's theory was not designed to undermine Marx's genius, but to establish a definite "pecking order," a hierarchy on the "Olympus" of socialist theory. Thus, the genius of these authorities had an absolute character only during their lifetime. In other words, Stalinist scholars believed in a certain "dialectic of genius," that rendered the work of the particular member of the Olympus beyond reproach during his lifetime, and yet would terminate this quality of infallibility thereafter. There could be a genius appropriate for a given stage of socio-economic development, and during this period, his genius would be unquestionable. A foundation for future theoretical development could be developed and to some degree, predictions regarding future development were accepted. However, such predictions were viewed as being subject to error and in this area, the theorist would be viewed as a "Great Man," or a Founding Father rather than an infallible visionary. New stages of socio-economic development bring new geniuses who build upon the foundations laid down by predecessors. Adjustments may be made, however, to encompass new realities to correct the mistakes made by these predecessors, and finally to offer a new theory. Thus, we may understand Rubinstein's observation that:

> The way to create the material and technological base for communist society was sketched in its general outline by Marx and Engels, however, its particular and comprehensive shape was worked out by Lenin and Stalin.   13

The principal implication of this dialectic of genius was that Stalin's infallability only applied to the period of his own rule and the contemporary phase of socio-economic development. Hence, implicit here is the idea that after Stalin there might emerge another authority who would be added to the socialist "Olympus" and whose reassessment of the teachings of the earlier geniuses and adaptation of them to a new period of social development would be viewed as fully legitimate. As a result of this dialectic of genius, early Soviet industrial theory manifested adaptability, flexibility and dynamism.

All in all, the role of early Soviet industrial theory was not to offer a critique of the party's industrial program, but to accept it without question and to popularize it. While the fundamental premises of Marxism-Leninism were repeated in a firm, but laconic way, without any elaboration, other aspects of Stalinist industrial theory were treated more specifically. Here, a clear tendency emerged: the more specific the subject, the more outspoken and creative

the Stalinist analysts became. There was a much greater
willingness to engage in creative discussion concerning
particular aspects of Soviet industrialization although
discussion of this subject never took on the character of a
debate because Stalinist writers refused to acknowledge the
existence of other Marxist views in this area. Instead,
discussion involved only a repetition of Lenin's and Stalin's
opinions on this subject with the enthusiasm of the authors
and the vigor of their more elaborate treatment clearly
visible. When Kuznetsov wrote that:

> The idea of genius which called for the technologi-
> cal reconstruction of Soviet industry, also
> pointed to concrete ways of acquiring contemporary,
> advanced, industrial technology for all of the
> branches of the economy, [14]

his enthusiasm stemmed from his unconditional acceptance of
Stalin's Marxism-Leninism. This enthusiasm was expressed as
follows:

> Stalin's having raised the question of the level
> of technological development and industry's
> saturation with new technology creates a picture
> of the creative transformation and enrichment of
> Marxism. It signifies a new step in the develop-
> ment of Marx's theory of productive forces. [15]

The first pillar of theoretical support for this program
was created by the elevation of Lenin and Stalin to the level
of genius which was shared with Marx and Engels. A second
pillar of support was provided by Soviet scholars, armed
with the logic of Stalinist Marxism-Leninism, who returned

to Marx's philosophy to generate as much support as possible for Lenin's program of Soviet industrialization. We see Kuznetsov, then, actually embarking upon his own interpretation of Marx's theory in search of greater support for the propagated doctrine. For example, he argues that the central message radiating from Capital was that:

> Therefore, to address the problem of the
> technological development of the society,
> it is necessary to begin first with machine
> technology, with production machinery.   16

In a further interpretation of Marx's theory, Kuznetsov added:

> Marx understood his concept of the development
> of industrial technology as the improvement of
> the tools of labor. The industrial technological
> level--it is the degree of the development of the
> tools of labor. For defining the level of tech-
> nological development of industry, the size of
> the industry, or the quality of the material goods
> production is not actually important. Instead, it
> is important for him how the material goods are
> produced, by what means of production, how developed
> are the means of production, to what degree has
> the society substituted the old tools of labor by
> the new ones. According to Marx's teachings, the
> level of industrial technology and the degree of
> the development of the means of production is the
> more important factor in the economic development
> of the society.   17

Continuing the analysis of Capital,[18] Rubenstein concludes the following:

> In a genial way Marx foresaw the basic directions
> of the further development of technology in
> socialist society. He characterized the features
> of the automated system of machine production,
> which 'without human assistance fulfills all the
> tasks necessary for the processing of raw

materials, and needs only control and super-
vision on the part of the worker.' Marx showed
the importance of the mechanization of industry,
the continuity of the productive processes, the
prospects for the development of electrification
and chemistry which, then, were in their very early
stages of development. Marx and Engels foresaw
that technological development in socialist conditions would lead to a deep transformation of the
productive forces, would abolish the contradiction
between the city and the village, would liquidate
'the idiocy of rural life,' and finally would
transform the very essence of work in industry
and in agriculture.   19

The goal of these interpretive efforts was to unequivo-

cally demonstrate that Soviet society was triumphantly

creating the socialist system:

The high level of the technological development of
the USSR, a level higher than that of other countries, occurred as a result of the completion of
the technological reconstruction of Soviet industry and agriculture. Lenin and Stalin put in
front of the Soviet nation the task of transforming all of the branches of the economy from
its backward technological base to a new, contemporary, industrial-technological base, which
itself creates the material foundations for the
creation of socialism. Right now, we have tamed
the very advanced technology, and in our society
it has saturated industry to a greater degree than
in the West. The saturation of industry with contemporary advanced technology, the creation of the
new technological base witnesses the achievements
of the economic goals of the second five-year
plan.   20

Markus was even more enthusiastic in his assessment of

Soviet industrial development than Kuznetsov. He maintained

that:

After fulfilling the second five-year-plan,
the USSR began constructing the classless
socialist society and embarked on a gradual

transformation from socialism to communism.
We are fighting to outstrip the most advanced
capitalist societies in industrial production
per capita in the next 10-15 years.   21

It is apparent that in their effort to muster support
from Marx's works for Stalinist Marxism-Leninism, Kuznetsov,
Rubinstein, Markus and virtually all other Stalinist theoreticians did not hesitate to bluntly misinterpret Marx's
philosophy. Thus, Marx's moral indignation toward the
alienating, mechanized industrial system was mysteriously,
without any further elaboration, transformed by the early
Soviet industrial theoreticains into an alleged adoration of
it. One had little reason to believe that their enthusiasm
for the industrial system created by advanced capitalist
societies was hypocritical or pretended. Like Lenin and
Stalin, they most probably considered the reconstruction
of this type of industrial system in Soviet society to
provide the only real possibility for the creation of
socialism there.

Soviet industrial theoreticains explored subjects which
in the West would be considered the domain of the applied
sciences. Here, no effort was spared to carefully analyze
such subjects as "underground gasification," or "chemization,"
or the "automation of industry," or "new thermo-energetics,"
or the "goals of transportation." Analyses of these subjects constituted the core of the work done by Soviet
industrial theoreticians and on first sight they really
appeared to be the products of specialists in the applied

sciences. However, under more careful scrutiny, they took
a much different form. Instead, Soviet theoreticians were
attempting to apply Marxist-Leninist theory to the applied
sciences in order to demonstrate that Marxism-Leninism was
as much a general theory of the social sciences as it was
of the applied sciences. Stalinist theoreticians attempted
to achieve this goal by advancing their argument in a very
characteristic way, with the analysis of each particular
topic exhibiting the same logical scheme. This logical
scheme was religiously repeated and was most apparent in
Rubinstein's work. Each chapter was devoted to a specific
subject within the area of the applied sciences and opened
with a statement outlining Marx's opinion (deduced or real)
on this subject. In view of the nineteenth century's level
of technological development, such "opinions" were usually
very general in character. Subsequently, Lenin's argument
on this subject was introduced and exhibited much greater
specificity. Next, Stalin's opinion on the subject would
follow and usually had a very specific and concrete character. Finally, the writer himself spoke on the subject and
offered a kind of follow-up development of Stalin's argument.
Thus, Rubinstein began his chapter on electrification by
stating that:

> During the first attempts of the industrial
> utilization of the electric energy, still in
> the middle of the XIXth century, Marx and
> Engels saw in it the buds of the technology
> of the future communist society. 22

Then, after a page of further elaboration of Marx's and Engels' ideas on electric energy, he turned to Lenin, where he began by pointing out that:

> Lenin's theses on electrification as the technological base of communism are an inseparable part of the body of Lenin's teaching about the victory of the proletarian revolution and the construction of communism.   23

The discussion of Lenin's ideas on electrification made the argument more specific and concrete, thus making it possible to introduce Stalin's ideas: "Comrade Stalin emphasized the meaning of Lenin's theses on electrification."[24] The man of practice--Stalin--brought the discussion to a very concrete level:

> At the XVIth conference of the Bolshevik party, Comrade Stalin pointed out that when we will have 10-15 regions with electrified agricultural industry, then the electrification of agriculture would stand on solid and real ground. We should reach the achievement of this goal in the coming five-year plan.   25

Only after introducing Stalin's ideas on the subject of electrification could Soviet industrial scholars engage in a very specific discussion of particular aspects of the Soviet program of electrification.

The early Soviet industrial theory not only emerged as a fully developed entity at the end of the Great Purge, but also it appeared at that time in its final form. Although the early industrial theory (as well as the rest of the body

of the Marxist-Leninist social disciplines) could be
readily changed at Stalin's instigation, few modifications
were made until after Stalin's death. Thus, one of the
most popular subjects of early industrial theory--the liqui-
dation of the essential difference between manual and mental
work in socialist society--was discussed in the same way by
the very pioneers of the Soviet early industrial theory such
as Rubinstein, Markus and Kuznetsov and those who worked on
this subject during the last years of Stalin's life. Here,
Kudravtsev and Fedorova opened their article on this subject
by stating that:

> Comrade Stalin points out in his work of genius
> The Economic Problems of Socialism in the USSR
> that the problem of the contradiction between
> manual and mental labor poses a well-known
> problem, which was introduced a long time ago
> by Marx and Engels. The coryphaeus of the
> Marxist-Leninist science--J.V. Stalin, analyzing
> the laws governing the transformation from the
> first phase of communism into its second phase,
> put forward, stemming from that, an utterly
> new problem--the problem of overcoming the
> essential difference between mental and manual
> labor. [26]

Even the appearance of Stalin's later work on the
subject of socialist industrial theory--The Economic Problems of Socialism in the USSR--did not change the repetitious and schematic character of the early Soviet industrial
theory because Stalin's work itself did not contribute in
any way to its advancement. Nevertheless, Stalin's latest
work on this subject was followed by a number of articles
published in Soviet scholarly journals where the industrial

theoreticians paid due tribute to Stalin's genius and also, with all due humility, offered their modest analyses of the teachings of the "Great Man." However, even Stalin's later work did not alter in any way the pattern and the logic of writing established in the late thirties. Hence, Konstantinov opened his article with the familiar tribute to Stalin's genius:

> The problem of the development of the forces of production and of the development of the relations of production, the question of their mutual interrelationship, their mutual correspondence, the contradictions and the conflicts between them which disappear and are solved in the process of historical development, occupy a very important place in the science of historical materialism. The new J.V. Stalin's work of genius The Economic Problems of Socialism in the USSR gave particular attention to those problems. 27

Also, between this unconditional pronouncement of Stalin's genius and the actual discussion of his work, there was the customary prelude of quotations from Marx and Lenin which introduced the subject further developed by Stalin himself.

The only meaningful change that occurred within Soviet early industrail theory during the last period of Stalin's life was caused by the objective change in the geopolitical situation of the Soviet Union. Due to the fact that after the Second World War the Soviet Union gained control of the vast empire of the subjugated Eastern European countries, the Stalinist Marxism-Leninism effectively became an international doctrine. The Soviet imposed and directed transformation of these societies was accompanied by

the introduction of Marxism-Leninism there. Consequently,
the Soviet Union became the director of their industrial
transformation and early Soviet industrial theory served
as the accompanying music of this transformation.

However crude the original melody, when directed
toward external societies, the themes took on a cruder,
more schematic and repetitious form. Here, the theoretical
efforts of the Soviet writers greatly diminished and their
efforts were concentrated on a persistent repetition of
the most basic, practical conclusions derived from the
Soviet industrial effort. In discussing the Soviet
industrial effort, the early industrial theoreticians
were very willing to indulge themselves in a very detailed
discussion of the natural sciences most relevant for the
industrial transformation; then, while discussing the
industrialization of Eastern Europe, this style was abandoned. Instead, stress was placed on just one aspect of
socialist industrialization--heavy industrialization.

Perhaps the most classic example of the way in which
the early industrial theoreticians dealt with Eastern Europe
was I.V. Dudinskii's article. Here, the early Soviet industrial theory's version of the general socialist theory
(i.e., some discussion of Marx's and Lenin's ideas) did not
appear at all. While Marx's name was not mentioned, Lenin's
appeared adjacent to Stalin's name. Thus, extreme emphasis
was placed upon Stalin's genius. The only innovation was
that now, for the Soviet authors, Stalin's genius had

already gained so much international recognition that pronouncements regarding his genius were now emanating from the countries in question, i.e., Eastern European societies. Hence one of the pronouncements of Stalin's genius took the following form:

> The Bolshevik Party and Comrade Stalin personally, helped the communist and the workers parties of the national-democratic countries to leave behind the class maintenance of national democratic types of regimes there and they were aided in this transformation toward the socialist system according to scientific laws. The Politbureau of the Central Committee of the Polish United Workers Party concludes that: 'The tremendous experience of Lenin's-Stalin's party and the extremely wise advice of Comrade Stalin, the great friend of our nation, who answered the main questions concerning the development of Peoples Poland, helped our party to achieve clear perspectives for the construction of socialism. That advice also helped our party to lead the Polish nation on the way to political and economic victories.' 28

The goal of this article was the propagation of the idea of heavy industrialization as the only way leading to socialism. The idea was propagated by the repetition of basically the same message throughout the pages of the article. A classical example of this style of writing can be found in the following paragraph:

> The main link of the long range plans for the development of the national economy of Peoples Democracies on which depends the success of the entire undertaking, is socialist industrialization. On the other hand, it is fully proven by the successful practice of socialist construction in the USSR. Thus, the basis, the key to the construction of the

new social system is socialist industrialization. However, during socialist industrialization, there emerges the importance of the power
of heavy industry, which is the only element
which could serve as the foundation of
socialism.   29

If the international subfield of the early industrial

theory did not contribute in any way to the advancement

of the early industrial theory itself, it made some attempt

to originate a new conceptualization of the newly emerging

community of socialist nations:

> The facts bear witness to the brotherly
> collaboration of the countries of the camp
> of democracy and socialism--this is the new
> system of the international economic inter-
> relationship. This was created by the great
> Stalin. This new system assures the contin-
> uous economic growth of these societies, which
> are stepping into the path of socialist
> development. It is the very innovative, the
> very progressive system of the interrelation-
> ship between the nations.   30

Concluding the discussion on the Stalinist period of

the early Soviet industrial theory, it should be underscored

that the theory reflected the interests of the political elite

and would change in accordance with perceived needs. In

fact, the theory remained unchanged during Stalin's tenure

and was only radically altered after Stalin's death. The

early industrial theory thus entered a new period--the

period of gradual transformation. The new "transformed"

version held sway for a period of three years, and following

this period, another sudden and abrupt change occurred and

Soviet industrial theory entered the period of its "mature"

development.

The main characteristic of the "transformation" period of the early industrial theory was the erosion of Stalin's role as a founding father of Marxism-Leninism. Although Stalin was not removed de jure from the "Olympus" of the principal socialist theoreticians, i.e., none of the writers of this period openly stated that Stalin was not equal to Marx, Engels and Lenin; he was treated in a de facto manner as if he were no longer a member of the socialist "Olympus." Not only did the word genius never again appear beside Stalin's name, but the entire logic used in constructing the argument changed. While the existence of the "Olympus" of socialist theory and its unity still were the logical cornerstones of the argument, the concept of hierarchy within the socialist "Olympus" disappeared entirely. That is, the elaborate logic which gave the right to each new genius to correct and adjust the theories of the geniuses preceding him to the needs of the newest stage of socio-economic development, was abandoned entirely. Also, the rights stemming from the "law of hierarchy" which belonged to the individual geniuses and hence, allowed them to use freely their common sense in making these adjustments and adapta-tions, (without the need for some theoretical elaboration on the subject, or even merely diligent explanations) were abandoned too. Thus, the writers of the "transformation" period of the early industrial theory ended all discussion of Lenin's right to update Marx's philosophy, as well as

Stalin's right to adapt and unify Lenin's controversial
theory.

The disappearance of the "Olympus" of socialist theory,
changed the character of the "Olympus" itself. The "Olympus"
effectively lost its immediate, overshadowing connection with
the contemporary period and became an institution of a
decisively historical, although still theoretically fundamental character. However, it hardly could be said that
Stalin's removal strengthened the early industrial theory.
Regardless of how preposterous Stalin's elevation to the
role of looming genius might seem to be, for those who believed in its premises it was still a logical and coherent
way of solving the inherent contradictions between Marxism
and Leninism. As a result, the Stalinist theory of Marxism-
Leninism had emerged. However, work on industrial theory in
the period of "transformation" separated Stalin himself from
this distinctive Stalinist theory. Stalin began to be isolated from both fundamental creations of the Stalinist
period: the theory of Marxism-Leninism and the socialist
"Olympus." How could both of these creations last without
Stalin's crucial genius? This question, which was fully
answered by the "mature" Soviet industrial theory, was
addressed during the "transformation" period of the early
industrial theory.

Among the Soviet industrial theoreticians, one of the
first to utilize the new style was A.A. Zvorikin who published
his pioneering article at the end of 1953.[31] The most

innovative part of his article concerned the treatment of the "Olympus" of the socialist theory. The hierarchy of the "Olympus" not only was no longer stressed, but was not even mentioned. The hierarchy of the socialist "Olympus" became obsolete because Zvorikin, as well as the other writers of this period, no longer devoted any attention to the differences between the theories of Marx and Lenin. That is, in this period Marx and Lenin began to be treated as if there were no differences between their philosophies. Hence, if the writers on the industrial theory did not mention any differences between these two systems of thought, then the theoretical institution of the socialist "Olympic" hierarchy, which regulated these very same differences, was no longer needed. Marx, Engels and Lenin began to be treated as some kind of general "founding fathers" of socialist doctrine, and if the writings of the "transformed" industrial theoreticians were to serve as one's only reference to these theorists, one would be left with the strong impression that there existed little difference between them. To give to a reader just this kind of impression, in support of his argument theoretically, Zvorikin quoted Marx, Engels and Lenin in a decisively random fashion. The rigid order of the early industrial theory thus disappeared. Zvorikin not only quotes the geniuses of socialist theory in a random fashion, but effectively removes Stalin from the position of parity with the other members of the socialist "Olympus." The vacuum created by the removal of Stalin as both a contemporary and an "Olympic" authority was now filled by stressing the authority and the role of the party.

> The economic policy of the Communist party,
> which is based on the firm ground of Marxist-
> Leninist theory concerning the Soviet economy,
> gives great meaning to the development of
> technology during the creation of the material
> base of socialism and communism. [32]

Following this statement, Zvorikin cites Lenin's opinion on this subject. However, the general theoretical introduction to the works of the "transformed" period of industrial theory differs from early industrial theory not only because of the random treatment of the socialist authorities and the specific emphasis placed upon the party, but also by allowing its writers a much greater degree of creative freedom. Thus, the hierarchical ritualism of the general theory of the early school was not replaced by a new, now random, ritualism of the "transformed" school. Instead, the authors actively partici- pated in a general theoretical discussion by offering their creative interpretations of statements emanating from the "Olympic" level. In this vein, Zvorikin formulated the fol- lowing bold statement:

> In the conditions of socialism, technology
> is the powerful means of satisfying the growing
> needs of all parts of society and of guarantee-
> ing the undisturbed growth of the welfare of
> the nation. [33]

Considering the fact that right after Stalin's death, discus- sion about the balance between the development of heavy and light consumer industry did not have yet a public character

and was reserved for the highest echelons of the elite,
Zvorikin's boldness in speaking out for balance in "satisfying
the growing needs of all parts of society" bears witness to
the obviously growing role of the industrial theoreticians in
planning Soviet industrial development. Undoubtedly, this new
boldness in the discussion of industrial development stemmed
from the replacement of Stalin's genius by party authority.
While the existence of a single, individual genius had an
intrinsically unifying quality, its replacement by the collective authority of the party brought about a degree of
disunity. After more than twenty years, the problems of
Soviet industrialization had begun to be discussed again, but
now in a very different society. The human fabric of the
society had already changed substantially. The politically
independent social milieus of yesteryear had disappeared completely; generations of new people socialized in the new
atmosphere had moved into positions of power. Finally, from
the point of view of the fundamental character of Soviet
industrial development "the die was cast" already. Even if
there had been some hypothetical social group striving for an
entirely different industrial path toward the construction of
socialism, it seems that the industrial development of Soviet
society according to Lenin's and Stalin's schemes had gone too
far to allow for any fundamental alterrations without a new
"Great Revolution". Thus, the new Soviet reality, constructed according to the spontaneous beliefs of the old Bolshevik

leaders, began itself to determine the new social rationality of the Soviet society. Now, discussion about the balance between the development of heavy and light industry, or about the proper utilization of the Machine-Tractor Stations, or about the proper application of material incentives for the workers, created the framework and the horizons for the industrial debate. This was the case because the political elite as well as the industrial scholars themselves were already products of the Soviet system. Clearly, questioning the very foundations of the system that had socialized them was outside of the realm of rational thought.

After Stalin's death, the atmosphere changed considerably. Even those industrial scholars who wished to remain within the rationality of the system, found that there existed the possibility of a real debate on the subject of the particular aspects of the Soviet industrial system. However, even though the scholars of the period of "transformation" were much more independent than those of the early period, they showed much less interest and much more timidity in the area of the fundamental problems of the socialist doctrine, because they were so much the product of the system. Radical criticism fell beyond the scope of their thinking. Thus, while on the one hand, they began to participate in a revival of the industrial debate in a much more independent and bold manner than their predecessors, on the other hand, their treatment of the general industrial theory was logically inferior. Instead of engaging in efforts to improve and refine the basic foundations of the Soviet industrial doctrine, the writers of the period of "transformation" abandoned it entirely. They neither repeated nor criticized the canons of the early theory on the subject, but instead they suggested, without any attempt to be precise, that there existed a valid and true theory of Marxism-Leninism. Thus, for the Soviet industrial theory of the "transformed" period, the method of coping with the inherent contradictions of the socialist doctrines lay in entirely avoiding the subject, or in being very vague while suggesting that the problem really never existed.

The pioneering Zvorikin created just such a vague picture of the unity of the socialist theory by opening his article with reference to Lenin's opinion on the role of technology in the socialist transformation. Then, after discussing some of his own thoughts on the subject, he reached the profound conclusion that:

> Only the Marxist analysis of the problems of technology is capable of discovering the long range laws of technological development. 34

Zvorikin then spent two pages analyzing Marx's opinion on the subject[35] and then, briefly presented and sharply criticized the individualistic attitudes of the bourgeois theoreticians who

> regard technological discoveries and explorations as the revelations of the human brain, and ignore the requirements stemming from the economic level of social development.   36

Also, in his criticism of bourgeois theories, Zvorikin
supported his own contentions with Lenin's authority.
Finally, criticism of bourgeois theories brought the discussion back to the socialist societies:

> Unlike the capitalist societies, in the USSR
> and in the states of People's democracy, the
> new technology is developed expeditiously
> without neglecting any part of the national
> economy.   [37]

His discussion took on the form of a dialogue between
himself and Marx, Engels and Lenin. Most importantly,
there was never the suggestion of even a trace of any
disagreement between the philosophies of Marx and Lenin,
which implied some state of harmony and unity at the foundations of socialist theory.

Almost an identical pattern of argument was exhibited
by another pioneer of the "transformed" style of the Soviet
early industrial theory--D.M. Troshin. He opened his article[38] with a tribute to Marxism-Leninism, because it
"considers science as s specific social phenomenon."[39]
Although the theory of Marxism-Leninism was such a classical
Stalinist creation, Troshin did not associate Stalin's name
with it, and instead, after leaving it enigmatically unasso-
ciated with its creator, he followed by introducing Engels'
opinion on the social role of science.[40] He then sharply criticized the bourgeois sciences of the imperialist societies:

> Only in the conditions of socialism does science
> achieve the truly limitless scope of its develop-
> ment, in the same way that the liquidation of

the exploitative classes abolishes all the
barriers and obstacles of scientific exploration. The particular factor in the development
of science in socialist conditions is the
socialist method of production. The socialist
relations of production are the main force which
carries forward the forces of production...
Marxism-Leninism established the social function
of science, revealed its role in the process of
social development, established the place for
science among other social phenomena, and finally,
delivered a crushing blow to the idealistic
interpretations of science.   41

This conclusion let him return again to the criticism of

bourgeois scholars whom he treated with a great degree of

harshness--as for example--"Bertrand Russell, the ideologue

of nuclear blackmail and the propagator of war..."[42] Again,

although the criticism of bourgeois science was based on

Marxism-Leninism, Stalin was not associated with it. Instead,

throughout the rest of the article the Marxist-Leninist

argument was supported with quotations from Marx, Engels and

Lenin.

A.M. Rumiantsev's article, which appeared two years

after these pioneering works, exhibited an identical style

in treating the foundations of socialist theory.[43] Here,

again quotations from Marx, Engels and Lenin helped the

author to substantiate his points concerning the political

economy and the character of the laws determining socio-

economic development. Again, the randomness that charac-

terized Rumiantsev's use of arguments gleaned from the works

of the "Olympic" authorities, suggested nothing else but

what for him was their obvious unity on the subjects in

question. Other strict adherents to this style were Gak,[44]

Soboliev,[45] Sadykov,[46] and Zauzolkov,[47] whose article, although one of the last to be written in this style, did not yet hint at the drastic transformation of Soviet industrial theory that would soon occur.

In this way, the writers of the "transformed" period of the early industrial theory ignored the problem of the obvious contradictions between Marx and Lenin. Undoubtedly, it was a step backwards, a true degenerating regression in comparison with the early industrial theory, which, regardless of how we assess it presently, made a genuine effort to unify these two philosophies. By contrast, the writers of the "transformed" period did not acknowledge that a problem existed. In no way did they suggest that their predecessors had already solved this problem and that it was time to theoretically "march ahead," as Lenin had done with the Proletcult, but instead, an attempt was made to relegate this problem to oblivion by ignoring it entirely.

The most obvious consequence which stemmed from ignoring the contradictions between Marx's and Lenin's theoretical systems was the disappearance of the theoretical need to maintain Stalin, or possibly his successor, in a position not only equal to that of Marx and Lenin, but even somewhat more important due to the fact that he would be the supreme and unchallengeable authority who would unify the socialist doctrines. Stalin's removal from the socialist "Olympus" was probably the most striking characteristic of the "transformed" period of the early industrial theory. In this point, the difference between the early industrial theory and the theory of the "transformed" period was the most apparent. The early industrial theory was built around the person of Stalin and propagated the theory officially ascribed to him. Although nominally Stalin was just another member of the socialist "Olympus," his person not only dominated the other founding fathers of the socialist theory, but also, virtually every theoretical claim had to be either supported by a statement of Stalin's or somehow derived from it. However, within a few months after his death and without any official explanation, the entire school of thought exhibited by the early industrial theory vanished. Subsequently, the new "transformed" theory emerged. The most peculiar thing here was that the new theory did not address this stunning and radical transformation in any formal way. It could be easily said that Stalin, and with him the Soviet early industrial theory, had departed through the "back door," and that a fundamental theoretical change had occurred in a public atmosphere as if little of note had taken place.

Although the "transformed" industrial theory had appeared suddenly in its fully developed shape, initially it was quite difficult to understand what Stalin's position in Soviet theory had really become. That Stalin had been removed from the socialist "Olympus" did not mean that his name had entirely disappeared from the literature. Actually, one could find only a handful of publications from this period where Stalin's name was not mentioned. However, Stalin was

no longer listed as one of the most important contributors
to the development of Soviet theory, but instead, his name
was usually mentioned when some minor point was being discussed, thus, reducing his opinion to a kind of footnote.
For the pioneering Zvorikin, it proved necessary to mention
Stalin's name only once, noting his opinion on the relationship of capitalist society to new technology:

> Capitalism, as pointed out by J.V. Stalin,
> supports new technology only if it offers
> the biggest profits in return, capitalism
> is against the new technology and fights
> to maintain the manual type of labor if
> new technology does not assure it the
> maximum profit return.   48

Considering the fact that in this article Zvorikin energeti-
cally searched for support from Marx, Engels and Lenin, the
lack of attention given to Stalin was probably the most
meaningful message flowing from his work. However, regardless of how clear the message was that Stalin was no longer
considered equal to the other "Olympic" figures, there was
no word of explanation in Zvorikin's work about it. One
would also look only in vain for an explanation of this
radical change in the work of the other pioneer of the new
style--Troshin. He too, searching for support for his own
argument, widely discussed the works of Marx, Engels and
Lenin, but mentioned Stalin's opinion only once, again in
a very laconic and footnote-like fashion and, purposefully
or not, illustrated the perversely ironic character of
Stalin's work. Stalin was quoted here in support of the

argument that science should be boldly critical and unafraid
to attack the old truths in spite of those authorities that
might support them.[49]   Again, neither this perverse irony,
nor Stalin's demise from the socialist "Olympus" were explained in any way.

Quite fortunately, however, the next year brought a full
explanation of the position given to Stalin by the "transformed" industrial theory. Basically, the style of Maslin's
article is the same as those of Zvorikin and Troshin, i.e.,
his argument is supported by the extensive citation of the
work of Marx, Engels and Lenin, with Stalin's opinion on
the subject being mentioned only once. In this case, it
served almost as a true footnote to the extensive analysis
of Lenin's theory, but again the subject on which Stalin
was quoted appears as the ultimate irony:

> Undoubtedly, the political liberties, the
> genuine democracy, achieved by our nation, have
> created a great good, but in this regard, the
> tasks of our revolution were not, and are not
> completed. 'Unfortunately,...pointed out J.V.
> Stalin in the year 1935,...still one liberty is
> in an insufficient amount. If there is not
> enough bread, and not enough butter and lard,
> and not enough manufactured goods, and the
> apartments are miserable, then this one free-
> dom would not carry the society too far...
> it is necessary for the political liberties to
> be supplemented with the material goods.'   50

However, this time, the reader was not left without
some hints as to Stalin's place in the "transformed" industrial theory. In a way similar to that by which Stalin's
argument was presented, Maslin introduced three other

opinions to support his thesis, those of Malenkov,[51] Khrushchev,[52] and Mikoyan.[53] Thus, on the one hand, there were the founding fathers of socialist doctrine--Marx, Engels and Lenin. All of these authorities were treated by the "reformed" authors with all due respect and their opinions were elaborated diligently. On the other hand, there was a group of important, contemporary party leaders-- Malenkov, Khrushchev and Mikoyan--whose authority was limited compared to that of the "Olympic" figures or the collective authority of the party, and thus, their opinions were treated merely as footnotes to the discussion. In the work of writers of the reformed period, references to Stalin's opinions would be grouped together with contemporary party leaders rather than being highlighted along with the Olympic authorities. Clearly, Stalin had been demoted from that most prominent place in Soviet theory that he had occupied shortly before.

In the case of Zausolkov's article, Stalin's degradation from the "Olympus" took on a very perfidious character. While one's position in the socialist "Olympus" had a strictly theoretical and abstract character, and thus, was purely dependent on theoretical and philosophical arguments, one's position in the ruling elite and one's accomplishments in performing practical leadership tasks are, to a great extent, empirically measurable. Thus, if Stalin's Olympic position is considered a matter of theoretical and philosophical judgement, his accomplishments as a political leader belong,

in general, to the world of concrete reality. [Among these
concrete aspects of Stalin's leadership were his actions
leading to the creation of a new technocratic and managerial
sphere in the Soviet Union, as well as the pragmatic utilization of engineers and managers "left over" from the pre-
revolutionary society.] How astounding then is Zauzolkov's
article which for the most part discussed the problem of
engineers and managers during the industrial drive of the
nineteen-twenties, thirties and forties, because in not even
mentioning Stalin's role during this period, it plainly dis-
torts the historical reality. Even Zauzolkov's insistence on
stressing in a very persistent but also very vague way the
party's role in this process cannot hide successfully his
determination to alter the historical facts.

This pattern of dealing with Stalin by redefining his
position in socialist theory and by undermining his historical role in the Soviet leadership persisted throughout the
entire period of the "transformed" industrial theory.
However, there could be observed definite irregularities in
treating this subject, undoubtedly demonstrating the degree
of disunity and uncertainty present during the "transformed"
period. Most characteristically, these irregularities became
more apparent towards the end of the "transformed" period,
which suggests that while the "transformed" period of Soviet
industrial theory was an adequate scholarly answer to the
transformation of Soviet society, it could not decisively
conclude and address the earlier period--the early industrial

theory. The irregular tendencies in treating Stalin's position within socialist theory broke down along two lines. On the one hand, there were those who still attributed to Stalin more theoretical prominence than was typical for the transformed industrial theory, and on the other hand, there were those, like Gak and Sadikov, who in their works ignored Stalin's role in Soviet theory entirely, and thus, did not even mention his name.

An example of the first style is found in Rumiantsev's article. Although his style basically corresponded with the general style of the transformed period, i.e., his argument was supported by Lenin, Marx and Engels; Stalin's role there was substantially greater. Although Rumiantsev clearly did not consider Stalin to be on the same level with the other supreme authorities, in the conclusion of his article, he not only put Stalin back in the socialist "Olympus," but also, he did it in a way reminiscent of the works of the early industrial theory:

> The political economy, developed by the geniuses of Marx, Engels, Lenin and Stalin, is the powerful theoretical arm of the working class and the broad working masses who utilize it in their victorious fight for communism. 54

The other example of this group could be found in Kurakov's article which had appeared virtually at the end of the transformed period. Kurakov's article had the flavor of an earlier epoch of industrial theory. Kurakov was almost as specific and diligent in his examination of the subjects

appropriate to the applied sciences as the first masters of
the early industrial theory. Moreover, he too, included
Stalin in the Olympus of socialist theory:

> As is pointed out in the works of Marx, Lenin and
> Stalin and in the instructions given by the Party's
> congresses, success in the introduction of
> technology, is measured by, most of all, the growth
> of productive labor and the lowering of the costs
> of production.
> 55

However, even those transformed industrial theoreticians,
who on some points almost returned to the style of the early
industrial theory, shared a distinctive characteristic that
sharply separated them from their predecessors. As was
touched upon earlier, one of the crucial differences between
the writers of the early industrial theory and those of the
transformed industrial theory was the capacity to independently take sides during the industrial debate taking place in
this period. Moreover, the writers of the transformed period
not only took sides in this debate, but also propagated their
ideas boldly and with an unambivalent commitment. Unfortunately, this heated debate concerned only the very particular
and isolated problems of industrialization there, totally
ignoring fundamental problems that had never been answered.

The underlying weakness stemmed from the lack of a
fundamental, clear socialist theory which could provide a
basis for constructing more specific arguments. When the
fundamental socialist theory was reduced to a vague myth
lingering somewhere, beyond the reach of theoreticians
interested in closer examination, the theoretical efforts

of the transformed period indeed became futile. That is,
the theoretical debate began to be reminiscent of the early
post-revolutionary industrial debate, when independent
clusters of Bolshevik elites disputed each other's industrial
programs and easily found support for their position in
Lenin's works, who was the source of the general, but very
inconsistent, socialist theory. Now the situation was com-
pounded, not only due to the fact that the "transformed"
theoreticians, contradicting each other in their industrial
debate, felt free to "raid" Marx's, Engel's and Lenin's
writings in search of assertions that could be construed as
being supportive, but also, there was a vague, and amorphous
argument which asserted that the given author derived his
argument from Marxism-Leninism. Of course, that, as well as
the frequently pronounced faith in the omnipotence of the
Communist Party, provided a clear indication that the scholars
of the transformed period shared a belief in the need for
philosophical and political unity. Nonetheless, even this
consensus on the ultimate need for a unified philosophy and
a unified political rule could not overshadow the fact that
the "transformed" theoreticians were in a difficult situation.

The true bone of contention lay in the discussion surrounding one particular aspect of Soviet industrial develop-
ment--the balance and the direction of its further development.
Theoretical work from this period reflected the fundamental
division in the Soviet political leadership on this issue.
On the one hand, a kind of modified Stalinism _sans_ Stalin

called for a continuation of the policy of placing the priority on heavy and military industrial development with a correspondingly minimized emphasis on light and consumer industries, as well as the policy of the internal colonization of the peasantry. On the other hand, there were those within the political leadership who wanted to strike more of a balance between these competing options. Like the political leadership, the "transformed" industrial theory became polarized in this debate. The attack on the Stalinist policy regarding the placement of emphasis on heavy and light industry began with the emergence of the "transformed" theory. Initially, pioneering efforts in this direction were quite general as was mentioned earlier with respect to Zvorikin's call for satisfying the growing needs of all parts of society. Despite their vagueness, they constituted a great breakthrough compared to the style of the early industrial theory. Over time, the "transformed" theory embodied even bolder and more and more precise attacks on Stalinist policies. Of course, the "transformed" theory never really crossed the invisible barrier, i.e., it never attacked Stalin himself and the Stalinist policies openly and by name. For example, taking his cue from the intra-party debate on agricultural policies, Gak states that

> The old order of planning, which allowed the
> central planners to give particular orders con-
> cerning future crops, livestock and cattle,
> without taking into consideration the conditions
> of the soil and the climate, did not promote the
> development of initiative on the part of agricul-
> tural workers. The new order will better serve

their interest by increasing productivity and
the harvest yield of agricultural crops and
livestock.   56

Moreover, the party needed to deal with the problems created

during the last period by "fighting with aspects of poor

management, red tape, negligence, and sometimes, indeed,

stupidity."[57]   In addition, Gak severely criticized such

arch-Stalinist agricultural organizations as the Machine-

Tractor Stations.[58]   Continuing, he effectively turned the

tables on the Stalinist industrial program:

> As long as it was impossible to develop light
> industry and agriculture at the same speed
> as heavy industry, human material interests
> were directly contradictory to the comprehensive
> effort in the development of heavy industry.
> However, the erection of the powerful industrial
> base allowed for the elevation of the society to
> a higher level of development, and thus, it
> facilitated the broadening of the production of
> items satisfying the needs of the population
> while still maintaining the primary principle of
> developing the production of the means of
> production.   59

Finally, he concluded by calling for balanced industrial

development.[60]   A year earlier, Soboliev had pointed out

that:

> The struggle against the formal-bureaucratic
> methods of production needs stern observance
> and the further development of democratic
> centralism, which was created by Lenin.   61

On the other side of the debate on these issues could

be found defenders of Stalinist industrial policies such as

Ostrovitianov, who by virtue of the logic of their argument

54

were also members of the transformed school.

> Without the primary development of the branches
> of the production of the means of production, it
> is impossible to assure the undisturbed growth
> of production on the base of high-technology and
> to systematically realize reproduction on an
> expanded scale. The proper inter-relationship
> between the two subdivisions of socialist pro-
> duction therefore needs the primary growth of the
> production of the means of production and above
> all, heavy industry and the production of machinery,
> and then, only on this base, to develop agriculture,
> light industry and the food industry in the
> dimension necessary to satisfy the growing needs
> of the society. Meanwhile, some economists
> have attempted to revise the most important
> foundations of Marxism-Leninism on the subject
> of the development of production and they put
> the need for the same or even greater speed
> of the development of the second subdivision
> (i.e., the light and the consumer industries*--
> V.Z.) above all else. In so doing they link
> themselves to the most vulgar interpretations of
> the economic laws of socialism. The home-grown
> 'theories' of the primary development of those
> branches of industry which produce goods for
> the satisfaction of consumer needs, are them-
> selves, in essence, a variety of right wing
> deviation and also, are the basis for anti-
> mechanization tendencies, and also, they play,
> in this way, into the hands of the incompetent
> managers who are devoid of understanding of new
> technologies, to the managers who are not
> capable of utilizing these enormous, new
> possibilities which open up the socialist system
> to technological development and the fullest
> growth of the productive forces. Those econo-
> mists greatly harm the effort to construct
> communism and the effort to further the well-
> being of the Soviet nation, and to provide for
> the security of our country.   62

In this point the transformed industrial theory entered

an ironic vicious circle: the openness and the creativity

of the renewed debate on the particular directions of Soviet

industrialization, at first sight, constituted a stunning

advancement over the slavishness and the indolence of the

early industrial theory, however, the very strength of
the transformed theory, under more careful scrutiny could
be easily considered its greatest liability. Its total
neglect of any attempt to reorganize the Stalinist foundations of industrial theory in order to transform society,
or to create entirely new foundations for industrial theory,
resulted in the transformed theory having a vague, distant
myth to serve as its fundamental theory. As a result, this
vague mythology allowed the most mutually contradictory
policy options to utilize the very same theoretical foundations as their justification.

The abrupt end to this phase of the development of
Soviet industrial theory was caused by Khrushchev's decision to openly attack Stalinism and never really permitted
an answer to the question of whether there was something
substantially transforming in the transformed theory; and
whether in the long run this theory would fully develop
and thus solve its intrinsic paradoxes. Instead, the new
phase in Soviet industrialism unfolded and the "mature"
industrial theory emerged.

56

ENDNOTES

.   L. Trotsky, <u>Lenin</u>, (New York: 1971, G.P. Putnam)
    p. 16.

2.   The Fifteenth Party Conference, (Moscow: 1927) pp. 519-
    520.

3.   Ibid., p. 721.

4.   J. Stalin, <u>Leninism</u>, (New York: 1928, International
    Publishers) p. 251.

5.   See: K.E. Bailes, <u>Technology and Society Under Lenin
    and Stalin</u>, (Princeton, N.J.: 1978, Princeton Univ.
    Press).

6.   Modest I. Rubinstein, <u>O Material'no-Tekhnicheskoi Baze
    Perekhoda ot Sotsializma k Kommunizmu</u>, (Moscow: 1940,
    Politizdat) p. 3.

7.   Boris Kuznetsov, <u>Kommunizm i Tekhnika Budushchego</u>,
    (Moscow: 1940) p. 6.

8.   Boris L'vovich Markus, <u>Trud v Sotsialisticheskom
    Obshchestve</u>, (Moscow: 1939, Gosudarstvennoie Izdatel'stvo
    Politicheskoi Literatury), p. 22.

9.   Ibid., p. 23.

10. Kuznetsov, pp. 5-6.

11. Rubinstein, p. 8.

12. Ibid., p. 7.

13. Ibid., p. 5.

14. Kuznetsov, p. 20.

15. Ibid.

16. Ibid., p. 21.

17. Ibid.

18. Rubinstein, pp. 5-8.

19. Ibid., p. 7.

20. Kuznetsov, p. 30.

21. Markus, p. 302.

22. Rubinstein, p. 18.

23. Ibid., p. 20.

24. Ibid., p. 21.

25. Ibid., p. 23.

26. I.S. Kudravtsev and A.T. Fedorova, "O Likvidatsii
Sushchestvennogo Razlichia Mezhdu Fizicheskom i
Umstvennom Trudom," Voprosy Filosofii, 1, (1953),
p. 47. See also: V.I. Kovalenkov and A.V. Khramoi,
Avtomatika i Telemekhanika v Narodnom Khoziaistve
SSSR, (Moscow: 1948, Gosplanizdat).

27. F.V. Konstantinov, "Glavnyi Dvigatel Razvitia Proizvodi-
el'nykh Sil," Voprosy Filisofii, 1, (1953), p. 29.

28. I.V. Dudinskii, "Industrialiatsia", Voprosy Filosofii,
No. 5, (1952), p. 135.

29. Ibid., p. 136.

30. Ibid., p. 148.

31. A.A. Zvorikin, "O Nekotorykch Voprosakh Istorii
Tekhniki," Voprosy Filosofii, No. 6 (1953), pp. 32-45.

32. Ibid., p. 32.

33. Ibid.

34. Ibid.

35. Ibid., pp. 33-34.

36. Ibid., p. 35.

37. Ibid., p. 37.

38. D.M. Troshin, "Ob Osobennostiakh Razvitia Nauki,"
Voprosy Filosofii, No. 6 (1953), pp. 46-62.

39. Ibid., p. 46.

40. Ibid., pp. 46-47.

41. Ibid., p. 48.

42. Ibid., p. 49.

58

43. A.M. Rumiantsev, "Predmet Politicheskoi Ekonomii i
    Khrakter Zakonov Ekonomischeskovo Razvitia Obschestva,"
    Voprosy Filosofii, No. 2 (1955), pp. 88-104.

44. G.M. Gak, "Obschestvennyi i Lichnye Interesy i Ikh
    Sotchetane pri Sotsializmie," Voprosy Filosofii,
    No. 4, (1955), pp. 17-28.

45. A.J. Sobolev, "O Zakonomernostiakh Perekhoda ot
    Katpitalizma k Sotsializmu v Evropeiskikh Stranakh
    Narodnoi Demokratsi," Voprosy Filosofii, No. 1,
    (1956), pp. 30-46.

46. F.B. Sadykov, "Podem Kul'turno-Tekhnicheskogo Urovnia
    Trudiashchykhsia pri Sotsializmie," Voprosy Filosofii,
    No. 2, (1956), pp. 35-48.

47. F.N. Zauzolkov, "Ob Opyte USSSR po Sblizheniu
    Umstvennogo i Fizicheskogo Truda," Voprosy Filosofii,
    No. 5, (1956), pp. 32-45.

48. Zvorikin, p. 36.

49. Troshin, p. 56.

50. A.N. Maslin, "Printsip Material'noi Zainteresovannosti
    pri Sotsializme" Voprosy Filosofii, 4, (1954) p. 6.

51. Ibid., p. 7.

52. Ibid., p. 9.

53. Ibid., p. 13.

54. Rumiantsev, p. 104.

55. I.G. Kurakov, "Nekotorye Voprosy Razvitia Tekhniki pri
    Sotsializme," Voprosy Filosofii, 1, (1956), p. 16.

56. Gak, p. 25.

57. Ibid.

58. Ibid., p. 26.

59. Ibid., p. 27.

60. Ibid., p. 28.

61. A.I. Soboliev, "Velikaia Sozidatiel'naia Rol'
    Sovietskogo Gosudarstva," Voprosy Filosofii, No. 5,
    (1954), p. 41.

62. K.V. Ostrovitianov, "Ispol'zovanie Ekonomicheskikh
Zakonov Sotsializma v Praktike Kommunisticheskogo
Stroitel'stva," <u>Voprosy Vilosofii</u>, 4, (1955), p. 10.

Chapter III

The Mature Industrial Theory (1956-1965)

The transformed period of Soviet industrial theory ended almost as abruptly as it began. Khrushchev's famous "secret speech" ended the uncertainty surrounding the role of the creator of the myth of Marxism-Leninism...Stalin...in the further development of Soviet industrial theory. Khrushchev's blunt criticism of Stalin's rule opened a true Pandora's box of social criticism of Stalinism. Many Eastern European social milieus, especially artistic and journalistic, excelled in the refutation of Stalinism and with great hope considered the late nineteen-fifties as "the spring" which was supposed to lead toward a radical transformation of social systems there. At the same time, the circle of Soviet industrial theoreticians exhibited an unusual degree of restraint and selectiveness in their treatment of Stalinism. This cautious attitude was shared also by other groups of social scientists and by many politicians. In retrospect and with the arrogance endowed by historical perspective, we may observe that these people, so passionately hated by many there, exhibited nothing else than learned judiciousness (in the case of the academicians) and true statesmanship (in the case of the politicians).

While perhaps shocking for some, this statement can be readily justified. Throughout history, every social system has operated on a very basic and demonstrable premise-- slavery, feudalism, laissez faire capitalism, welfare state capitalism and of course, the Soviet social system also had

a clearly identifiable premise. For Soviet society, the
operative premise consisted of a combination of an industrial system adapted from the most advanced capitalist
societies coupled with a political system based on Lenin's
idea of a vanguard party-led state apparatus. However, the
sheer scope of Lenin's writings and their apparent inconsistency would make very unlikely their "unadapted" use
as the fundamental philosophy of the new society. Thus
emerged what was Stalinism's true historical mission--
to adapt Lenin's writings to the needs of Soviet society,
and most of all, to enforce this common-sense blueprint
with all the means available.

Without a doubt, the greatest strength of the new
fundamental theory of the Soviet society lay in its name--
"Marxism-Leninism"--which in itself had a distinctively
perverse character due to the inherent contradiction
existing between these two philosophies. Otherwise,
Stalinist "Marxism-Leninism" was an exceedingly crude and
simplistic theory which, from the scholarly point of view,
could not hold its ground against any kind of criticism.
However, the new fundamental theory was not subjected to any
kind of criticism, scholarly or otherwise, because it was
protected by the colossal political power amassed in the
hands of Stalin and the Stalinists, and by the aura surrounding Stalin himself--the personality cult. On the other
hand, the "noble lie" of the improbable unification of
Marxism and Leninism served as well the new, Soviet society

as other noble lies have served other societies throughout history. In particular, it prevented the international isolation of the Soviet brand of "socialism," the avoidance of which was of great importance for the international communist movement, and also, for the state of the subjective feelings of the Soviet elites, who as was the case with other Eastern European elites, were paranoically afraid of a situation in which their society might be considered as anything short of an advanced, Western, modern society.

In the immediate aftermath of Stalin's death, the greatest problem in Soviet society was caused by the massive resentment caused by the ruthlessness by which the Stalinist elites implemented the program of Soviet transformation. Measured along a number of other dimensions, however, the program was stunningly successful. The dreams of the early Bolsheviks were being fulfilled with the Soviet Union on its way to becoming a giant of heavy industry. Leaving aside for the moment the brutality and oppressiveness of the system, its other serious shortcomings--pathetically inefficient agricultural sector and weakness in the area of light, consumer industries--although very painful, were considered then, and in fact were, nothing other than well-planned, calculated risks--the price of rapid development in the heavy industry sector.

From the vantage point of these learned Soviet industrial scholars and other similarly learned and judicious scholars as well as politician-statesmen, it would be quite

easy to understand why those who actively propagated the
Eastern European, post-Stalinist "spring appeared as
shallow, overly vengeful and ignorant thinkers who would
throw out the proverbial baby with the bath. Moreover, the
propagators of the anti-Stalinist "spring" did not present
any viable alternative to the existing system. Those who
based their critique on Marx's work, obviously did not com-
prehend how tremendously different and contradictory to
Marx's ideals was the Soviet social system. They either
failed or preferred not to acknowledge that Marx's goals could
be reached only through a true workers' revolution. Other
critics plainly did not have in mind any general program for
change, and still others (especially in Eastern European
societies such as Poland and Hungary, only recently introduced to the Soviet brand of socialism) simply sought to
restore capitalism in some form.

Hence, if the Soviet Union wanted to remain after
Stalin's death what it had become after WWII, then the
Stalinist system had to be retooled so that it could function without the deceased genius. The criticism of some
selected, particularly outrageous aspects of Stalinism
without a doubt greatly modified this system and adapted
it to the new reality. However, the broadly based and
comprehensive criticism of Stalinism undermined the very
theoretical foundations of Soviet society which were
already precariously vague and inconsistent, regardless
of whether the critics actually meant to achieve such a

result, or even whether they realized the consequences of
their actions. The choices thus were as follows: either to
proceed with the well tested and apparently successful
approaches which would be only somewhat modified, or to
step into the unknown. Of course, this question is purely
academic as the responsible political elites as well as the
majority of the scholarly milieus recognized the appropriate
path right from the outset.

From the beginning of the official criticism of
Stalinism, i.e., from Khrushchev's famous secret speech,
Soviet industrial theoreticians evidenced a great degree of
restraint and moderation, while at the same time actively
pursuing a theoretical redefinition of Stalinism and Stalin's
role in it. Although instances of unbalanced criticism of
Stalinism occurred, they were quite rare. An example of
such unbalanced criticism was the early article by Konnik
"O Protivorietchiakh Sviazanykh a Dieistviem Ekonomitcheskikh
Zakonov"[1] which, despite its bold and innovative argument,
was "hidden" well in the back of the particular issue of
Voprosy Filosofii in which it appeared. Despite the humble
way in which Konnik's article was published, it consisted
of a powerful and a quite comprehensive critique of
Stalinist industrialization. Analyzing the working of
economic laws during the process of Soviet industrialization,
Konnik divided his analysis into three parts: the pre-war
period, the war period and the post-war period. He concluded that very fundamental and drastic mistakes were

committed during the process of Soviet industrialization.
Remarking on the pre-war period, Konnik noted that:

> It is not necessary to say, that during that
> period, the economic laws of the planned and
> balanced development of the national economy
> were violated. Rather, the requirements of
> these economic laws called, in these complex
> concrete-historical conditions of that period,
> for the rapid development of heavy industry.
> However, the requirements of the law of value
> entered into an antagonistic relationship with
> the requirements of the law of the planned
> and balanced development of the national
> economy and the requirements of the concrete
> realization of these laws in that particular
> stage of transformation. The products of that
> contradiction were: the "card" system of dis-
> tribution which to a great extent contained
> the spontaneous revelation of the law of value,
> and the lowering of the level of the popula-
> tion's living standard.   2

During the war period, further manipulations of prices
and wages resulted in the situation where

> in the complex conditions of the war period,
> the requirements of the fundamental law of
> socialism entered into a clear contradiction
> with the requirements of the law of value and
> the requirements of the law differentiating
> wages according to the different character of
> labor.   3

Finally, after the war, fundamental mistakes were committed
with regard to the balance between the development of heavy
industry on the one hand, and light, consumer industries
and agriculture on the other hand. Although Konnik agreed
that even after the war there still remained the paramount
need to develop heavy industry because it was implicitly
understood as being most beneficial to the development of

Soviet society, in the long run, he pointed out that
excessive imbalance proved to be counterproductive. Here,
Konnik identified a true paradox contained within Soviet
industrial development policy: the exaggerated development
of heavy industry had resulted in the neglect of agriculture and light industries which in turn impaired the
development of the entire society, and thus ultimately,
the development of heavy industry.

> However, during the rapid and intensive period
> of our development, this situation resulted in
> the agricultural sector's inability to suffi-
> ciently satisfy the national economy's demand
> for agricultural raw materials and food. As
> a result, the insufficient growth in the
> circulation of commodites, the partial deficit
> of commodities, the growth of prices on the
> disorganized market, speculation and other
> phenomena of hidden tendencies of the law of
> value have occurred. Consequently, the
> requirements of the law of value in those
> conditions entered an antagonistic relation-
> ship with the realization of the requirements
> of the law of planned, balanced development of
> the national economy, and caused a whole range
> of unfavorable consequences for the national
> economy.   4

This general criticism of Soviet industrial development
set the stage for Konnik's attack upon the chief director of
this process of industrial transformation. Here, he quoted
Stalin on the fundamental premise of the Marxist-Leninist
theory of industrial development which maintained that the
growth of consumption, i.e, purchasing power, should decisively outstrip the growth of production. For the Stalinists,
this was one of the crucial theoretical premises

differentiating socialist industrial development from
capitalist industrial development. However, Konnik
sharply disagreed here:

> We cannot agree with that premise, because the
> growth of consumption cannot always outstrip
> the growth of the production. If we view
> purchasing power as a human need (certainly
> not the lone aspect of human needs), then the
> tendency for purchasing power to constantly
> outstrip the growth of production would mean,
> indeed, that the socialist system of economy
> would suffer a chronic deficit of merchandise.
> In such a case, it would mean an unexplainable
> contradiction between the growing purchasing
> power of the population and the constantly
> lagging development of production. Without
> any doubt this contradiction has some positive
> impact, that is, it pushes ahead the develop-
> ment of production. However, the conditions
> of merchandise starvation, indeed, are charac-
> terized by all kinds of irregularities of the
> planned range of production, its quality, etc. 5

Moreover, Konnik delivered a further blow to the
Stalinist theory of Soviet industrialization. This time
the attack was really pitched at the very theoretical
foundations of the Soviet brand of "socialism"--Marx's
theory was contrasted with the particular canon of Marxism-
Leninism:

> If under consumption we understand the growing
> needs of the masses (and this is also not its
> only aspect), then, this contradiction, as Marx
> pointed out, is inherent to the general dialec-
> tical unity of production and consumption,
> and as such cannot be considered as a specific
> contradiction which is only inherent in the
> socialist economy.   6

Not surprisingly, Konnik's article was published in

January of nineteen fifty-seven, in the immediate aftermath
of Khrushchev's open attack on Stalinism in his "secret
speech." Had the type of criticism exhibited in Konnik's
article been allowed to continue, then a theoretical avalanche would have resulted, threatening to destroy the
entire theoretical foundation of Soviet "socialism." Had
this been allowed to occur, it would not have been due to
any determination on the part of the Soviet scholarly
milieus to undermine the theory, but rather it would have
been the consequence of the inherent weakness and inconsistency of the Stalinist Marxism-Leninism. The fundamental
Soviet social theory was just too much of a "noble lie,"
too much of a "house of cards" to withstand any kind of
serious criticism. The most obvious points of vulnerability were the glaringly apparent differences and the
mutual contradictions existing between Marxism and Leninism.
If Stalin's precarious "unification effort" had been
entirely annihilated, what then would really have held
together these two mutually contradictory theories?
Together with Stalin, the "house of cards" of the fundamental Soviet social theory could collapse as well. The
next consequence would be the total separation between the
components of Soviet theory, i.e., Leninism, and Marxism.
How otherwise the constant pitching of Marx's theory
against Leninism could be tolerated during the future public
policy debates? Of course, Soviet ideology would have
found itself in a very precarious situation: isolated in

the international "communist" movement and reeling from the internal shock of having repudiated both Stalin and Marx.

It would be ludicrous to imagine that such theoretical turmoil could cause the Soviet society to collapse, and that, in the short run, it would be capable of eroding the political power and the corporate consciousness of the new elites produced by the Soviet social system. However, in the long run, without any doubt, it would greatly undermine the mass belief system in Soviet society, which in turn, would have enormous consequences for the social system there. To question the importance of the mass belief system as a pillar of Soviet society, is to commit an analogous mistake to that of the Stalinist theoreticians who maintained that the mass belief system was not one of the pillars of Western societies because it was irrelevant due to the overwhelming political role of the "conspiracy of the capitalist ruling class." In the long run, the mass belief system is equally vital to both types of societies.

The publication of as controversial an article as Konnik's in the official, prestigious scholarly journal, Voprosy Filosofii was possible in the confusion and intellectual turmoil of the immediate period following Khrushchev's secret speech. However, it seems that the Soviet elites, both political and academic, were then too much crystallized to allow these first proverbial "stones" to turn into a landslide. In order to guarantee that such would not be the result, the "mature" Soviet industrial theory began to be built.

In laying the foundation for the new period in the development of Soviet industrial theory it was crucial, of course, to establish a "final solution" for the problem of Stalinism. The Soviet industrial theoreticians belonged to the "vanguard" of those who began to experiment with the new theory. By mid 1957, Voprosy Filosofii afforded the prestigious place of its opening article to V.V. Nikolaev's "O Glavnykh Etapakh Razvitia Sovietskogo Sotsialisticheskogo Gosudarstva."[7] This was the first article which dealt with the problem of Stalinism in the spirit of the "new epoch" and thus contributed to the establishment of the foundations of the "mature" Soviet industrial theory.

In the comparatively lengthy introductory section of his article,[8] Nikolaev restated the basic principle of the Stalinist "Marxism-Leninism" which had established Lenin's theory as the only true continuation and advancement of Marx's theory. Unlike the earlier period, the restatement of such a principle did not make incumbent upon the writer any appeal to higher political or personal authority. The theory would stand upon its own merits without any kind of "outside" help. Of course, Nikolaev never entertained, even for a moment, the idea of suggesting that there existed somewhere a serious theoretical justification for this premise, but instead he made his point as if there were something intrinsically obvious about it, so obvious and well under- stood by everybody that it was not necessary to marshall a theoretical argument of any kind behind it.

After removing Stalin in this "matter of fact" way from the foundations of Soviet socialist theory, Nikolaev addressed a topic from which Stalin could not as easily be dismissed from all discussion, i.e., the implementation of Marxism-Leninism during the transformation of Soviet society. Here, Stalin (and by implication, Stalinism) was presented as a controversial and highly inconsistent figure who had committed grave errors in guiding the socio-economic transformation of Soviet society under the rubric of Marxism-Leninism.

> It must be admitted that the cult of Stalin's personality found its expression in that after Stalin's speech on the theoretical problems of the state during the XVIIIth Party Congress, we paid very little attention to the enrichment and treasuring of Lenin's ideas on the state generally speaking, and his ideas on the socialist state in particular. We also paid very little attention to Lenin's splended theses and laws and the periods of the development of the state during the dictatorship of the proletariat.
>
> Stalin's statement in his lecture during the XVIIIth Party Congress on the main periods of the development of the Soviet socialist state and of its fundamental goals and functions can be now interpreted as being to a great extent dogmatic. At that time, what had not been kept in mind was the fact that the teaching of Marxism-Leninism on the socialist state was a living, developing teaching, which was being enriched through the experience of the revolutionary struggle of the masses and through the experience of the construction of communism in the USSR and socialism in the countries of People's Democracy. The metaphysical belief that Stalin had presented the full and finished teaching on the subject of the socialist state became very widespread in our literature. [9]

However, in so arguing, Nikolaev did not mean to reject
entirely the Stalinist theory of the state. Actually,
after acknowledging the superiority of Lenin's teaching on
this subject--"However, the genuine creator of the teaching
on the socialist state is Lenin"[10]--it could be admitted
that Stalin was an important contributor to the advancement
of Marxism-Leninism:

> Nevertheless, J.V. Stalin has great achieve-
> ments in the development of the theory of the
> socialist state (especially on the subject
> of the problems in strengthening the Soviet
> state in the conditions of the encirclement
> by the capitalist states and the struggle of
> the two social systems for supremacy, and
> also, on the subject of the necessity to
> preserve the state apparatus under the com-
> munist system which was created in the con-
> ditions of capitalist encirclement, on the
> subject of the main periods and functions of
> the Soviet state during its development, and
> other subjects).   11

Moreover, he maintained that Stalin's contributions on these
subjects constituted the historical-dialectical development
of Lenin's theory:

> In his lecture during the XVIIIth Party Congress,
> J.V. Stalin outlined the characteristics of the
> main periods in the development of the Soviet
> state, and its fundamental goals and functions.
> Stalin's solution to the problem of the main
> periods in the development of the Soviet state
> constitutes, in itself, the advancement of Lenin's
> theses on this subject. That is, it is based on
> the Leninist theses on the necessity to explain
> the main periods in the development of the state
> apparatus and the necessity to apply it to the
> process of the development of the Soviet state.
>
> Forty years of experience in the development of
> the Soviet Union shows that the theses on the
> main periods, fundamental goals and functions

of the Soviet state should be considered, with
some corrections and supplements, as reflecting
the objective, concretely-historical process of
the development of our state. [12]

Further, Stalin was credited with declaring a decisive

war against the remnants of the capitalist period in the

aftermath of the Revolution, and he theoretically concep-

tualized this struggle as one of the fundamental functions

of the young socialist society. The result of this strong

drive was the total socialization of the means of produc-

tion, especially the collectivization of agriculture. As

a result:

> The victory of socialism in the city and the
> village directly resulted from this work.
> Already in the year 1930 the socialist sector
> of the economy concentrated in its hands the
> key sectors of the national economy. The USSR
> entered the period of socialism. [13]

Here, too, Stalinism's great successes were accompanied,

according to Nikolaev by some very serious mistakes. The

strong Stalinist leadership totally concentrated on the

economic and organizational aspects of social life there,

greatly neglecting in the meantime the social and educa-

tional aspects of social life, which according to Nikolaev

were as important.

The goal of Nikolaev's theoretical effort was to achieve

a general, balanced picture of the Stalinist period, a

picture in which Stalin would be seen as a very important

leader who greatly contributed to the Soviet transformation, as both the theoretician and implementator of Marxism-Leninism. According to Nikolaev, Stalin's contributions to the construction of socialism in the USSR were not only of a fundamental and lasting nature, but also, they were based upon the implementation and the continuation of Marxist-Leninist theory. However, there were mistakes. Those mistakes were obviously much less substantial when compared to the achievements of Stalinism. Mainly, they fell into the category of over-zealousness and a certain singlemindedness in the implementation of the program of socialist transformation, in addition to the category of the errors of the cult of Stalin's personality. For Nikolaev, it was obvious that Stalinism's achievements greatly outweighed its shortcomings, which basically had a superficial, easily rectified nature. Thus, the general message flowing from Nikolaev's article maintained that the mistakes of Stalinism, although indeed painful in many cases, should not overshadow its "scientific," constructive and fundamentally positive role for the construction of socialism in the Soviet Union.

From the theoretical point of view, Stalin had become totally and finally separated from his own creation--the theory of Marxism-Leninism. He was clearly presented as a very important contributor to the development of the doctrine, but the idea of the existence of the theory of Marxism-Leninism which first had appeared in Stalinist writings, now was implicitly based on the apparent, for the Soviet theoreticians, continuity of Marx's and Lenin's philosophies. As such, the existence of the theory of Marxism-Leninism resulted from a natural progression rather than being a Stalinist creation.

The importance of Nikolaev's article lies in the fact that it was one of the first publications espousing the views of the newest, and in a way the final, paradigm of Soviet socialist theory. We shall designate this paradigm the "mature" theory because it exhibited a striking consistency in its conceptualization of the most fundamental principles of the Soviet brand of "socialism" from its origin until the present time. The views expressed in Nikolaev's article were consistently espoused in numerous publications throughout the entire period. As might be expected, the first works of this paradigm were considerably simpler and less elaborate than the later works, however, their theoretical foundation was virtually the same. Although it took years for the "mature" industrial theory to develop fully, the problem of Stalinism was tackled immediately and hence a "final solution" emerged much earlier than was the case of other theoretical problems tackled by the "mature" industrial theory. The general character of the "final solution" to this problem was fairly well foreshadowed by Nikolaev's article, but the following few years saw the publication of a number of other works which further contributed to the exploration of this subject and thus, according to the Soviet point of view, the subject was exhausted.

A multitude of opinions eventually contributed to solving the problem of Stalinism in Soviet industrial theory. Thus, there were voices which had only criticized Stalinism without mentioning its positive aspects. However, those voices were extremely restrained and criticized only certain aspects of Stalinism, avoiding the impression of having undermined the entire system based on Marxist-Leninist theory.

Chagin's and Kharchev's article "O Kategoriakh 'Proiz-voditel'nye Sily' i 'Proizvoditel'nye Otnoshenia"[14] was representative of this strain. Here, the attack was concentrated on the arch-Stalinist principle that under the conditions of Soviet socialism, a full harmony exists between the forces and the relations of production:

> On the basis of that which was written above it is possible to make the argument that the full harmony between the productive forces and the productive relations, in all of its totality, is practically impossible. Only the prolonged compliance of the productive forces of one or another form of property with the appropriate form of the relations of production might take place. Thus, there is the possibility that other aspects of the productive relations might lag behind in the given socio-economic formation. On the thesis of the full harmony between the forces and the relations of production under socialism is theoretically mistaken because it contradicts the thesis of the continuous development of the productive forces of society, and also, it is harmful from the practical point of view because it appeases people and renders them complacent. Therefore, to discover these contradictions, it is necessary to comprehensively approach the analysis of the

interrelationship between the forces and the
relationship of production, and to uncover the
contradictions existing between the elements of
the productive forces themselves and their
internal dialectics as well, without which the
concrete role of the relations of production
cannot be finally explained.   15

This particular Stalinist principle was attacked severely,

but the attack was limited only to this particular tenet.

However, such attacks on Stalinism were a rarity indeed.

Moreover, the strength of such criticism was normally

greatly diluted by the praise showered upon certain aspects

of Stalinism in other works. Such praise usually had a

onesided character without any indication of even the most

general criticism of the period. Also, in some other cases,

while some aspects of Stalinism were lauded, they were

accompanied only by general and very vague criticism of the

period.

An example of such onesided but very cautious and

specific acclaim for Stalinism could be found in Smirnov's

article.[16] Here, Stalin was presented as the important

propagator of Marx's philosophy who had contributed to its

development especially on the subject of interrelationship

between different social groups:

When we are talking only about the situation
of the social groups and do not mention the
transformation of occupational activities,
then in so doing, the characteristics of the
given aspect of the productive relations
becomes obfuscated in its relationship to
the particular forms of social ownership of
the means of production. What is meant by
the interrelationship between social groups

in the process of production? Are not the forms
of the social ownership of the means of production or the forms of the social division or the
fruits of production really the forms of the interrelationship between the social groups? You know
that J.V. Stalin, on the basis of Marx's words,
inserted a perfectly concrete meaning into these
interrelationships: the self-transformation of
the occupational activities. Thus, by omitting
Marx's words on the transformation of the occupational activities, we impoverish the forms of
understanding the productive relations. 17

Another example of such a style could be found in

V.V. Nikolaiev's second article[18] which again prestigiously

opened the particular edition of Voprosy Filosofii. Atten-

tion was paid not so much to the judicious search for a

balanced approach to Stalinism, but rather to the vigorous

defense of the integrity and supremacy of Soviet Marxism-

Leninism against the assorted attacks of the "revisionists,"

i.e., in this case, mainly the Yugoslav and the Western

Marxists. Here again, Stalin was portrayed as an important

contributor to the development of Marxist-Leninist theory:

As was already stated above, V.I. Lenin created
the theory dealing with the strengthening and
development of the Soviet socialist state.
J.V. Stalin's contribution lies in what he
demonstrated about Engel's theory of the
withering away of the state apparatus in the
conditions of socialism. Hence, if Engels'
theory were to have maintained its validity in
the conditions of the victory of socialism in
all societies, or at least in the majority of
societies, this theory would be inapplicable
when socialism is victorious only in one society,
or only in a few societies. J.V. Stalin
developed Lenin's theses on strengthening the
Soviet state and his activities underwrote this
achievement. 19

In discussing the early development of the Soviet "mature" industrial theory and the creation of its theoretical foundation, one notes the striking similarity between this stage in the development of the "mature" industrial theory and the "transformed" theory which preceded it. Both of them appear to be in an unsettling state of shock after the collapse of Stalinism. In both cases, the lack of a firmly established theoretical foundation was clearly evident, which caused the respective authors to, on the one hand, cautiously "chip away" at some of the Stalinist premises, and on the other hand, to attempt to preserve the integrity and the continuity of Soviet "socialist" theory. In the conditions of the apparent absence of a firm and clear theoretical foundation, the writers of both periods had to resort to alluding to their "apparent" existence and in the meantime, to attempt to rescue themselves in any way deemed safe and possible, i.e., by presenting tidbits of this supposedly existing theory, which were essential for their more particular arguments.

There was, however, a substantial difference between the "transformed" and the "mature" stages in the development of Soviet industrial theory. This difference was derived from the degree of theoretical insecurity. During the "transformed" period, the degree of insecurity about the fundamental premises of the Soviet brand of "socialism" was more severe, and most of all, was far more realistic because while the foundations of the Stalinist theory had been weakened, there was deep insecurity about the direction of post-Stalinist development. By contrast, after the consolidation of political power in the hands of the Khrushchevites, the political elites called upon academic officialdom to reestablish the theoretical foundations of Soviet "socialism." Of course, an enterprise of such magnitude could not be accomplished overnight, so the new principles of Soviet social theory were simply "missing" during the first few years of the new period. However, during the first few years of the new period, Soviet scholars were no doubt perfectly aware that the great endeavor of creating the new theoretical foundations for Soviet social theory was in the making. During this period, there were apparently several very definite "leaks" on the general characteristics as well as on many particulars of this effort. Thus, although the writers of the early period of the "mature" theory still were somewhat insecure because they did not have any clear cut theoretical fundamentals to build upon, they, nevertheless, produced works which were consistent with those written after the fundamental theory was published, and hence belonged to the same theoretical period as the later authors.

Finally, the new fundamental theory of Soviet "socialism" emerged. The main outcome stemming from the development of the new fundamental tenets of Soviet "socialist" theory was the fact that the industrial theoreticians obtained the solid clear cut theoretical foundations for their work and

could focus their attention on issues addressed by industrial theory rather than having to create tidbits of
theoretical fundamentals in support of their particular work.
Of course, with the creation of the new theoretical fundamentals the development of the Soviet social theory, in
a way, had gone full circle, i.e., it had found itself in a
position very much reminiscent of the early Stalinist period.
That is, the Soviet theory again took the shape of the
pyramid with the "supreme" fundamental theory at the summit.
However, now the "supreme" fundamental theory, to maintain
its position, no longer needed the supreme genius-political
leader to stand behind it, but instead, the bureaucratized
"vanguard-party" and the bureaucratized academia were able
to generate enough power to support the new "supreme" fundamental theory of Soviet "socialism." In effect, the Soviet
academic elite was in fact trusted with the creation of the
new "supreme" fundamental theory.

The society was no longer in a state of turmoil due
to socio-economic transformation, where the narrow vanguard
elite played the pivotal role. Instead, now the system was
run by a monumental bureaucracy, and, of course, Soviet
academia was a highly bureaucratized and hierarchical body
as well. Moreover, by then Soviet academia was already a
stable, well entrenched and large body which greatly contributed to the socialization of the masses of educated
Soviet citizens. It should also be noted that higher
echelons of the bureaucratized and hierarchical Soviet

academia belonged to the Soviet elite in the broad sense
of the word. Hence, it could be trusted by the narrow
party elite, because it was immediately controlled by this
elite. All in all, the full weight of the party authority
standing behind these new theoretical fundamentals transformed them into a new "supreme" fundamental theory of
Soviet "socialism."

The advantages stemming from such an approach were
colossal. First of all, by separating the origins of the
fundamental socialist theory from the narrow political
elite, the theory gained more respectability and consequently appeared to have originated more independently and in a
more scientific fashion. On the other hand, perversely
enough, it gave more credibility to the political elite
which now was supposedly following a scientific theory of
quite "neutral" origins, indeed. Moreover, this situation
somehow united political ideology with scientific doctrine.
This advantage constituted only the tip of the iceburg in
terms of the benefits stemming from the fact that the new
theory enjoyed a scientific-academic genesis.

The new fundamental theory of Soviet "socialism" was
in fact developed by two teams of top-notch Soviet scholars
and as a result of their work, two complementary works were
published successively in the years 1958 and 1959.[20] Each
work had a truly collective character and was comprised of
a large number of different pieces written by a variety of
authors. The collective character of these works had two

important beneficial characteristics: first, for all intents and purposes, it harmonized the variety of official Soviet schools of academic thought; and also, by the virtue of such massive participation, it instantly familiarized a large number of the Soviet academicians with the new theoretical fundamentals.

However, on purely theoretical grounds, the appearance of the new Soviet fundamental theory of socialism was very anticlimactic. That is, the new fundamental theory was basically nothing other than another adaptation of Lenin's philosophy to the Soviet reality. Once again, the adaptation of Marx's philosophy had only a marginal character, and then, only when it could be presented as totally harmonious with Lenin's system of thought. What then was so new about the new Soviet theoretical fundamentals?

First of all, Soviet society now had a different character when compared with that of thirty years earlier. In short, then, it was basically a pre-industrial society... now it was decisively an industrial one. Secondly, there was the entire experience of Stalinism, i.e., the implementation of the Leninist scheme for the transformation of Soviet society which although, according to Soviet theory, undoubtedly was a stunning success, nevertheless, has caused some negative developments which, in turn had to be dealt with. Thirdly, the international scene had changed dramatically. Considering that all of these factors had to be dealt with theoretically, there was some degree of

newness in the new fundamental theory of Soviet
"socialism."

Moreover, there was another marked difference between
the new theory and its predecessor--it was much more
erudite, scholarly and "professional." Most of the crude
and simplistic arguments of the Stalinist theory either
disappeared entirely, or were improved by a great deal of
modern scholarly erudition, certainly an important advantage derived from entrusting this kind of enterprise to
professional academicians.

From the logical point of view, however, it would be
very hard to find anything new in the "new" fundamental
Soviet theory, just as difficult, perhaps, as any effort to
integrate two contradictory philosophies, those of Marx and
Lenin. However, its form was decisively improved, becoming
more elaborate, more erudite, and covering a much greater
range of topics, inasmuch as it constituted the fundamental
theory for all the social disciplines as well as the guiding
light for the natural sciences.

In providing the new theoretical foundations for the
industrial theory, the new fundamental theory essentially
did not add anything that had not already been discussed
by the Soviet industrial theoreticians during the "transformed" and the early "mature" periods. However, the
points made during these periods were not presented in an
orderly and comprehensive manner, and above all, as now
presented, were devoid of any degree of controversy,

(assuming that there had been some degree of real controversy to begin with). Also, the new theory was written
in a very confident and definitive style which left
virtually no room for discussion. An example of this new
style can be found in the discussion of the balance in the
development of the different branches of industry, a
crucial subject within the area of industrial theory:

> Let us consider for a moment that society or
> its state organs guided by the best intentions
> wanted suddenly to increase sharply the volume
> of consumption omitting, however, to arrange in
> good time for a corresponding increase in pro-
> duction. As a result, the existing stocks of
> commodities would be rapidly exhausted. The
> same would happen if the relationship between
> the consumption and accumulation of resources
> earmarked for the expansion of production were to
> be arbitrarily changed. A reduction in the share
> of accumulation will inevitably slow down economic
> development and subsequently bring it to a halt,
> leading to the rapid consumption of basic capital
> and to the disorganization and decline of economic
> life. An excessive increase in the rate of accumu-
> lation, however, may weaken the material incentive
> of those engaged in production and ultimately
> affect the rate of growth of labour productivity.
> Nor can one disturb with impunity the proportions
> between wage rates and the level of labour pro-
> ductivity, between the total monetary income of
> the population and the volume of trade, etc.
>
> In addition to those already enumerated, many
> other branches of production and distribution
> exist which cannot function normally unless
> certain proportions are observed. Thus, a
> balance must be maintained between the basic
> branches of the national economy, such as
> industry, agriculture and transport. Incal-
> culable difficulties threaten if any of them
> falls behind.
>
> Definite relationships are required in the
> development of heavy and light, extractive and
> manufacturing industries. A faster rate of
> development for heavy industry ensures the
> advance of all branches of the economy. Similarly

> the raw-material and power industries must expand
> faster than the manufacturing industries, and
> create the necessary reserves for their advance. 21

The difference between the points of the argument made
above and the same points which were made during the
"transformed" and the early "mature" periods was that during
the earlier periods the points of the argument were based
upon and frequently illustrated by the often very painful
mistakes committed during the Soviet process of industrial
transformation. However, the fundamentals of the new
theory of Soviet "socialism" were typically presented to the
reader as some kind of supreme truth which inhered in the
theory of Marxism-Leninism. The particular arguments of
the new fundamental theory usually began with a statement
from Marx and Engels, and then included supporting material
from Lenin's writings, and finally, these arguments were
skillfully correlated with Soviet social practice. Rarely,
however, was there ever any admission of the mistakes committed during the Soviet transformation, indicating little
recognition of the principle of learning from one's mistakes.
Of course, in some cases the mistakes were too infamous to
be discretely whitewashed, as in the case of some of the
more preposterous and outrageous aspects of the personality
cult. These errors in fact had been exposed and their
condemnation had become an integral part of the body of
Marxism-Leninism. Thus, the general Marxist-Leninist principle now maintained that:

Marxism-Leninism proceeds from the fact that
the decisive role in history is played by the
activity and struggle of the classes, the
activity of the masses of the people. The
real part played by leaders can be understood
only when it is related to the class struggle,
the activity of the masses, to the social demands
created by this struggle. Such an understanding
of history is incompatible with the cult of the
individual--the worship of an outstanding leader,
to whom superhuman merits and virtues are
ascribed. The cult of the individual is an
ideology contrary to Marxism, an ideology that
has its roots in the world outlook of feudalism
and bourgeois individualism.   22

Applying this newly discovered fundamental principle

of Marxism-Leninism to the particular case of Stalin, was

to underline his positive personal characteristics which

led him to such political prominence, and also, to underline

the negative side of his personality which led to its cult.

However, what most characterized the new fundamental theory

was the way in which it placed into systematic and histori-

cal perspective as shocking and outrageous a phenomenon as

the personality cult:

These negative phenomena did not, of course,
change the socialist nature of Soviet society.
During that period, too, it continued to develop
along the socialist path, the path of consolidating
socialist ownership of the means of production,
rapid growth of the productive forces, and raising
the standard of life, culture and consciousness
of working people. In spite of all the negative
consequences of the cult of Stalin's personality,
the peoples of the Soviet nation achieved in that
period outstanding victories. However, their
success would have been ever greater but for
Stalin's mistakes and the cult of the individual. 23

All in all, the new version of Marxism-Leninism was

as full of devastating loopholes as the early, Stalinist

version, with the difference deriving almost entirely
from the professional jargon of the scholars of the Soviet
academic establishment and of course, from the newly gained
confidence stemming from the apparently successful industrialization of the country and from the new, now imperial
role played by the Soviet Union in the international arena.

The final crystallization of the Soviet fundamental
social theory freed the industrial theoreticians from the
need to construct the theoretical foundations on their own.
Now, able to point to the clearly established set of fundamental premises for their general guidance, they could set
off into the theoretical exploration of the particular
problems of Soviet industrial development.

After publication of the fundamental theory of Soviet
socialism, an incredible wave of enthusiastic optimism
swept the literature on the industrial theory. Of course,
the publication of the fundamentals was not the only reason
for this great optimism, but it certainly was one of the main
reasons. The fundamentals of the Soviet socialist theory
beamed with the steady glow of the confidence and optimism
exuded by the academic elites. It was with this self-
assured confidence that the transformation of Soviet society
was portrayed as a steady chain of successful events.
According to this perspective, the success of the Soviet
transformation was caused not by luck but by the rigorous
application of the scientific doctrine which stood behind
it. Moreover, the success of the Soviet industrial

transformation did not have an esoteric character--it could be measured empirically and when such measurements were made, the data generated compared favorably with the most advanced capitalist societies. What was even more important, it was argued that the apparent mistakes of the Soviet industrial transformation did not seem to be caused by the faults inhering in the scientific doctrine itself, but by mistakes and excesses in its application which in turn were ascribed to Stalinism. However, such apparently subjective problems seemed to be very easy to overcome, and finally were overcome by the collapse of Stalinism.

The atmosphere of optimism stemmed not only from the theoretical assessment of the general dialectics of the Soviet industrial transformation, but also, from a very particular, "scientific" premise of the Soviet industrial theory which identified the development of heavy industry as being of a paramount and "determining" character in the industrial process. According to Soviet scholars, the difficulty in achieving industrialization lay in the development of the heavy industry sector. The development of light and consumer industries, as well as the development of agriculture was supposed to be the natural consequence of having developed the heavy industry sector. Moreover, there was something obvious, intrinsically easy, and logically and practically simple and natural in the development of light industry following the construction of the heavy industrial sector. Considering the astounding success registered in their society in the development of heavy industry, Soviet scholars were virtually certain that the industrial and agricultural development of their society, and the resultant abundance of consumer goods which was supposed to lead it to communism, was just around the corner. At this point, Soviet theory--from the early Stalinist period to the emergence of the "new" fundamentals of the late nineteen fifties--was confirmed by the apparent achievements of industrial development, which caused a wave of optimism about the future of the social system, which had spread widely in the intellectual milieus in general, and amongst the industrial theoreticians in particular.

By the end of 1958, and continuing for the next six years, scholarly works of an ultra-optimistic character were being published. Shershunov and Shcheglov in their "O Svoeobrazzi Protivorechii Stroitel'stva Sotsializma v SSSR"[24] point to the industrial backwardness of the pre-revolutionary Russia:

> One of the negative consequences of the under-
> development of the material-industrial base of
> the country was the low level of the industrial
> production per capita. The Russia of the year
> 1913 produced less per capita than the U.S.: raw
> steel--ten to eleven times less, coal--twenty-five
> times less, crude petroleum--six times less,
> electric energy--nineteen times less. The First
> World War and especially the Civil War which
> followed as well as the resulting foreign inter-
> vention threw the industry of our country back
> to the level of tzarist Russia in the second half
> of the nineteenth century.[25]

The Bolshevik Revolution created a new ruling class
which as its paramount goal saw the industrial development
of the country:

> The main means of overcoming the contradiction
> between the advanced form of political power
> and the backward material-industrial base of
> the society was the creation of the large machine
> industry, and especially heavy industry, and in
> so doing, the achievement of such a level of
> production per capita and such productivity, that
> the level already achieved by the main capitalist
> societies would be excelled.   26

The fact that by the end of the nineteen-fifties the
Soviet Union had achieved the second industrial output in
the world bore witness to the success of the Bolsheviks'
plans:

> Presently, the Soviet Union possesses large-
> machine productive capacity in the areas of
> industry and agriculture. The characteristic
> of the present level of the development of our
> productive forces is the fact that in the area
> of industrial production our country ranks
> second in the world.   27

However, there still existed an important contradiction
in the development of the world forces of production--the
much more dynamically developing "socialist" Soviet Union
still lagged behind the "decaying" U.S. in the production
of consumer goods per capita. Thus, to overcome this
dialectical and historic-philosophical contradiction:

> Our party in its practical activities based its
> stand on the necessity of overcoming this contra-
> diction. Efforts are now being made to achieve
> in the next four to six years, the production per
> capita of butter, milk and meat equal to the U.S..

> Also, during the nearest fifteen years, our
> nation is geared to achieve the U.S. level of
> production per capita in the industrial sphere.
> The fulfillment of these goals will mark the
> solution of the contradiction between the
> advanced economic and political system of our
> society and its material-technological base
> which still is insufficiently developed to
> satisfy the growing needs of the members of
> socialist society.

At the end of 1958, another Soviet industrial theo-

retician--Dvorkin[29]--showed even more optimism about the

future of Soviet industrial development. He saw the Soviet

Union as already being superior to the U.S. in the area of

applied sciences, and thus as having by far, much greater

potential in the development of high technology:

> The great number of accomplished foreign
> engineers, after acquainting themselves with
> the industry and the accomplishments of the
> applied sciences in the USSR, admits that the
> Soviet Union stands ahead of the capitalist
> societies in its achievements in the field
> of automation, and as a matter of fact, only
> the U.S. could be compared to it.   [30]

As it turned out, the optimism expressed in 1958 was

only a prelude to the optimism of the following years.

First of all, the glorification of technological growth

under the socialist system emerged as a consistent feature

of the works on industrial theory and ultimately became

a very important logical premise for these works. Socialism

was conceptualized by the Soviet industrial scholars as

the only system which could lead and consciously facili-

tate the further technological progress of humanity.

Finally, this theoretical "truth" became so entrenched that for any practical purpose it had departed from the realm of theory (i.e., that realm where it could be analyzed and discussed with the marshalling of some empirical evidence to support it) and it entered the realm of political beliefs, where it became the unquestionable ideological "truth."

This assertion was often coupled with another vigorously repeated ideological "truth"...the one that maintained that although the capitalist system was the crib of modern technology, it also is the coffin for its further advancement. Of course, it must be pointed out that these two claims are classical theses of Soviet Marxism-Leninism, and their roots reach deeply into the early Stalinist period. However, at that time, these claims had a purely theoretical and speculative character and were mainly based on the works of Marx and Lenin. Now, theory and speculation were traded for certainty as these assertions took their place among the "fundamentals" of Marxism-Leninism, thus freeing the industrial scholars to concentrate on other activities.

These profound statements regarding the different dynamics of technological development within socialist and capitalist systems were based upon what was indeed a very selective marshalling of empirical evidence. Undoubtedly, there existed a serious danger that a broadening of their empirical argument could lead to conclusions contradictory

to the fundamentals of the Soviet theory of socialism.
For example, Kurakov quoted a U.S. economic journal to
demonstrate that most of the resources generated in the
capitalist economy which could be channelled into the
development of technology were parasitically used by the
capitalist class there.[31] By contrast:

> The socialist system of production is saved
> from the necessity of channelling a great part
> of the national revenue to the rulers of
> capital. This situation allows the socialist
> system of production to assure a rapid and
> steady speed of growth for the national economy.
> Capitalism cannot separate itself from paying
> the capitalist rent, the interests from borrowed
> capital and the dividends, because all of that
> would mean the liquidation of the capitalist
> system. Socialism will always have the great
> advantage in the resources destined for the
> development of technology.   [32]

To support his thesis, Kurakov examined the rates of
industrial growth of the leading capitalist societies and
compared it to the Soviet rate of industrial growth. Finding
the Soviet rate of industrial growth to be a number of
times greater than the growth rate of the already industrially well advanced capitalist societies, he concludes
that the socialist system is intrinsically superior.
Moreover, his confidence also derived from the comparison
of a number of statistics in the areas of the applied
sciences:

> We have also all the potential for the rapid
> multiplication of the quantities of our
> scientific-exploratory, construction and
> planning cadres. The basis for that is the
> number of specialists already working in the

national economy. If we look only at the
certified engineers, we have almost two times
more of them than the U.S.   [33]

For Mendel'son, the main industrial goal of the Soviet

Union ("The main goal of the USSR in contemporary period is

to achieve and then to exceed the U.S. level of industrial

production per capita.")[34] will be surely achieved because

of the superior Soviet social system which allows for

much greater speed in the development of the productive

forces than the capitalist system. To prove this claim,

Mendel'son points to a number of "proven" examples of some

aspects of the development of high technology. Thus,

> the USSR was the first one to construct a
> nuclear power plant, the first one to construct
> ballistic rockets, the first one to send
> into space artificial satellites of the earth
> and artificial planets themselves.   [35]

Mendel'son addresses the important issue of labor,

arguing that the harmony existing in the socialist condi-

tions between mental and manual kinds of labor elevates

the labor process to a level unachievable in the conditions

of the capitalist system of production because of the

contradictions existing in the latter system between the

mental and the manual types of labor.

> Under capitalism, there are tremendous contra-
> dictions existing between the manual and mental
> types of labor. In turn, these contradictions
> greatly limit the process of the socialization
> of labor there. On the other hand, in socialist
> society, during its movement towards communism,
> the socialization of labor enters a higher phase
> which is unreachable for capitalism...the

harmonious combination of the mental and the manual types of labor in the activities of every part of the society.   36

Sometimes the optimism exhibited when making comparisons between the Soviet Union and the advanced capitalist societies exceeds even the most liberally understood borders of rationality and takes the shape of blunt self-aggrandizement. Illustrative of this phenomenon is the following passage, gleaned from the most prestigious, semi-official, Soviet philosophical journal:

> In the contemporary period, the USSR substantially overcame the most industrially developed capitalist society...the United States of America...not only in the tempo of the growth of production, not only in the tempo of the growth of productivity, but also in the size of the absolute growth of the most important products of industrial production. Our recent technological and scientific achievements eloquently bear witness to the fact that the Soviet Union has substantially overcome the U.S. in the development of contemporary technology and science in the most important, key directions.   37

Continuing in this vein of irrational self-aggrandizement, another author, O.G. Iurovitskii, went so far as to argue that the Soviet Union had overcome the U.S. in the field of individual consumption. While he points to the quantity and quality of popular consumption in the USSR, he also quotes American authors on the unevenness of the slicing of the "social pie" in the U.S. He implicitly leads his reader to believe that from the point of view of consumption, the population of the Soviet Union is better off than the population of the U.S. because in the U.S. the statistics for consumption per capita are very misleading due to the fact that the rich there are consuming disproportionately more than the poor: "According to the American statistics, the rich are eating 3.6 times more meat and fish, 2.8 times more milk products, 4 times more fresh fruits, 7.5 times more citrus fruits and tomatoes than the poor."[38]

The ultra-optimism of the Soviet industrial theoreticians bloomed in larger and more elaborate works where support was garnered through the selective use of documentation. Unfortunately, the quantitative growth of this type of argument did not bring much change in its quality.

Thus, already in the year 1959, Osipov published Tekhnika i Obshchestvennyi Progress[39] which still is considered in the Soviet Union as a classic in the field of industrial theory. His work, which was highly touted among Soviet industrial scholars, did not really contribute anything new to the subject, but rather it eloquently wove together the arguments already made in numerous articles in the field of industrial theory during the "mature" period of its development. As a result, he was able to conclude his more comprehensive work with the identical ultra-optimistic conclusion exhibited in earlier articles:

> The fulfillment of the seven year plan for
> the development of the national economy will

mean a great victory for the Soviet Union in its
competition with the capitalist societies. In
the year 1965, our country will overcome the
current production of the United States of
America in terms of the absolute production of
some central aspects of production, and in the
production of other aspects, will equal the U.S.
Moreover, the production of the most important
agricultural products, both in the absolute
numbers and on a per capita basis will rise above
the contemporary level of agricultural production in the U.S.

The Soviet Union's superiority in the rate of
growth of production will be the real base for
exceeding the general level of the U.S. production per capita during the five years following the year 1965. Therefore, at that time, and
possibly sometime earlier, the Soviet Union will
gain first place in the world in the absolute
size of its production, as well as in the amount
of production per capita, which will assure the
highest standard of living for the population
here. It will constitute the paramount historical
victory of socialism in its peaceful competition
with the capitalist system.   40

The same year saw publication of another work--

Strumlin's Na Putiakh Postroenia Kommunizma[41]--which also

in time gained recognition as a classic in the field of

industrial theory. If one, would expect to find, based

upon the title of this work, a discussion of the paths

leading to communism, then, one would be very disappointed.

Instead, one encounters a very general and vague discussion

about the anticipated progression from Soviet "socialism"

to a communist system, but the level of generality was so

great that it would be very difficult indeed to learn

anything from it, unless, for example, one were to find

the quotation of such profound statements as Khrushchev's

"communism--This is Science"[42] as sufficiently precise.

With a highly selective use of empirical evidence, Soviet
scholars produced what they considered to be a devastating
critique of the capitalist system. As a result of these
efforts, the economic superiority of the Soviet system was
proclaimed once again and this assertion came to be a fundamental premise utilized by Soviet industrial theorists.
More and more inventive varieties of this type of argument
appeared, but the conclusions always remained the same, as
is exemplified by Shemenev's work:

> With the enormous economic accomplishments of
> the USSR serving as a background, the limits
> of the capitalist system were definitively
> exhibited both in the general and the particular
> aspects of technological progress, and also the
> solution of all kinds of technological problems
> wholly (tsielikom) depends on socialist condi-
> tions.   43

By 1961, the ultra-optimism exhibited by the Soviet
industrial theoreticians took on a repetitious character.
Kurakov, for example, repeats the argument that the Soviet
Union was superior to the U.S. in the field of science.[44]
Kukin predicted that during the nineteen-sixties, the USSR
would decisively overcome the U.S. in industrial production
and also added that:

> All the population will be assured of material
> affluence. The problems of everyday life will
> be radically solved, and heavy physical labor
> will be a thing of the past.   45

Moreover, after examining some statistical data, he authoritatively assured his readers that during the nineteen-sixties the Soviet Union would overcome the U.S. in agricultural production as well, and during the nineteen-seventies, it would become a truly communist society. Further exhibiting this strain of repetitious ultra-optimism, Fedoseyev assured his readers that communism would be achieved in the Soviet Union during the following twenty years.[46] Stepanian, in turn, restates the claim of Soviet economic superiority over the U.S., and also depicts Soviet society in the year 1980:

> Until the year 1980, that is during the next twenty years,...the central role will be played still by the socialist principle of distributing material goods according to one's work. However, during this time, the communist principle of the division of material goods will steadily grow in importance. Right now, seventy-five percent of the entire socialist pie is sliced according to the socialist principle, and the remaining 25% of it is divided according to the communist principle, that is, independently from one's working input: this part includes the free system of education, health services and so forth. At the end of the twenty year period, the entire half of the social pie still will be divided according to the input of one's work, but already, the other half will be distributed freely. Only after twenty years will the time come when the communist form of the division of labor will begin to play an increasingly more important role than the socialist form...the division according to labor. [47]

To justify this ultra-optimism even more, Shukhadrin ventured into the writing of an elaborate treatise Osnovy Istorii Tekhniki where he marshalled massive

historical evidence in support of his argument.[48] In
the same year, Strumlin created a monumental work, Problemy
Sotsializma i Kommunizma[49] where the length of the argument
about the superiority of the Soviet brand of socialism over
the advanced capitalist system and about its immediate
glorious future, was reversely proportional to its
innovativeness.

The years 1963-1965 were the last years in which this
ultra-optimism prevailed and during this period the work
of Soviet industrial scholarship produced an immense number
of basically very repetitious arguments. Those who excelled
in this ultra-optimistic repetition were Naumova,[50]
Manevitch,[51] Strumlin,[52] Novoselov,[53] Kozlova and Fainburg,[54]
Sukhomlinskii,[55] Shemshev,[56] Belozertsev and Fomina,[57]
Marakhov;[48] and in their more substantial, lengthy publications, Karpov in his Osnovnyie Zakonomernosti Razvitia
Estestvoznania,[59] Rachkov in his Nauka i Obshchestvennyi
Progress,[60] and Kudrashov in his Sovremennaia Naucho-
Tekhnicheskaia Revolutsia i ee Osobennosti.[61] These
theorists sought to assure their readers that the new high-
technology was the missing link between the Soviet brand
of socialist society and the communist system as outlined
by Marx himself. Communist society would then emerge
immediately following the full incorporation and utilization of this advanced technology. Riding a wave of enthusiasm, Soviet theoreticians claimed to have developed

a complete understanding of the course of humanity's
development. Moreover, they believed that their society
was on the verge of entering the last stage of human
development and, thus, was infinitely superior to capitalist society which was ready to sink into chaos and degener-
ation under the pressure of the growth of technology.

Of course, during the "mature" period in the development
of the Soviet industrial theory, there were subjects other
than the comparison of the industrial dynamic of the
Soviet Union and the advanced capitalist societies which
were addressed and analyzed.[62] However, the discussion of
other subjects was totally overshadowed and dominated by
the ultra-optimism generated by the newly mastered art of
the selective marshalling of empirical evidence. As
a result, the entire industrial theory of this period was
permeated with arrogance. Soviet scholars were sure that
their society had mastered the dynamics of human development. From an historical perspective, the coup de grace
was supposed to have been delivered to the capitalist
societies in almost no time at all. This euphoric
enthusiasm and arrogance in effect rendered all other
discussions meaningless and irrelevant. The work on other
traditional subjects of Soviet industrial theory still
continued to be produced but lacked a balanced or consistent character because it was so dominated by the feelings
of ultra-optimism. The literature of this period reveals
an attitude among Soviet scholars that the consistence,

balance and even the responsibility of their arguments did
not matter much, because in any event, their society would
quickly prove to the world that it had already mastered
"The Great Scientific Truth about Humanity" and in comparison to this great historical achievement the exaggerated
preoccupation with creating the details of their theory--
the fundamental socialist theory, or just the particular
industrial theory was really of minor importance. After
all, nobody judges the absolute winners, and they expected
to be the winners very soon indeed. However, the ultra-
optimistic period of the Soviet "mature" industrial theory
ended abruptly as the great dreams of overcoming the most
advanced capitalist societies collapsed.

Before we begin our discussion of the next stage in
the development of Soviet industrial theory, we will turn
first to another phenomenon born during those euphoric days
of ultra-optimism: the rejection of the concept of post-
industrial society by the mature Soviet industrial theory.

ENDNOTES

1. I.I. Konnik, "O Protivorechiakh Sviazanykh s
    Deistvem Ekonomicheskikh Zakonov," Voprosy Filosofii,
    1957, No. 1, (174-181).

2. Ibid., p. 174.

3. Ibid., p. 175.

4. Ibid.

5. Ibid., p. 176.

6. Ibid.

7. V.V. Nikolaev, "O Glavnykh Etapakh Razvitia Sovietskogo
    Sotsialisticheskogo Gosudarstva," Voprosy Filosofii,
    1957, No. 4, (10-26).

8. Ibid., pp. 10-13.

9. Ibid., p. 14.

10. Ibid.

11. Ibid.

12. Ibid., p. 15.

13. Ibid., p. 17.

14. B.A. Chagin and A.G. Kharchen , "O Kategoriakh
    'Prozvoditel'nye Sily' i 'Proizvodstvennye Otnoshenia'",
    Voprosy Filosofii, 1958, No. 2, (9-20).

15. Ibid., p. 16.

16. G.L. Smirnov, "Razdelene Truda i Obmen Deiatel'nos-
    t'ii v Sistemie Proizvodstvennykh Otnoshenii,"
    Voprosy Filosofii, 1958, No. 5, (27-40).

17. Ibid., p. 39.

18. V.V. Nikolaev, "Protiv Revizionistskikh Iskodzenii
    Marxistskogo-Leninskogo Uchenia o Gosudarstve,"
    Voprosy Filosofii, 1958, No. 11, (3-17).

19. Ibid., p. 11.

20. Osnovy Marksistskoi Filosofii, 1958, and Osnovy
    Marksizma-Leninizma, Gospolitizdat'.

21. Fundamentals of Marxism-Leninism, 1961: Moscow, Foreign Languages Publishing House, second edition, p. 705.

22. Ibid., pp. 226-227.

23. Ibid., pp. 229-230.

24. A.D. Shershunov and A.V. Scheglov , "O Svoeobrazii Protiviorechii Stroitel'stva Sotsializma v SSSR," Voprosy Filosofii, 1958, No. 11, (32-43).

25. Ibid., p. 33.

26. Ibid.

27. Ibid., p. 34.

28. Ibid., pp. 34-35.

29. I.N. Dvorkin, "O Reformistskikh Teoriakh 'Vtoroi Prommyshlennoi Revoliutsii," Voprosy Filosofii, 1958, No. 12, (39-53).

30. Ibid., p. 41.

31. I.G. Kurakov, "Razvite Tekhniki na Baze Sotsializma," Voprosy Filosofii, 1959, No. 1, (15-31).

32. Ibid., p. 16.

33. Ibid., p. 24.

34. A.S. Mendel'son, "O Proizvoditel'nykh Silakh," Voprosy Filosofii, 1959, No. 1, (157-166), p. 158.

35. Ibid.

36. V.Ia. El'meev, "Vozrastanie Roli Umstvennogo Truda v Razvitii Proizvoditel'nykh Sil Sotsializma," Voprosy Filosofii, 1959, No. 8, (33-44), p. 39.

37. V.I. Evdokimov, "Polnaia i Okonchatel'naia Pobeda Sotsializma v SSSR," Voprosy Filosofii, 1959, No. 11, (16-26), p. 22.

38. O.G. Iurovitskii, "Obschestvennoe Proizvodstvo i Lichnye Potrebnosti," Voprosy Filosofii, 1959, No. 11, (27-40), p. 35.

39. G.V. Osipov, Tekhnika i Obshchestvennyi Progress, 1959: Moscow, Izdatel'stvo Akademii Nauk SSSR.

40. Ibid., pp. 208-209.

41. S.G. Strumlin, Na Putiakh Postroenia Kommunizma,
    1959: Moscow, Gospolitizdat.

42. Ibid., p. 299.

43. G.I. Shemenev , "Indzhinerno-Tekhnicheskaia Inteli-
    gentsia v Period Razvernutogo Stroitel'stva Kommuniz-
    ma," Voprosy Filosofii, 1960, No. 8, (25-34), p. 33.

44. I.G. Kurakov, "Rol' Nauki v Sozdanii Material'no-
    Tekhnicheskoi Bazy Kommunizma," Voprosy Filosofii,
    1961, No. 6, (18-32).

45. D.M. Kukin, "Vdokhnovliaiuschies Znania Borby za
    Kommunizm," 1961, No. 8, (28-39), p. 29, Voprosy
    Filosofii.

46. P.N. Fedoseev, "Dialektika Pererastania Sotsializma
    v Kommunizm," 1961, No. 10., (28-42). Voprosy Filosofii.

47. Ts.A. Stepanian, "Osnovnyie Zakonomernosti Stroitel'-
    stva Kommunizma," 1961, No. 12, (3-11), p. 9,
    Voprosy Filosofii.

48. S.V. Shukhadrin, Osnovy Istorii Tekhniki, 1961: Moscow,
    Izdatel'stvo Akademii Nauk SSSR.

49. S.G. Strumlin, Problemy Sotsializma i Kommunizma, 1961:
    Moscow, Ekonomizdat.

50. N.F. Naumova, "Dva Mira--Dva Otnoshenia k Trudu,"
    1963, No. 1, (15-23), Voprosy Filosofii.

51. E.L. Manevitch, "Rasperedelene po Trudu i Printsip
    Material'noi Zainteresovannosti v Period Perekhoda
    ot Sotsializma k Kommunizmu," No. 2, (15-25), Voprosy
    Filosofii.

52. S.G. Strumlin, "Kommunizm i Razdelenie Truda," 1963,
    No. 3, (37-49). Voprosy Filosofii.

53. N.S. Novoselov, "Razdelenie Truda pri Kommunizme ne
    Iskliutchaet Vozmozhnosti Peremeny Truda i Vsesto-
    ronnego Razvitia Lichnosti", 1963, No. 3, (49-55).
    Voprosy Filosofii.

54. G.P. Kozlova and Z.I. Fainburg, "Izmenene Kharaktera
    Truda i Vsestoronene Razvite Cheloveka," Voprosy
    Filosofii, 1963, No. 3, (55-62).

55. V.A. Sukhomlinskii, "Trud--Osnova Vsestoronnego
     Razvitia Cheloveka," 1963, No. 4, (54-63), Voprosy
     Filosofii.

56. G.I. Shemshev, "Sviaz Nauki s Proizvodstvom i Vsestoron-
     zee Razvite Lichnosti," 1963, No. 9, (29-35),
     Voprosy Filosofii.

57. V.I. Belozertsev and V.A. Fomina, "Kommunisticheskoie
     Razdelenie Truda ne Iskliuchaet Vsestoronnego
     Razvitia Tcheloveka," 1963, No. 9, (35-39) Voprosy
     Filosofii.

58. V.G. Marakhov, "Nauka i Proizvodstvo," 1963, No. 10,
     (3-12). Voprosy Filosofii.

59. M.M. Karpov, Osnovnyie Zakonomernosti Razvitia Estes-
     tvoznania, 1963: Rostov, Izdatel'stvo Rostovskogo
     Universiteta.

60. P.A. Rachkov, Nauka i Obshchestvennyi Progress, 1963:
     Moscow, Izdatel'stvo Moskovskogo Universitieta.

61. A.P. Kudrashov, Sovremennaia Nauchno-Tekhnicheskaia
     Revoliutsia i ee Osobennost, (Moscow: 1965, Izdatel'stvo
     Mysl').

62. See especially the collection Sotsial'no-Ekonomicheskie
     Problemy Tekhnicheskogo Progressa, (Moscow: 1961,
     Izdatel'stvo Akademii Nauk SSSR), and S.G. Strumlin,
     Na Putiakh Postroenia Kommunizma, (Moscow: 1959,
     Gospolitizdat), S.G. Strumlin, Problemy Sotsializma
     i Kommunizma, (Moscow: 1961, Ekonomizdat).

Chapter IV

The Mature Soviet Industrial Theory

and the Concept of Post-industrial Society (1956-1965)

The emergence of post-industrial society had meant the radical transformation of advanced capitalism. The post-industrial transformation of the advanced capitalist societies was accompanied by a radical change in their ideology, i.e., generally speaking, the ideology of "welfare state" capitalism gradually pushed out of the "mainstream" the ideology of the laissez faire society. In the particular field of industrial theory, the body of work on the "second industrial revolution" had emerged. However, the Soviet industrial scholars obviously did not grasp the full implications of the post-industrial transformation. Thus, while many Western scholars were engaged in the analysis of the radical systemic changes that the "second industrial revolution" had introduced in their societies, analysis which had led them to the conclusion that the entire mode of production and with it the entire industrial society was entering a new stage of its development, by contrast Soviet industrial scholars understood the "second industrial revolution" in basically very narrow and strictly technological terms. That is, for the Soviet industrial scholars of that period, post-industrialism was not so much the new mode of production which gradually transforms the social system as it was a new technological advancement in the industrial mode of production which resulted in nothing more than the further facilitation of basic industrial development. In other words, according to Soviet industrial scholars, the post-industrial mode of production would not bring the post-industrial type of society, but instead it would hasten and bring to full bloom industrial development. Hence, the advent of the analysis of the new phenomenon of post-industrialism did not cause any reevaluation of the most fundamental assumption of Leninism, i.e., that the combination of the industrial system, borrowed from advanced capitalism, with the "vanguard party" type of political superstructure would create a communist society in the Soviet Union.

If both the emerging post-industrial mode of production in advanced capitalist society and the related theory of the "second industrial revolution" were to be seriously considered by the Soviet industrial scholars, then, indeed, a serious new debate on the foundations of the Soviet brand of socialism would be unavoidable. However, such a proposition would undoubtedly sound grotesque to a Soviet academic establishment fresh from having completed its work on the new foundations of Marxism-Leninism. If the post-industrial type of society were to be conceptualized as advanced in comparison to the industrial type of society, then it would have very serious implications for the recently overhauled theory of Marxism-Leninism.

First of all, it would mean that either Lenin's blueprint for the road to communism was fundamentally wrong or that this blueprint was of some historical value and would have to be supplemented because the industrial mode of production proved to be nothing other than a stepping

stone for the advancement to post-industrial society.
Before advancing to communism, the Soviet Union would
have to achieve a post-industrial type of society. In
the second option, the implicit dialectical unity between
Lenin's conceptualization of industrialization and the
oncoming post-industrial society would have to be argued,
in which case Lenin would be put in the same position as
Marx had been put by the Soviet theory of Marxism-Leninism.
Of course, either line of thought would require a theoretical effort of a scope comparable to Lenin's adaptation of
Marxism to the Russian reality, or the Stalinist adaptation
of Leninism to Soviet reality. Such an effort would dwarf
the so painfully laborious undertaking by which Stalinist
Marxism-Leninism was adapted to the new, post-Stalinist
reality.

All in all, even the most superficial speculations
about the consequences of a possible serious treatment of
post-industrialism by Soviet scholars would suggest that
a serious, analytical treatment of post-industrialism
would surely result in a powerful intellectual tremor.
Yet even the most cursory examination of the chances that
such an enterprise would indeed be undertaken, indicates
how hopelessly "academic" are such speculations. In light
of the fact that the Soviet economy moved in the <u>direction</u>
designed by the political elites, the proper understanding
of post-industrial development could not come from "within"
the Soviet political and academic elites, given their

unabashed enthusiasm for the continuation of industrial
development in the post-Stalinist period.

As a result, Soviet societal development continued to
be dominated by extreme bureaucratization, and as such was
extremely well insulated from influences that were disap-
proved of by the elites. The sluggishness of Soviet
bureaucratic responses to internal stimuli had already
been widely criticized in many Soviet and non-Soviet
quarters. Here, however, our interest focuses on the
possible response of the Soviet bureaucracy to external
stimuli. In the case of emerging post-industrialism, their
response was only possible so far as this phenomenon could
be proven by clear cut, demonstrable and convincing
examples. Unfortunately, inasmuch as post-industrialism
was only emerging, there were only a few examples which
were of a rather technological character. Because of that,
the post-industrial theories which were so disturbing from
the standpoint of Marxism-Leninism could be discarded as
confused and mistaken speculations. On the other hand,
these technological features of the post-industrial mode
of production which already were proven to constitute a
technological advancement in comparison to the industrial
period, were easily classified by Soviet industrial scholars
not as features of the new stage of social evolution, but
as new aspects of the still evolving industrialism, and
as such, were assimilated into the body of Soviet industrial
theory. Thus, enthusiasm for the mature industrial theory

remained undisturbed and the Soviet industrial scholars
were entombed in an outdated intellectual paradigm,
despite their passionate desire to be the theoretical
pathbreakers of humanity's industrial development.

When in the late nineteen-fifties, they came in contact
for the first time with post-industrial developments and
theories that sought to explain these developments, they
were absolutely confident that, regardless of contemporary
developments in the most advanced capitalist societies,
their Stalinless and rejuvenated industrial program was
just about to procure communism in the foreseeable future.
Thus, the Soviet brand of socialism was supposed to
unleash an unparalleled productive potential and, in this
way would bring the development of humanity to its conclusion, i.e., communism regardless of the emergence of a
post-industrial order or other possible developments
within decadent capitalist societies.

Although it is understandable why the Soviet industrial scholars who were so enthusiastic about the further
industrial development of the Soviet Union would not pay
much attention to the just emerging post-industrialism,
nevertheless, some attention was directed towards dealing
with this new phenomenon. Post-industrialism, both as a
mode of production and as a body of theory, had already
appeared and hence, posed a problem which the exquisitely
bureaucratized Soviet academic establishment could not
ignore without formulating a proper solution.

In this chapter, we will examine the works of those among Soviet industrial scholars who, amidst the enthusiasm for the mature period of Soviet industrial theory, decided to undertake what was indeed the very ungrateful task of dealing with the newly emerged phenomenon of post-industrialism. During the undertaking of this endeavor, there occurred an instant and categorical division of their effort into two directions. On the one hand, efforts were mounted to address theoretical works on the "second industrial revolution," and on the other hand, there were efforts to assimilate the technological and scientific aspects of the post-industrial mode of production into the body of Soviet industrial theory.

From the outset, the Western theories of the "second industrial revolution" were sharply attacked, and it became obvious that the Soviet industrial theoreticians were not interested in attempting to undertake any kind of dialogue with their Western counterparts. Instead, their apparent goal was to produce a wholesale refutation of the post-industrial theory and in so doing, remove it as promptly as possible from the realm of Soviet academic concern and interest. Thus, the theoretical assault had a very sharp, almost brutal, but very general character. Apparently, there was nothing for Soviet scholars to learn from Western post-industrial theory as the general character of these theories was contradictory to the teachings of Marxism-Leninism and quite simply, they did not deserve any further exploratory treatment.

A good example of such an approach could be found in
I.N. Dvorkin's article, "O Reformistskikh Teoriakh Vtoroi
Promyshlennoi Revolutsii."[1] For Dvorkin, the Western
theories of "the second industrial revolution" were basically
nothing more than the latest assault by revisionists upon
the true Marxian theory--Soviet Marxism-Leninism. According
to him, Western theoreticians of post-industrial society
represented not so much the new and "oncoming" type of
society, but in fact were the intellectual representatives
of the last stage of capitalist development--imperialism,
which in any event was already decadent and dying. Post-
industrial theories, in this view, served as a defense
of the already decadent social system and a rather desperate defense at that. The crisis of imperialist society
which had pushed desperate theoreticians to construct
false theories of the "second industrial revolution" was
made particularly evident by the unparalleled triumph of
the "new" and most progressive type of society--the Soviet
brand of socialism. Thus, post-industrial theories were the
product of a "reformist" imperialism, shaken by the successes of Soviet development:

> As a matter of fact, this crisis is the reflection
> of the failure of reformism when facing on the one
> hand, the great victories of socialism in the USSR
> and the countries of People's Democracy and on
> the other hand, the growing demise of imperialism.
> The reformist economists attempt to overcome this
> crisis by creating a new "social base" for their
> ideology. Therefore, during the post-WWII years,
> the reformist leaders wrote about the necessity

for a 'new spiritual orientation' and ideological
retooling. This is the source of the imperialist
propaganda's present overflow of the new reformist
theories. However, under close scrutiny, those
new theories turn out to be a fusion between the
old Bernsteinian-Kautskian conceptions and the
newer theories of the bourgeois economists. Thus,
Hilferd's old theory of 'organized capitalism'
harmoniously blends with the Keyesian theories of
the regulated input of capital and of 'full
employment'; further, Bernstein's theses of the
global 'growth' of capitalism into socialism
harmoniously blends with the theory of the with-
drawal of the means of production from the
capitalist class. Also, the reformist theory
of the collaboration between the classes unites
the newer bourgeois theories of the 'proletariani-
zation' of the bourgeoisie and the 'bourgeoisation'
of the proletariat.

One of these theories--the theory of the 'second
industrial revolution' which sprang up 5-6 years
ago is very intensively propagated by the bourgeois
economists who hope that it will serve them as the
escape from their ideological 'blind alley,' which
reformism must always be.   2

Dvorkin and other Soviet scholars who were interested in

the refutation of the Western post-industrial theories,

were particularly alarmed by those theories which predict-

ed that the "second industrial revolution" would bring

about a dramatic improvement in the life of the working

masses under the capitalist system. The argument of the

post-industrial theoreticians that the new technology

would greatly diminish the hardship of the labor process

itself, became the object of particularly ferocious cri-

ticism by Soviet writers. The reasons for this are quite

obvious. While Soviet Marxism-Leninism effectively pre-

vented Marx's philosophy from influencing the Soviet

transformation, Marx's passionate critique of the capitalist system was fully incorporated into the very same body of Marxism-Leninism. As long as Marx's critique of laissez faire capitalism could be applied to the further stages of capitalist development, the Soviet theoreticians had no problem. However, the advent of capitalist post-industrial society promised to make many of Marx's predictions of the future development of capitalist society quite obsolete.

Of course, the solution to this problem was not only quite obvious, but already well established by the independent Western Marxists, i.e., Marx's philosophy was considered not so much as untouchable dogma, but rather as a fundamental philosophy which provided its adherents with the general logic of thinking, but did not require them to follow its every detail. Perversely enough, for Soviet Marxism-Leninism which itself was born as a very "liberal" adaptation of Marx's and Lenin's philosophies, the attitude of Western Marxism was anathema. The key to this puzzle is quite simple. If there were a very few limitations which Soviet theory would consider while adapting Marx's philosophy for its uses, these adaptations had to be accomplished in a strictly bureaucratized manner. That is, there had to exist a "social need" as defined by the Soviet political elite, which consequently would provide the academic bureaucracy with the directions for the desired changes in social theory. In turn, the academic milieus were supposed to respond with a vigorous effort, and finally, the new paradigm could emerge. However, once

the new paradigm was finally set and approved by the
elites, Soviet scholars were sternly discouraged from
further work on its fundamentals, and instead, were
supposed to implement the new theory in their work on the
more specialized subjects.

Of course, during the stormy beginnings of the Soviet
society, this just sketched, "ideal model" proved to be a
poor reflection of reality. Even when after the Great
Purge Soviet reality was being increasingly drawn closer
and closer to this ideal, the exceptions consistently
persisted. However, it could be safely argued here that
the fundamental Soviet social theory had developed through
definite "leaps," as compared to Western Marxist theory
which had advanced by the constant unfolding and subsequent clashing of new interpretations of Marx's philosophy.

As a result, nothing was more abhorred by the followers
of Soviet doctrine than the independently developing
schools of Marxian thought. For those "infidels," Soviet
theory aptly spewed forth the highly contemptuous term
"revisionism" which in itself wielded highly discriminating
and disqualifying powers. If a theory were classified
by Soviet scholars as "revisionist," and even if the
most superficial and general analysis had led to such a
conclusion, then, from the point of view of Soviet academia,
it was relegated into a kind of theoretical morgue where
it was buried and forgotten.

Undoubtedly, such would have been the fate of the

post-industrial theories after they had been labeled
"revisionist" by Soviet academe, if it were not for the
fact that they so persistently claimed the emerging post-
industrial society as their base. This claim provoked
Soviet scholars to treat Western post-industrial theories
in a somewhat more diligent manner. The goal of the Soviet
argument was very simple: they wanted to disprove the
claim of Western post-industrial theories that the emerging
post-industrial mode of production causes the structural
transformation of the entire capitalist society. In so
doing, the logic of their argument was based on Marx's
critique of <u>laissez</u> <u>faire</u> capitalism. Further, the
quintessence of their argument was based upon the assumption that Western post-industrial theoreticians were wrong
about the further development of the capitalist system
because their theories were in disagreement with many of
Marx's predictions about the future dynamics of capitalist
society. Of course, there was preciously little room for
any other kind of approach to the post-industrial theories
than that of extreme bias and prejudice, because the newly
reestablished fundamentals of Soviet Marxism-Leninism had
again readapted Marx's critique of the early capitalist
system as the universal means of criticizing capitalist
society regardless of the actual dynamics of its development. Thus, it was not enough to dismiss Western post-
industrial theories as "revisionist," because they derived
from the empirically observable phenomenon of the

post-industrial mode of production. Here, Soviet industrial
scholars decided to apply the canons of Marx's criticism
of the early capitalist system, which were incorporated
into the "scientific body" of Marxism-Leninism, to prove
that these already existing and observable aspects of the
post-industrial mode of production not only did not
advance the capitalist system into the next stage of its
development, but instead, that they actually would bring
upon capitalist society its final demise.

If the prelude to Soviet scholarly criticism of Western
post-industrial theories--the statement of their intrinsically "revisionist" character--had basically a very
schematic, repetitive and virtually ritualistic character,
then the subsequent argument which pointed to the demise of
the capitalist system which was supposed to be caused by
the advent of the new, post-industrial technology, was
pursued in a very vigorous and inventive manner. Thus
Osipov in his _Tekhnika i Obshchestvennyi Progress_[3] which
with time came to be revered by Soviet scholars as a
classic in the field of industrial theory, pointed out
that high-technology and automation "_also_" develop in
advanced capitalist societies--"Great attention is given
to automation with programmed self-management in the USSR,
Czechoslovakia, East Germany, Hungary, and also in the
U.S., England and West Germany."[4] However, the most
immediate consequence of the development of high-technology
in capitalist conditions was considered to be rapidly

growing unemployment:

> In capitalist society, in the conditions of its
> constant chase for the maximizing of profits,
> technological progress and the growth of pro-
> ductivity unavoidably brings the growth of unem-
> ployment. Thus, the introduction of electronic
> machines in Cleveland's factories diminished ten-
> fold the need for the labor force. Presently,
> the prior amount of work is performed by 250
> workers instead of 2500. As a consequence, 2250
> workers became unemployed. In the year 1956,
> the tractor factory in Coventry (England) increased
> its productive output from 7,000 to 10,000
> tractors in one year. In so doing, 3500 workers
> were thrown out of their jobs.
>
> A current publication of the University of
> Chicago states that in 12 cases of automation,
> beginning with a candy factory and concluding
> with railway transportation, the economy of
> the utilization of the labor force increased on
> the average from between 13% to 92%. As a result,
> the firings of the workers in those enterprises
> are reaching, on the average, 63.4% of the labor
> force.
>
> In the contemporary bourgeois society, the workers
> see the danger of unemployment embedded in the
> growth of automation.   5

While at first sight it would appear that this argument

of Soviet industrial scholars was based upon hard empirical

data, instead, it really stemmed from the "knowledge" of the

capitalist system which was derived from the "science" of

Marxism-Leninism. In other words, the argument which

maintained that the post-industrial mode of production

would destroy the capitalist society was only marginally

supported by empirical data, and the backbone of this

argument was derived from the strictly theoretical funda-

mental premises of Marxism-Leninism. Thus, if the Soviet

fundamental theory saw capitalist society as only oriented

towards profit-making, then, of course, the advancement of

the post-industrial technology depended only on its

profitability:

> Under the capitalist regime, the new technology
> is employed only if it gives maximal profits to
> the capitalists. Therefore, the advancement of
> technology does not bring any relief to the
> toiling masses. When some new aspect of advanced
> technology is introduced to the process of
> production, then it drags with itself unemploy-
> ment, and for those who still remain employed,
> it brings the growth of their physical strain. [6]

Capitalism was portrayed by the Soviet industrial

scholars as a brutal, "bare knuckles" system which was

still under the strong influence of Taylorism--"The

influence of Taylor's system is still very strong."[7]

As a consequence, the consideration of the human factor

in industrial production, so hypocritically advertised,

in reality, was completely ignored under capitalism:

"The rulers of the capitalist enterprises and the

engineers in their practical activities really ignore

the so widely advertised 'human factor'."[8] Thus, if some

of the accomplishments of the advanced capitalist methods

of management cannot be ignored, nevertheless,

> In the conditions of capitalism, the great
> accomplishments and successes on the field of
> the organization of production transform them-
> selves into the means of intensifying the
> exploitation of the working masses. [9]

Moreover, the exploitativeness of the relations of

production under capitalism was accompanied by the
inherently exploitative character of the very technique
of the labor process--the machine itself--in capitalist
society: "The machine constantly rushes the worker, it
does not allow him to lower the tempo of work, threatening
him with death and mutilation."[10]

Now, the logic of Marx's critique of early capitalism
could be transplanted and applied to speculations about
the dynamics of contemporary capitalist society. Hence,
under capitalism, the advancement of the post-industrial
mode of production sharpens and deepens the contradictions
between the social classes:

> In the conditions of capitalism, the transformation
> of methods for the management of production causes
> the sharpening of contradictions between management
> and the process of production itself and the
> strengthening of the autocracy. [11]

As a result, the new post-industrial technology caused the
rapid spread of misery among the working masses in capitalist societies:

> After finishing the regular day of labor, millions
> of American workers have to work overtime just to
> assure themselves of the minimum necessary to sur-
> vive. The price for it is being paid by the
> extreme exhaustion of one's strength. [12]

Thus, the predictions for the workers' revolution which was
supposed to annihilate capitalism were gradually being
fulfilled through the rampant spread of unemployment, the
misery of those who still worked and the general atmosphere

of crisis and chaos:

> The entire social production begins to be
> dominated by growing chaos which leads to crises
> when there is a lack of buyers for all these
> riches which are being produced. In this chaos
> and crisis, millions of workers are dying and
> starving because they cannot find employment.   13

In this light, Western post-industrial theoreticians
were not only mistaken and misguided "revisionists" who
as such, should be ignored and their theories discarded,
but rather, they were "wretched"[14] and dangerous hypocrites who wanted to confuse the working classes by
spreading mystifying and harmful beliefs that the supposed
post-industrial society would create the objective conditions necessary for easing the class struggle. Because of
such villainy they deserved as diligent a reprimand as was
in fact being administered to them by the Soviet industrial
theoreticians.

This pattern of critique of Western post-industrial
theories which was so clearly exhibited in Osipov's
classical work was perhaps the only possible way of dealing
with the post-industrail theories for those who seriously
had considered Soviet Marxism-Leninism as their fundamental
theory. Thus, Osipov could hardly be considered as the
originator of this particular theoretical approach, although he presented it so clearly, because other Soviet
theoreticians who had dealt with this problem at the same
time presented a variety of arguments exhibiting virtually
the same type of logic. This logic had been established

in the fundamental body of the "science" of Marxism-
Leninism and, for those who attempted to deal with the
post-industrial theories, Marxism-Leninism provided such
strong directions that their arguments had amazing consistency. Thus, if according to the logic of "scientific"
Marxism-Leninism, any differing theory was just "revisionist" and thus, unworthy of any serious attention, then all
of the work of Soviet scholars who dealt with the Western
post-industrial theories would necessarily be classified
as the product of revisionist minds. However, because
there were reasons to give a somewhat more serious treatment to these particular theories than to other products
of revisionism, those Soviet scholars who forged ahead in
this area had no other choice but to use the tool for
dealing with contemporary capitalist society which had
been provided to them by the fundamental doctrine of
Marxism-Leninism which applied Marx's critique of early
capitalism to the present dynamics of the advanced capitalist system. As a result, Soviet critics of the Western
post-industrial theories began to present arguments of
astounding consistency.

Thus, not only was it Osipov who saw the greed for
profits as the only reason for the introduction of high
technology into the capitalist process of production, but
also Dvorkin who pointed out that:

> While adapting the new technological inventions
> the capitalists are not directed by the social
> needs of their societies, but only by their
> concern for and their interest in profits. The
> introduction of automated technology advances
> there in the conditions of the brutal struggle
> of competition.   15

For Kurakov,[16] on the other hand, the fact that profits
were the only reason for the introduction of advanced
technology into the capitalist process of production
greatly impaired the advancement of this type of technology because a great chunk of these profits was being
parasitically consumed by the capitalists instead of being
reinvested to prompt technological advancement. Further,
El'meyev pointed out that those who follow Western post-
industrial theories forget that profit-making based upon
class-exploitation was still the main feature of
contemporary capitalism:

> The followers of the 'technocratic' theories
> ignore the fact that, under capitalism, special-
> ists in productive technology are being used
> by the bourgeoisie to enlarge their profits
> and to increase the exploitation of the working
> masses, and that the higher echelons of the
> technical intelligentsia live off the growing
> accounts of capitalists' profits.   17

Moreover, Stepanian[18] argued that advanced capitalism
was capable of developing some elements of modern
technology which were so advanced that some Soviet
scholars who were very impressed by these achievements
came to the conclusion that they could be termed true
elements of a communist type of technology.

Nevertheless, those who claimed that the U.S. already possessed the economic base for a communist system could not have been more wrong, because they ignored the inherently profit-seeking and exploitative character of capitalist society which gives its economy an extremely uneven character and which in turn, is incompatible with the communist system. In the work coauthored by Osipov and Maslin,[19] a quotation from Marx on exploitation under the capitalist system was unabashedly applied to the "conditions of imperialism" which enabled the authors to conclude that:

> The contradiction between the mental and manual types of labor takes exceptionally sharp forms in the conditions of imperialist society. It is connected most of all with the appearance and the development of monopolies, and with the further strengthening of capitalist exploitation of the working masses which is being pursued now on the basis of the growth and development of technology and also by bringing to perfection the capitalist technology of production. All powerful 'scientific' systems and technological methods and devices for strengthening the exploitation of the working masses, are most developed in the U.S.. [20]

These examples of the consensus existing among Soviet industrial theoreticians on the subject of the inherent exploitativeness of advanced capitalist society could be multiplied almost ad infinitum.

What is most important here is that this critique of the modern capitalist system was pursued not so much by applying Marx's dialectical method to the analysis of the

dynamics of contemporary capitalism, as was done by
independent Western Marxists, but by the literal application of Marx's critique of the early capitalist system
to the conditions of contemporary capitalism. Such a
crude and simplistic method of analysis resulted in the
painfully inadequate conclusions reached by Soviet
theoreticians. Thus, their literal application of Marxism-
Leninism to the analysis of advanced capitalism resulted
in their creation of a caricature-like image of the
system.

Like every caricature, this caricature too consisted
of some real elements. That is, the advent of post-
industrialism had caused a degree of unemployment, some
of it of a structural nature, which in turn had produced
some degree of relative misery. When Soviet industrial
scholars fed these and other similar data on the problems
of post-industrialism into their "omnipotent computer of
scientific wisdom--Marxism-Leninism," they arrived at the
conclusion that capitalism was facing its ultimate demise.
Had this been a deliberate caricature, then it would have
served the purpose of entertaining Soviet citizens.
However, for many years, it was held to be the unquestionable truth, and given the virtual monopoly which was
enjoyed by Soviet industrial scholars on this subject,
entire generations of the Soviet population were socialized to believe this image of capitalism.

In this situation, not only were the industrial

scholars prevented from gaining any degree of real understanding of the advanced capitalist systems, but so too
were Soviet intellectual elites. Thus, they were seemingly
rendered incapable of noticing the most rudimentary
dynamics of the post-industrial society, e.g., that most
of those who became unemployed because of the advancement
of the post-industrial mode of production eventually
gained employment in the post-industrial society's
rapidly growing "tertiary" sector. They also failed to
notice that "welfare state capitalism" was characterized
by an amazing capacity to neutralize the potential revolutionary zeal of its chronic lumpenproletariat. Finally,
they were unable to notice that even the lumpenproletariat
which is so psychologically and socially deprived, is
deprived materially in only a relative way, because of the
increased productive capacities of post-industrial society.
Thus, the overwhelming majority of the lumpenproletariat in
the advanced capitalist societies materially fares better
than the average worker in the Soviet Union.

The general picture of contemporary capitalism, which
was established in such a peculiar way by the Soviet
scholars, produced amazing consistency in discussions of
much more particular aspects of capitalist development.
For instance, their analysis of the introduction of automation into the process of production in advanced capitalist society showed such consistency. The consensus was
that automation in production processes should produce

catastrophic unemployment in the conditions of advanced capitalist society. Although Soviet scholars had an extremely meager amount of empirical evidence to support such a contention, nevertheless their confidence about the correctness of their conclusions on this subject was unshakeable. This confidence, of course, was not based primarily upon empirical evidence, but on the unswerving belief in the "scientific" truthfulness of the Soviet fundamental theory. Conclusions about the actual dynamics of the advanced capitalist system were really derived from the canons of Marxism-Leninism with only the pretense of empirical evidence. Thus, for Dvorkin and Osipov, automation was supposed to spell disaster for advanced capitalist society despite all the hopes which were being placed upon it by the revisionist theoreticians:

> The automation of production brings a great change into the relationship between the monopoly sector on the one hand, and the small and medium sized non-monopolistic enterprises on the other hand. Some reformist economists pronounced automation as the anchor of rescue for small and middle sized enterprises. In so doing, they base their claims on the supposed evidence that, in many cases, partial automation does not require special losses of capital, and brings a meaningful growth of production, as well as a lowering of the costs of production. On such a basis, the argument was being made that the small and middle sized enterprises which do not have a great amount of capital at their disposal are gaining the upper hand in their competition with the monopoly sector and will squeeze it out.
>
> This argument has nothing in common with real social relations...The automation of production will cause a great increase in the concentration

of capital and will squeeze out the small and
medium sized enterprises and they will be substituted for by the monopoly sector. As a
result, the contradiction between the monopoly sector and the free, competitive market
will grow stronger.

Further, the unquestionable consequence of
automation in the conditions of capitalism
will be the great elimination of workers from
the production process and consequently, the
unyielding growth in unemployment. It would
mean the growth of pressure by unemployed
workers on that part of the working class
which will be still employed and also, it
would mean the strengthening of the tendency
toward the absolute and relative pauperization
of the proletariat. Growing automation would
cause the growth of the volume of production
which in turn would clash with the tight situation of the market. This will produce the
unavoidable strengthening and deepening of the
crisis.   21

On the other hand, Leontyev maintained that the new

post-industrial technology was inherently contradictory to

the capitalist relations of production. Hence, automation

proceeds in these societies in an extremely uneven,

spasmodic manner. Thus, its

deformed development puts fear in the working
masses which is fully justified because the
working class sees, for example, that in the U.S.
this kind of development of automation leads to
the growth of chronic unemployment which con-
demns millions of people to deprivation and
suffering. The introduction of contemporary
computerized technology holds Democles' sword
over the heads of the broad masses of clerks.   22

Similarly, El'meyev did not see anything else resulting

from the automation of the capitalist production process

but the growth of chronic unemployment and misery.[23] Even

the experience which was brought by the passage of a few
years did not change the attitudes of Soviet scholars on
this subject. Thus, Ukraintsev stated in the year 1962
that:

> Capitalism turns technological progress against
> man. Even if contemporary technology could
> serve as the means of domination over nature
> and the means to free the workers from heavy
> physical labor, as a result of its introduction
> in capitalist societies, advanced technology
> turns into the force which enslaves man. Only
> during the last eight years of the introduction
> of automation in the U.S., the number of workers
> who were employed in industry has shrunk by
> better than a million which even further sharp-
> ened chronic unemployment. Presently, on average,
> every ninth worker is unemployed in the
> developed capitalist societies.   24

Moreover, a year later Volkov still maintained that:
Complete and full automation would mean the transformation
of the majority of the population of the capitalist world
into the army of the unemployed."[25]

This consensus among Soviet scholars on the disastrous
consequences of the introduction of advanced technology
into capitalist societies led them to pronounce, as
Osipov had, that the final collapse of the capitalist
system would be caused by the advancement of technology.
Thus, Dvorkin observed in a very authoritative manner
that:

> It is a different matter with contemporary
> capitalism. It finds itself at the end of
> its historical development. Right now, the
> bourgeoisie is no longer the ascending social
> class but the social class in eclipse.

> All of the actual breakthroughs in contem-
> porary technology which occur in contemporary
> capitalist society cannot result in the over-
> throwal of the relations of production without
> abolishing the rule of capital and establishing
> the dictatorship of the proletariat.   26

Ermoliayev, on the other hand, stated that while the
socialist economies vigorously advance toward communism,
"The capitalist system which is shaken to its foundations
by economic crises and by the competitive struggle and by
other obstacles continues its decline."[27]   Other Soviet
theoreticians claimed that the introduction of advanced
technology into the capitalist societies would result in
nothing other than "catastrophe."[28]   For still another
Soviet theoretician, the very advancement of science was
supposed to be the force which would dismantle capitalism:
"Capitalism freezes and obstructs the potentials of
science most of all, therefore, because science is not
only the means to multiply profits, but also, it is the
power which shatters the foundations of capitalist
society."[29]

It is essential to underscore the point that this
consensus among Soviet industrial theoreticians on the
inevitability of the demise of the capitalist system
ensuing from the advancement of technology, was the consequence of their unquestioning belief in the theory of
Marxism-Leninism which resulted in the slavish application
of Marx's critique of the early capitalist system to the
analysis of the contemporary capitalist system. Although

this was very apparent in all of the works in this particular field, rarely was it admitted as openly as was done
by Leontyev. He, as well as the rest of the Soviet
industrial theoreticians, was enraged that many Western
writers argued that the emerging post-industrial mode of
production would lead to the emergence of a new and more
advanced type of capitalist society, the post-industrial
society. He condemned the notion of the "second industrial
revolution" and rejected any suggestion that this development would be as system-transforming as the first industrial revolution, or for that matter as had been every
previous historical revolution in the mode of production.
Thus, he too pronounced authoritatively that such speculations were a-scientific:

> Reasonings could be found in the bourgeois and
> the social-reformist literature that the con-
> temporary technological revolution the contours
> of which are already becoming distinct, has the
> same meaning as mastery over fire, steam, or
> electricity. Such a conclusion is typical of
> the bourgeois mode of thought which is a-
> historical, and therefore is a-scientific and
> anti-scientific. [30]

Because the bourgeois mode of thought is anti-
scientific, then the "already emerging contours of the
technological revolution" lead the bourgeois thinkers to
construct absolutely false theories such as those of the
post-industrial society. If in turn these bourgeois
theories were dismissed as totally useless, then the new
emerging mode of production could be analyzed by the only

available scientific method--that of Marxism-Leninism.

> Thus, on the basis of the scientific analysis
> of the contemporary capitalist reality, Marxism
> discovers in an absolutely irrefutable way and
> reveals those previously unrevealed contradic-
> tions which still remain in the way of the
> development of the productive forces. Those
> contradictions witness to...the historically
> determined demise of the capitalist system. 31

After the final refutation of the bourgeois theories,
Soviet Marxism-Leninism could proceed with the interpretation of the emerging new mode of production, and this
interpretation would only spell doom for the capitalist
system.

What is most intriguing here is the fact that Soviet
industrial scholars did not hesitate to expose their
fundamental doctrine to radical testing. The puzzling
question is why they risked potentially enormous
embarrassment should their theory be proven wrong in the
case of the critique of Western post-industrial theories
and the emerging post-industrial mode of production, both
of which were so extreme and explicit. Even in the late
nineteen-fifties when they were establishing their
analysis of the post-industrial dynamics, the period of
time allotted for the testing of their theories was
extremely short. Moreover, the advancement of the post-
industrial mode of production and the demise of the
capitalist system were supposed to be synchronized. Thus,
to assure themselves and their readers that this synchron-
ization was occurring right from the beginning, they gave

examples of the destructive dynamics which were unleashed in capitalist society throughout the introduction of advanced methods of production. What is most important, the Soviet scholars decisively rejected any possibility of even marginally adjusting their newly emerged fundamental theory to the newest socio-economic dynamics. Of course, there could not exist much temptation to borrow Western Marxism's skillfull adoption of Marx's dialectical method which had offered new and very inventive avenues for criticizing the advanced capitalist system, because this line of thought could conceivably be viewed as being even more critical of Soviet society than of advanced capitalist society.

However, relatively small adjustments in the Soviet fundamental doctrine could have been countenanced which would have prolonged only a little its post-Stalinist "rebirth," but which would have allowed the Soviet scholars to adopt a much more flexible approach to post-industrial developments. Also, without any changes in their fundamental doctrine of Marxism-Leninism, the Soviet theoreticians could have taken a much more cautious stance towards post-industrialism, perhaps by maintaining that the post-industrial mode of production would inevitably destroy the capitalist system in the long run, for example, in the next century. Of course, these academic speculations could be entertained almost ad infinitum. Probably few would disagree that if the fundamental theory of Marxism-Leninism had been treated by Soviet scholars with a grain of salt or an ounce of caution, then, despite its tremendous shortcomings, they could have applied it without any special embarrassment. Many societies throughout history have relied upon as questionable and frequently inconsistent theories as Soviet Marxism-Leninism without particularly dramatic consequences for their policy-making. However, the whole difference in this instance stemmed from the staunchness and the zeal with which Soviet scholars professed acceptance of their fundamental doctrine.

As a result, another perversely ironic situation emerged. The doctrine of Marxism-Leninism which resulted from the "common sense" combination of Marx's and Lenin's philosophies with the reality produced by the Bolshevik revolution, now pushed the Soviet scholars into a pattern of thought which could hardly be described as exhibiting common sense. By the late nineteen-fifties, the uncritical and feverish belief in Marxism-Leninism had led the Soviet scholars into a virtual state of euphoria. They began to proclaim that communism would be achieved in the Soviet Union by the late nineteen-seventies and by approximately the same date, capitalism would finally crumble. These were not empty speculations, but in their own way, were very precise and well documented. Thus, the way to communism was supposed to lead through the last phase of socialism. The construction of this last phase of socialism, according to the Soviet scholars, had finally been undertaken. There was nothing vague or unclear about the last phase of socialism. According to Marxism-Leninism, it was supposed to be the society of material abundance. Literally understood, it was supposed to become a true "consumer paradise," to such an extent that the oversaturation with material goods would, in turn, alter human nature so much so that the new communist man would emerge, thus fulfilling one of the fundamental requirements of communism. The other variables, i.e., the social ownership of the means of production and the advanced superstructure already existed.

Thus, Soviet scholars, as well as the rest of the entire society, thought that only one step, only one serious effort divided them from communism. This step appeared to have a very simple and well-defined direction--simply to develop further the society's productive powers. This task had appeared for them as something of a strictly economic nature and considering the success that the Soviet economy had enjoyed thus far, it somehow had appeared to the Soviet theoreticians as a task substantially less difficult than those already achieved by Soviet society. On the other hand, the capitalist system's path of destruction was also described in a manner no less precise and clear than the Soviet advance into communism. Most importantly, there emerged a very characteristic harmony between the fundamental canons of Marxism-Leninism and reality as it was

perceived by Soviet scholars. All the pieces in the
"historical puzzle" of the development of humanity seemed
to fall right into place. Merely twenty years was supposed
to divide the Soviet Union from achieving communism and
during the same twenty years, the post industrial mode
of production, which according to the "revisionist"
scholars was supposed to advance the capitalist system,
actually was going to destroy it.

Thus, after such a diligent castigation, the Soviet
industrial scholars could finally discard the Western
post-industrial theories, never to pay them attention
again. However, there was a fundamental and crucial
element of post-industrialism which not only was not going
to be disregarded by the Soviet scholars, but vice versa
was going to be thoroughly absorbed and assimilated in its
entirety. It was the last "missing link," the last piece
of the historical puzzle--post industrial technology
itself.

The Soviet industrial theoreticians have dealt with
post-industrial technology in the most characteristic way.
First of all, according to them, the entire notion of post-
industrialism was already convincingly and finally refuted
as the anti-scientific fantasy of revisionist minds. That
which the mistaken Western scholars identified as the
post-industrial mode of production, in reality was nothing
else but advanced industrial technology. However, there
actually was a grain of truth in the mistaken speculations

of the "sick minds of the bourgeois revisionists" regarding the second industrial revolution. Of course, for the Soviet scholars the idea that this was another revolution in the mode of production comparable to the first industrial revolution and this that it would lead to the emergence of a more advanced type of capitalist society was labeled a complete absurdity.

On the other hand, the Soviet scholars also noticed a revolutionary element in the emerging new technology, but this revolutionary aspect was not in any sense comparable to the scope of the system-transforming industrial revolution. Instead, the revolutionary character of the emerging new technology existed only in its strictly technological dimension. According to the Soviet fundamental social theory of Marxism-Leninism, the industrial system was the avenue which was supposed to lead Soviet society, already possessing an advanced social superstructure, to communism. Post-industrial society did not fit anywhere into this scheme. However, post-industrial technology was classified as the technology of the last, the most advanced stage of industrial development. It had a revolutionary character only in the strictly narrowly technological sense, i.e., it was not supposed to alter in any special way the general character of the Soviet industrial system. Vice versa, the emerging new technology absorbed by the Soviet industrial system was supposed to contribute to the already awaited "productive outburst"

which was supposed to bring communism to Soviet society.
Hence, the emerging new technology which was understood
by the Soviet theoreticians as a strictly technological
aspect of the advanced industrial system was, in this way,
identified as the "missing link" between the Soviet
social system and communist society. The "puzzle" of the
particular character of the future advancement of humanity
was thus solved by the Soviet industrial scholars who
were armed with the fundamental science of Marxism-Leninism.

The first task which faced the Soviet scholars in their
dealings with the emerging new technology was to conceptualize it properly and in this way, to remove any
possible connotations with the theories of the "second
industrial revolution." Thus, the emergence of the new
technology was conceptualized as the "Scientific and Technological Revolution" (the STR), which instantly cast
it in the desired narrow and strictly technological dimension. This term came later to symbolize the fully
developed Soviet post-industrial theory, but in the first
period after its formulation it had meant something
diametrically opposed to that, i.e., it symbolized the
refutation of the Western post-industrial theories and
the apparently final triumph of Soviet socialist industrialization, a term which had evolved over time. This
evolution was, of course, caused by the evolution of
Soviet post-industrial theory itself, which, as we saw,
started as the total negation of post-industrialism and

as a continuation of classical industrial theory, but with
time experienced a dramatic transformation. However,
throughout the remainder of this chapter, we will focus
on the analysis of the concept of the Scientific and
Technological Revolution as it was used initially.

Among the first of those Soviet industrial theoreticians who began to master the new concept of the Scientific
and Technological Revolution were: Danilevskii,[32]
Stepanian,[33] and Osipov.[34] Especially in Stepanian's
work, the conceptualization of the Scientific and Technological Revolution (the STR) as the latest stage of
industrial development, which had been glorified by Soviet
scholars, was handled in a particularly clear and concise
way:

> [The communist] form of the property of the
> means of production is inextricably connected
> with the most advanced material-technological
> social base which is capable of subjugating the
> powerful forces of nature and satisfying the
> steadily growing material and spiritual needs
> of the masses. The heavily industrialized
> productive sector which is collectivised,
> mechanized and automated, which is also based
> on the utilization of electric, atomic, solar
> and other types of energy, and relies upon the
> utilization of all the new achievements of
> technology and science, creates this kind of
> social base. This kind of material-technological
> social base of the communist formation is being
> gradually created and developed in our country.
>
> The development of the productive forces of the
> contemporary society has laid the foundation for
> the new scientific-technological revolution which
> is in accordance with the communist formation.
> Human pre-history was indeed characterized by
> the discovery and the consequent mastery of fire.
> The genuine (sic) history of mankind is character-
> ized by the discovery and the full utilization of

nuclear energy and other new energy sources. 35

Osipov, too, had found the development of nuclear energy
as one of the main features of the STR and, in particular,
he claimed that nuclear energy would vitally contribute to
the further growth of humanity.[36] However, Osipov's most
meaningful and pioneering contribution to the discussion
of the STR was its extremely narrow technological conceptualization. Thus, for him, the Scientific and Technological Revolution was

> the revolution in the management of the tech-
> nological processes. The control panel is the
> main component of the machine. The machine
> operator sits at the central control panel and
> with one movement of his hand, he directs the
> work of the productive plants which are not
> situated in the field of his sight, but they
> are situated tens, and sometimes even hundreds
> of kilometers away. The control apparatus works
> instantaneously and, as a result, in distant
> industrial plants, tasks are performed which
> were dictated by the man at the control panel.
> With this transformation toward managerial
> control panels, the communal character of the
> technological processes which are utilized
> during the performance of a whole panorama of
> different tasks begins to be more and more
> clearly outlined. In this way, humanity will
> again return to the 'universal' tools of labor,
> but now, on a higher base. [37]

Also for Dvorkin the oncoming Scientific and Technological
Revolution meant just the technological improvement of
the already existing industrial system.

Although, right from the very beginning of the discussion on this subject, a very explicit consensus existed
amongst the Soviet scholars that the STR was nothing other

than the continuation of the basic industrial process in
the Soviet Union, a number of years passed before the door
was finally "slammed" on this issue, that is, before the
final conclusion was derived from the "science" of Marxism-
Leninism. Koval'tchyk placed the final "dot over the i"
in his article which prestigiously opened the particular
edition of Voprosy Filosofii.[38] Here, Koval'tchyk made a
very powerful point. Starting his argument, he pointed
out that a truly radical historical transformation had
occurred only after the socialist revolution when the
capitalist system was abolished and the socialist system
was beginning to be built. According to him, this was
the point in human history when the contradiction between
the old and the new was at its apex. On the other hand,
the transformation from the socialist system to the communist system would have no similarities with this earlier
revolutionary transformation because little real antagonism existed between the two systems. Thus, Koval'tchyk
proceeded to explain that:

> However, a totally different degree, a different
> depth of the negation between essential qualities
> is characteristic for the process of the construc-
> tion of communism. In the very basic foundations
> of the essential qualities of the socialist
> system, there are such aspects, such moments,
> which by the way are not of a secondary charac-
> ter, which, to the same extent will be inherent
> for the new social system--communism. In this
> case, there will be a different correlation
> between the negation and the continuation,
> between the liquidation of the inherent qualities
> and their preservation [than was the case of the
> transformation from the capitalist system to

148

the socialist system]* During the process of
the gradual transformation toward the higher phase
of the communist system, the negation will not
be applied to all of the foundations of the
essential qualities of the socialist system, but
only to some if its separate aspects and its
separate elements which are characteristic of
the socialist system as the lower phase of
communism. Therefore, this is why, according to
the very nature of this process in this given
instance, the very essence of the socialist system
cannot be annihilated or liquidated, because,
inherently, the socialist system is also a
communist system, although not sufficiently
developed or economically mature.

Socialism and communism--in principle these are
not different socio-economic formations, but
two phases of the same communist formation,
which, despite their qualitative differences,
have much in common from the point of view of
their crucial and fundamental features. The
social ownership of the means of production,
the relations of production, the mutual self-
help and cooperation of the working people who
are freed from exploitation, the domination of
Marxist-Leninist ideology as well as the whole
range of other crucial foundations of the social
system are as much characteristic of socialism
as of communism.
                                          39

To so argue was to openly make the claim that the contem-

porary social base of Soviet society, which rested upon

its industrial system, was nearly sufficient to serve as

the social base for communist society. One did not need to

resort to elaborate deduction to see that some strictly

technological improvements in the Soviet industrial system

would suffice to carry the society into the communist

system, because, not only had Koval'tchyk stated this

explicitly, but as well, he had placed the entire weight

of Marxism-Leninism behind this conclusion. He

*my explanation, V.Z.

interpreted Lenin's theory on this particular subject and

concluded that:

> Finally, V.I. Lenin taught that the difference
> between the socialist and the communist systems
> is in the degree of the maturity of the new social
> system [i.e., of the socialist system]* and most
> of all, in the degree of the development of the
> very same (for both of the social systems)* mode
> of production...In those very circumstances is
> rooted the cause of the fact that the transfor-
> mation towards the communist system excludes the
> necessity of upheaval in the economic system of
> the society. In this given case and in the most
> general view, we are witnessing the process of a
> gradual transformation from the socialist to the
> communist system, without any giant leaps.   40

Moreover, to even further strengthen his argument,

Koval'Tchyk extensively quoted Khrushchev on this issue,

thus presenting a conclusion that truly expressed both

the scholarly as well as the political consensus on this

issue. Thus, after the diligent refutation of Western

post-industrial theories, the Soviet theoretical inter-

pretation of the emerging new mode of production--the

theory of Scientific and Technological Revolution--finally

became incorporated into the body of the Soviet industrial

theory as an integral part. Koval'tchyk's work served

to finally "cap" what constituted a long and intensive

effort by many Soviet industrial scholars. Most importantly,

there appeared to have emerged an enduring consensus among

Soviet industrial theoreticians on this issue.

The consensus view that the emerging new technology

*my explanation, V.Z.

formed an integral part of the basic Soviet <u>industrial</u>
development harmonized extremely well with the consensus
among Soviet scholars which maintained that the technology
of the period of the Scientific and Technological Revolution creates a most obvious and clear avenue leading
towards the establishment of communism.

What is apparent, however, is that the consensus on the
capacity for technological breakthroughs to achieve
communism in the Soviet Union was typical for Soviet
socialist theory long before the post-industrial mode of
production and the Western post-industrial theory had begun
to emerge. The belief in technological discoveries as the
panaceum for problems surrounding the communist transformation was deeply rooted in the theory of the Soviet
type of socialism beginning with Lenin's own philosophy.
Later, throughout the nineteen-twenties, thirties and
forties, this belief coincided with Soviet self-assuredness
regarding the absolute perfection of their political
system in particular, as well as of the virtual perfection of the Soviet social superstructure in general.
If the Soviet social superstructure was already perfect,
i.e., if it were already tantamount to the superstructure
of a communist society, and if the Soviet social base
enjoyed the healthy communist foundations of the social
ownership of the means of production, then what was really
preventing this society from finally achieving communism?
Apparently, only a technological breakthrough. Considering

the fact that Soviet society was "planting the saplings" for this technological breakthrough right from the time of the Revolution by creating the monumental infrastructure of technological education and research centers, the emergence of the new technology was interpreted through the theory of the STR as the "full blooming and bearing of fruit of these trees."

Now, at the end of the nineteen-fifties, Soviet society was just supposed to patiently await the time when these technological "fruits" would ripen and would be ready to be harvested, thus achieving the communist system. Because of this traditional approach to prognoses concerning future development, Soviet industrial theoreticians maintained the unshakeable position that the Scientific and Technological Revolution constituted the rapid and most immediate avenue toward communism. Thus, Stepanian concluded that:

> The new law which emerges in the conditions of the Scientific and Technological Revolution gives an opportunity to a whole range of countries, of course in accordance with their economic system, to enter, almost in the same time into the epoch of communism. [41]

On the other hand, Dvorkin categorized the STR as the uniquely socialist industrial revolution which was going to result in the creation of the communist system.[42] For Leontyev, it was "beyond discussion that the contemporary technological revolution reveals gigantic new perspectives and possibilities, which only a few decades ago would have appeared as fantasy."[43] Of course, this new technological potential has nothing in common with fantasy and will be utilized to facilitate the communist transformation because:

> The construction of socialism and communism
> is distinguished by a splendid combination
> of a very sober calculation of the real con-
> ditions of fulfilling current economic goals
> with a correct and predictive estimation of the
> perspectives of economic and technological
> development.   [44]

Other Soviet theoreticians such as Fedoseyev chose the avenue of extreme specificity in discussing this subject. He states that:

> Under the leadership of the party, the Soviet
> nation pursues the task of creating the
> material-technological base of communism. This
> task will be practically achieved in the near
> future--during the next twenty years. In the
> next ten years, an enormous program to create
> the material-technological base of communism
> will be implemented. Of course, in so doing,
> the entire economy will not be transformed into
> one based upon the utilization of atomic and
> hydrogen energy during the next ten or twenty
> years. The material-technological base of the
> higher phase of social development bursts forth
> from the buds of the interrelated processes of
> technological progress which are already visible
> in the present conditions of the transformation
> towards communism. Those interrelated processes
> are: electrification and complex mechanization,
> automation and chemization of the process of
> production. However, these are augmented further
> by utilization of atomic energy and of isotopes
> in the national economy.
>
> All possible utilization and development of the
> achievements of contemporary science and tech-
> nology assures the real possibility of creating

the material-technological base for the communist
system in the outlined period.   45

For Marakhov, too, the further advancement of the contemporary Scientific and Technological Revolution was the
surest way of achieving the communist system.[46] Also,
Gapotchka spared no effort to demonstrate theoretically
that the Soviet scholars' consensus on this issue was
deeply rooted in the scientific theory of Marxism-Leninism.
In a very clear statement of this argument: he maintained
that:

> V.I. Lenin stressed many times that without
> the newest technology and without the new scien-
> tific discoveries the communist system will be
> impossible to construct.   47

Meleshchenko, similarly confident that the further advancement of the STR would lead to communism called upon Soviet
industrial theoreticians to advance the detailed theory of
its particular aspects.[48] Expressing the same overall
theme, Rachkov concluded his classical work by pointing
out that the only way to communism leads through rapid and
bold advancements in high-technology.[49]

Another subject addressed by the theory of the Scientific and Technological Revolution which greatly preoccupied
the Soviet industrial scholars was the influence of the
STR, or if we prefer, the influence of the post-industrial
mode of production upon the relations of production in
general, and upon the individual worker in particular. In
response to this question, Soviet industrial scholars

proceeded with the construction of a theoretical outline

of the relations of production of early communist society.

Predictably enough, the discussion on this particular

subject did not bring to the surface anything that would

change the general attitude of the Soviet industrial

theoreticians to the STR, or anything which could chal-

lenge their unshakeable belief that the STR was the

panaceum for all of the possible problems of industrial

society. However, the more detailed discussion of this

subject threw a very interesting and revealing light on

the thinking of the Soviet scholars, and, most of all,

touched a very important problem which later came to

haunt the already fully developed Soviet post-industrial

theory. Thus, Naidenov, while discussing one of the

crucial aspects of the post-industrial mode of production--

automation--found it to be particularly beneficial for

workers in the conditions of a socialist society. According

to his analysis, the introduction of an automated process

of production would, generally speaking, broaden the intel-

lectual horizons of a worker:

> A worker's range of activities greatly expands
> with the advancement of the level of mechani-
> zation and automation. The opportunity emerges
> for him to perform a few functions at the same
> time, and to operate a few machines at the same
> time. In turn, the system of enlarged circle of
> workers' functions gradually grows into the system
> of operating the automated lines and complexes.
>
> In the automated process of production, a worker
> does not have to specialize in performing one-
> sided and narrow functions. To the contrary, he

has to understand and serve an entire range of
the fields of the industrial process. To a great
extent, the universalization of the labor process
will occur instead of narrow specialization.   50

Moreover, the intensive automation of the process of produc-

tion, according to Naidenov, was supposed to greatly

increase the general culture of labor. In particular, the

collective character of the labor process was supposed to

be enhanced thanks to the growth of automation. Finally,

the further technological advancement of the process of

production was supposed to result in an increasingly more

social character of production. However, he pointed out

that the advancement of automation would bring with itself

some problems and shortcomings. Hence, Naidenov main-

tained that:

It must be admitted, that the process of automation has a complex character. At a certain
level of its development, it exhibits some contradictory tendencies. Thus, those facts which
show that in some cases the process of automation
results in increased monotony in the worker's
life and makes his work more simplistic, cannot
be disregarded. In automated production, some
groups of workers perform only the primitive tasks
which do not require any special qualifications...
Therefore, there sometimes appear speculations
that automation leads not to the broadening of
workers' functions, but to their narrowing.   51

However, Naidenov took very strong exception to this kind

of speculation. He answered such pessimism by stating

that the problems and contradictions of automation were

nothing but very temporary problems stemming from its

developmental period. The further advancement and

maturation of automation was supposed to inherently solve
these problems:

> Complex production equipment utilizing mechani-
> zation and automation removes any remnants of
> unskilled and monotonous manual labor.   52

On the other hand, Nikolaev argued that the development of
high technology would totally fulfill Marx's vision of a
communist society. Hence, all the differences between the
village and the city and manual and mental labor would
disappear. In turn, an entirely new, communist division
of labor would emerge which would be based on an incredible
growth of all kinds of personal liberties and where all
choices concerning one's career would be made according to
one's personality and talents.

> Communism will create previously unknown condi-
> tions for the harmonious development of the
> human personality. The tremendous development
> of the highly mechanized and automated production
> process will dramatically shorten labor time for
> members of communist society, and also it will
> assure every man of enough leisure time for pur-
> suing arts, sciences, literature, sports, tourism,
> etc.   53

In other quarters, a very interesting argument was made
which maintained that communism could not be achieved
without high-technology because man as a worker is full of
weaknesses and he really cannot work in a truly rational
and efficient manner. However, if the highly technological machine is the only avenue towards communism, the
future system was not envisioned as a society run by

robots, because the highly productive and efficient machinery was still supposed to be dominated by the human element.[54]

Finally, the definitive consensus on this subject was reached. The Soviet industrial scholars began to simultaneously proclaim that the Scientific and Technological Revolution would solve all of those problems of the communist transformation which had preoccupied them throughout history. Thus, the STR was supposed to finally eliminate all of the vices of the socialist labor process, such as for example, hard and monotonous labor or still persisting differences between mental and manual types of labor, while it would lead the communist transformation of the entire society.[55] The Soviet industrial theoreticians strenuously maintained that the communist system was already within reach and that the development of this process was well under way. The Scientific and Technological Revolution was already successfully transforming human labor and leading toward communism. Thus, it could be already stated that:

> In our society, labor is an important source
> of human happiness, the source of joyous
> creativity, the sphere of the fullest ful-
> fillment of human talents, abilities and
> propensities.   [56]

Generally, Soviet industrial theoreticians' early responses to the Western theories of post-industrial society, as well as their practice of the theoretical

incorporation of the elements of the post-industrial mode
of production into the Soviet industrial theory--the theory
of the Scientific and Technological Revolution--were only
small components of the general, post-Stalinist wave of
enthusiasm which had overwhelmed Soviet society in those
years. Although this powerful wave of enthusiasm served
as another mighty tool for social mobilization there, we
would not suggest even for a moment that the Soviet
industrial theoreticians were just another milieu of
hypocritical propaganda artists who cynically raised the
hopes of the masses in order to exploit them. Instead, a
more judicious conclusion would suggest that the Soviet
industrial scholars were an extremely sincere group of
zealots who staunchly believed in the science of Marxism-
Leninism. If they were hypocrites, then, undoubtedly,
they would not have established fifteen or twenty year
time limits for the fulfillment of their scientific predictions, but rather they would have maintained that
communism would be reached in the much more distant future--
perhaps sometime during the next century or centuries.

Of course, without any doubt, very substantial tangible
social benefits accrued from this post-Stalinist wave of
enthusiasm which was not limited only to the political and
the academic elites, but was intensively spread by the
communication and education media among the rest of Soviet
society. However, there remained the possibility that
those scientific theories were wrong, that no meaningful

transformation would occur in the Soviet context during
the next twenty years. In such a case, the collapse of
this wave of enthusiasm would contribute to the spread
of cynicism and nihilism among Soviet citizens. In
Soviet-style socialism, the social atmosphere generated is
one that promises to youth increasing benefits yielded by
the new model of development and to parents, psychological
satisfaction stemming from the knowledge that their own
sacrifices will contribute to the happiness of their chil-
dren. The dangers of widespread cynicism in this type of
society cannot be easily dismissed. This is a society
where the patriotism and the pride of the population were
among the main reasons for its very survival, where the system
of moral incentives for the workers was one of the main
reasons for its initial economic success and where even the
abundance of police and security forces was insufficient to
protect property which to an overwhelming degree has a social
or state character. Of course, Soviet society is emanantly
capable of dealing with individual or isolated group out-
bursts of cynicism, or alienated hooliganism. However,
widespread passive cynicism, nihilism and alienation would
in the long run hurt vital aspects of social life, such
as labor productivity, respect for social property, obedience
to law and patriotism, to name but a few.

There can be no doubt now that the scientific dreams
which predicted the achievement of communist society in

the Soviet Union by the end of the nienteen-seventies,
collapsed sometime during the second half of the nineteen-
sixties together with the wave of post-Stalinist
enthusiasm which had spawned it. It may be argued with
more than modest assurance that the Soviet Union presently
is no closer to communism than it was at the end of the
nineteen-fifties. Thus, in the following chapters we
will examine how Soviet industrial thought has adapted
itself to the collapse of its scientific dreams and how
it combatted the negative effects stemming from the
collapse of those dreams.

ENDNOTES

1. I.N. Dvorkin, "O Reformistskikh Teoriakh 'Vtoroi Promyshlennoi Revoliutsii'" Voprosy Filosofii, 12, (1958); see also: S.G. Strumlin, Na Putiakh Postroenia Kommunizma, (Moscow: 1959, Gospolitizdat); S.G. Strumlin, Problemy Sotsializma i Kommunizma (Moscow Ekonomizdat, 1961), S.V. Shukhadrin, Osnovy Istorii Tekhniki, (Moscow: Izdatel'stvo Akademii Nauk SSSR, 1961).

2. Dvorkin, ibid., p. 34.

3. G. V. Osipov, Teknika i Obstchestvennyi Progress, (Moscow: Izdatel'stvo Akademii Nauk SSSR, 1959).

4. Ibid., p. 20.

5. Ibid., p. 67.

6. Ibid., p. 63.

7. Ibid., p. 52.

8. Ibid.

9. Ibid., p. 57.

10. Ibid., p. 64.

11. Ibid., p. 59.

12. Ibid., p. 62.

13. Ibid., p. 57.

14. Ibid., p. 61.

15. Dvorkin, Ibid., p. 43.

16. I.G. Kurakov, "Razvitie Tekhniki na Baze Sotsializma, Voprosy Filosofii," No. 1, (1959), (15-31).

17. V.Ia. El'meyev, "Vozrastanie Roli Umstvennogo Truda v Razvitii Proizvoditel'nykh Sil Sotsializma", Voprosy Filosofii, No. 8, (1959), (33-44), p. 41.

18. Ts.A. Stepanian, "Osnovnyie Zakonomernostii Stroitel'stva Kommunizma," Voprosy Filosofii, No. 12, (1961), (3-11).

19. A.N. Maslin, G.V. Osipov, "Soedinenie Umstvennogo
    i Fizicheskogo' Truda--Odna iz Vazhneishikh Zadach
    Stroitel'stva Kommunizma," Voprosy Filosofii, No. 12,
    (1961), (12-23).

20. Ibid., p. 14.

21. Dvorkin, ibid., p. 52.

22. L.A. Leont'iev, "O Nekotorykh Osobennostiakh Sozdania
    Material no-Tekhnicheskoi Bazy Kommunizma," Voprosy
    Filosofii, No. 6, (1959), (3-16), pp. 14-15.

23. V.Ia. El'meev, "Vozrastanie Roli Umstvennogo Truda
    v Razvitii Proizvoditel'nykh Sil Sotsializma,"
    Voprosy Filosofii, 8, (1959).

24. B.S. Ukraintsev, "Novyi Tip Obshchestvennogo Progressa,
    Voprosy Filosofii," No. 1, (1962), (13-24), pp. 16-17.

25. G.N. Volkov, "Avtomatizatsia--Novyi Istoricheskii
    Etap v Razvitii Tekhniki," Voprosy Filosofii, No. 6,
    (1964), (15-26), p. 21.

26. Dvorkin, ibid., p. 49.

27. Voprosy Teorii Sotsialisticheskogo Obshchestva,
    (Moscow:Izdatel'stvo VPSH i AON pri CK KPCC, 1960),
    p. i4.

28. G.N. Filonov, "K Voprosu of Vsestoronnemu Razvitii
    Lichnostii," in Voprosy Teorii Sotsialisticheskogo
    Obstchestva, ibid., pp. 188-189.

29. P.A. Rachkov, Nauka i Obshchestviennyi Progress,
    (Moscow: Izdatel'stvo Moskovskogo Universiteta, 1963).
    p. 176.

30. Leot'iev, ibid., p. 7.

31. Ibid., p. 14.

32. V. Danilevskii, "Na Poroge Novoi Nauchno-Tekhniches-
    koi Revoliutsii," Neva, No. 4, (1956).

33. Ts.A. Stepanian, "Oktiabrskaia Revoliutsia i Stanov-
    lenie Kommunisticheskoi Formatsii," Voprosy Filosofii,
    No. 10, (1958), (19-36).

34. Osipov, ibid.

35. Stepanian, ibid., p. 26.

36. Osipov, ibid., p. 22.

37. Ibid., pp. 37-38.

38. A.S. Koval'chyk, "O Kharaktere Perekhoda k Vysshei
     Faze Kommunizma," Voprosy Filosofii, No. 11, (1961),
     (16-28).

39. Ibid., p. 18.

40. Ibid., pp. 18-19.

41. Stepanian, ibid., p. 34.

42. Dvorkin, ibid., p. 53.

43. Leontiev, ibid., p. 7.

44. Ibid., p. 8.

45. P.N. Fedoseiev, "Dialektika Pererastania Sotsializma
     v Kommunism," Voprosy Filosofii, No. 10, (1961),
     (28-42), p. 33.

46. V.G. Marakhov, "Nauka i Proizvodstvo," Voprosy
     Filosofii, No. 10, (1963), (3-12).

47. P.N. Gapochka , "Leninskii Podkhod KPSS k Resheniu
     Glavnoi Problemy Stroitel'stva Kommunizma,"
     Voprosy Filosofii, No. 4, (1964), (16-26).

48. Iu.S. Meleshchenko, "Teknika i Zakonomernostii
     ieio Razvitia," Voprosy Filosofii, No. 10, (1965),
     (3-13), p. 3.

49. Rachkov, ibid., pp. 277-310.

50. V.S. Naidenov, "Sotsial'no-Ekonomicheskiie Posledstvia
     Teknicheskogo Progressa pri Sotsializme," Voprosy
     Filosofii, No. 8, (1960), (14-24), p. 16.

51. Ibid., p. 17.

52. Ibid.

53. V.V. Nikolaev, "O Razvitii Sotsialisticheskoi
     Gosudarstvennosti v Kommunisticheskoe Obschestvennoe
     Samoupravlenie," Voprosy Filosofii, No. 12, (1960),
     (25-37), pp. 25-26.

54. D.A. Oshanin, D.Iu. Panov, "Chelovek v Avtomatiches-
     kikh Sistemakh Upravlenia," Voprosy Filosofii,
     No. 5, (1961), (47-57), especially page 48.

164

55. See especially:
A.P. Kudrashov, <u>Sovremennaia Nauchno-Tekhnicheskaia Revoliutsia i ee Osobennosti</u>, (Moscow: Mysl', 1965);

Ie.L. Manevitch, "O Likvitdatsii Razlichii Mezhdu Umstvennym i Fizicheskim Trudom v Period Razernutogo Stroitel'stva Kommunizma," <u>Voprosy Filosofii</u>, No. 9, (1961) (15-28);

and, M.I. Bobneva, "Tekhnika i Chelovek," <u>Voprosy Filosofii</u>, No. 10, (1961);

and, A.N. Leontiev, D.Iu. Panov. "Psikhologia Cheloveka i Tekhnicheskii Progress," <u>Voprosy Filosofii</u>, No. 8, (1962), (50-65);

and, G.P. Kozlova, Z.I. Fainburg, "Izmenenie Kharaktera Truda i Vsestoronnee Razvitie Cheloveka," <u>Voprosy Filosofii</u>, No. 3, (1963), (55-62);

and, V.A. Sukhomlinskii, "Trud--Osnova Vsestoronnego Razvitia Cheloveka," <u>Voprosy Filosofii</u>, No. 4, (1963), (54-63).

56. Sukhomlinskii, ibid., p. 55.

Chapter V

The Quasi-Pluralistic Theory, (1966-1973)

Even the most cynical critics of Soviet politics probably would admit that the work done in Soviet social theory during the late nineteen-fifties and the early nineteen-sixties not only exuded unabashed enthusiasm but also proved to be the most original and creative product of the development of social theory there. If for a moment we put to the side the scholarly craftsmanship and refined academic jargon of Soviet industrial scholars, we find in their writings echoes of the early enthusiasm of the Bolshevik leaders, especially Lenin and Bukharin, and we notice definite traces of the robust and feverish artistic enthusiasm such as that exhibited in the works of Mayakovskii.

The emotional-artistic enthusiasm of the post-Stalinist period converged with and complemented scholarly confidence which had been spawned by the conclusions of the industrial theory which was firmly based on the rejuvenated doctrine of Marxism-Leninism. A communist system was supposed to be achieved in the Soviet Union during the next twenty years and in a manner which was supposed to be very analogous to the way in which the country had become industrialized, i.e., the communist system was supposed to be erected there according to the rhythm of the five-years plans, in the same way as the steel mills and the tractor factories had been constructed earlier. If the brisk industrialization of the Soviet Union provided a solid base and enhanced the Soviet brand of socialism, the equally speedy development of high-technology was supposed to establish, in no time at all, a society of material abundance which would naturally transform Soviet society into a communist society. Thus, during that period of time, Soviet academic and social elites and with them, the entire society, came to believe that they had in fact mastered history and that the final and perfect form of social organization was soon to be erected there. This belief led Soviet society into a state of euphoria which was profusely expressed in the works of the industrial scholars. However, this enthusiastic anticipation was extremely short-lived. Its own demise was caused by its fundamental "strength," i.e., the fact that the argument that communist society was expected to come to fruition during the nearest twenty years, had caused a wave of heightened expectations to grip Soviet society which clearly could not be satisfied.

If communism was supposed to be achieved in the early nineteen-eighties, then the decisive steps leading toward it were supposed to be taken during the nineteen-sixties. Elements of communist society were supposed to burgeon during the nineteen-sixties in the Soviet Union in the same way in which steel mills had proliferated during the industrialization drive. However, after the road to communism had been laid out theoretically and fully endorsed by the political elites, in practice, not only did the Soviet Union not take its first steps towards communism, but _vice versa_, its rate of industrial growth began to steadily decrease throughout the nineteen-sixties. As a

result, in the second half of the nineteen-sixties, it
became brutally obvious that the entire construction of
Soviet industrial theory had been only a magnificent castle
built upon melting ice. Consequently, the great wave of
enthusiasm subsided and Soviet social theory in general,
and industrial theory in particular, faced the need of
still another transformation.

The first and most obvious conclusion to be reached
would be that if the Soviet industrial theory depended so
intimately upon the fundamental theory of the Soviet brand
of socialism--the theory of Marxism-Leninism--then its
failure had to constitute a severe blow to the fundamental
theory. As a result, it could be suggested that the transformation of Soviet industrial theory had to be accompanied
by the transformation of the fundamental doctrine as well.
However, during the late nineteen-sixties and early nineteen-
seventies, when Soviet industrial theory was fundamentally
transformed yet another time, this time the basic doctrine
of Marxism-Leninism was left alone. Although Soviet literature, scholarly and otherwise, never addressed the problem
of why this time the fundamental doctrine of Marxism-
Leninism was left untouched when its derivatives were being
subjected to serious changes (in some cases being almost
completely liberated from this dependence), we may
nevertheless surmise the reasons for this approach.
Marxism-Leninism and its derivatives had completely failed
as a blueprint for a speedy and effective transformation

toward a communist system. However, even if Soviet society were not a system which was progressing dynamically toward communism, nevertheless it still was a militarily and industrially powerful society which sustained a gigantic bureaucratic apparatus that was more capable of maintaining socio-economic stability, even if this meant inertia for many sectors of the society. The bureaucratized elites of the Soviet Union had no reason to undertake drastic changes in the basic social doctrine as long as the society remained relatively stable and the collapse of the wave of optimism did not result in the growth of instability. Thus, from the point of view of Soviet elites the solution was a very simple one. Precise discussions of the transformation toward communism simply ceased. In effect, communism came to be discussed by the elites in a very vague and non-committal way, so it would be impossible to deduce whether it was supposed to be achieved after an additional twenty years or perhaps after an additional two hundred years. If Marxism-Leninism had failed to serve as an effective guide toward achieving a communist system, it still was perfectly suitable for the Soviet brand of socialism even though it had not proved to be that social system which dynamically progressed toward communism. Hence, even if the post-Stalinist reality of Soviet society was not evolving into communism, still its elites were satisfied with it to the extent that it was a stable and functioning system, and no further plans for fundamental socio-economic changes were being pondered.

Consequently, the fundamental doctrine of Marxism-Leninism
was left untouched.

The case of industrial theory in particular was a much
different one. Here, the changes had to be undertaken
because given that the notion of a communist system had
been consigned to a vague and distant future, post-industrial
developments were apparently rooted in place for at least
the foreseeable future. They could not be discarded any more
than had been the case during the period of frenzied enthusiasm, thus making a serious revamping of Soviet industrial
theory essential. Now, some permanent form of Soviet
post-industrial theory had to be created which naturally
posed a great challenge to the Soviet industrial scholars.

First of all, this undertaking was a matter requiring
great subtlety and delicacy. While the fundamental doctrine
would remain untouched, its derivative (Soviet industrial
theory) would be subjected to radical revisions. Since an
open challenge of the old theory would inevitably lead to a
challenge of Marxism-Leninism itself, the new theory had
to maintain at least the appearance of continuity. This
chapter will investigate how such intellectual acrobatics
were in fact performed by the Soviet industrial scholars
in their quest to achieve some kind of theoretical response
to the emergence of post-industrial society.

The first step in maintaining the continuity was taken
in abiding by the concept of the Scientific and Technological Revolution (STR). Of course, the unbounded enthusiasm

of the earlier conception of the STR was inappropriate given

the requirements of the new situation. Initially, the theory

of the Scientific and Technological Revolution had been

formulated as a negation of Western post-industrial theories

and, in the view of Soviet industrial scholars, it was

supposed to conceptualize the last pre-communist stage in

the industrial development of the advanced socialist system.

Now, however, the theory was supposed to conceptualize the

Soviet version of a post-industrial society as one of

relative permanence without clear and precise references to

any speedy achievement of communist society. Moreover, it

was necessary to integrate into the body of Soviet post-

industrial theory some of the achievements of Western post-

industrial theories which had been categorically rejected

only a few years earlier. As a consequence, the theory of

the Scientific and Technological Revolution took on a meaning

which was something quite different from its initial charac-

ter. However, a mechanism was developed which prevented

the shifting theory of the STR from appearing to have changed

so radically that the fundamental integrity of the theory of

Marxism-Leninism might be endangered: the development of

the theory of the Scientific and Technological Revolution

proceeded in two quite different directions. One wing of

this theory began to assimilate some of the experience of

Western post-industrial theories and synthesize it with its

own conceptualization of post-industrial dynamics which

were very loosely and vaguely connected with the fundamental doctrine of Marxism-Leninism. At the same time another wing emerged which clung to an extremely conservative inter- pretation of post-industrial developments and maintained a strict relationship with Marxism-Leninism. However, the conservative wing of the theory of the Scientific and Tech- nological Revolution differed dramatically from the earlier period which had been marked by enthusiasm; the conservative wing entirely lacked this early enthusiastic bent. Although it was closely connected and dependent upon the doctrine of Marxism-Leninism, there was no discussion of any soon-to- emerge communist society.

Those who might have expected that such a diversity of views as expressed by Soviet industrial scholars would now undoubtedly put Soviet industrial theory into a state of schism and confrontation (as had happened during the Great Industrial Debate of the nineteen-twenties) could not have been more wrong. Astoundingly enough, no confrontation emerged between these two dramatically different wings of STR theory and, in fact, they coexisted harmoniously. Thus, the Soviet academicians had invented still another and very ingenious form of intellectual pluralism wherein contradic- tory doctrines were tolerated. Coexistence was achieved by having the two wings ignore each other. The theoreticians of each wing contained their activities within the secluded worlds of their own paradigms without admitting the existence of the opposite side. There were no noisy critical disputes, no confrontations and no intellectual exchanges between the two sides. Each paradigm existed independently of the other one and without paying even the slightest attention to the other school of thought. Moreover, the intellectual balance between these two paradigms was paralleled by a roughly equal attention to each strain in Soviet publications. All in all, this strange and inconsistent form which developed within Soviet industrial theory sent a very clear message to its students: a post-industrial theory had to be developed despite its inconsistency with the fundamental doctrine of Marxism-Leninism, which in turn, despite this challenge, would remain the ruling philosophy of the Soviet Union. Regardless of how bizarre this unlikely combination might seem to us, in the very specific conditions of Soviet society, the bifurcated theory developed undisturbed and could effectively perform its social function.

In the peculiar conditions of Soviet culture, the recognition of a theory depended first of all on its consistency with the dominant doctrine of Marxism-Leninism. If a theory happened to contradict some of the canons of Marxism-Leninism, then it had to be discarded and replaced by a more harmonious theory even if this were internally inconsistent or even bizarre. On this score, the emergence of these two wings of Soviet industrial theory was undoubtedly less bizarre than the earlier discarding of and forbidding of the study of genetics, or the substitution of Lysenkoite and Michurinist quackery for scientific agrobiology, or the Marxist-Leninist impositions which were made on the

theoretical physicists. Relatively, the industrial scholars'
achievements were substantial. Those who decided to experiment with the creation of a Soviet brand of post-industrial
theory had a relatively free hand to do so and could go so
far as to even assimilate some aspects of Western post-
industrial theories, as long as they did not openly challenge
the fundamental doctrine of Marxism-Leninism. The emergence
of the conservative wing served not as a constraint upon
their everyday activities, but rather as a general reminder
of the systemic limitations imposed on their activities or,
to put it differently, it was a general outline of the
theoretical "bottom line." Considering the fact that the
effective harmony of Soviet post-industrial theory was
achieved by combining the play of two completely different
instruments, it appears to be appropriate to divide this
chapter into two subparts where each of the two wings of the
Soviet theory of the STR will be discussed separately. Only
after we fully understand their separate identities, can we
analyze their combined effect upon Soviet society.

The Liberal Wing

The year 1966 brought the first attempts to establish
the new style, not by some new generation of Soviet scholars
which began experimenting with post-industrial theory, but
rather by the very same academic establishment which during
the earlier period had actively participated in the creation
of the hyper-optimistic paradigm of Soviet industrial theory

and which had categorically rejected the concept of post-industrial society. Thus, I.G. Kurakov, the distinguished theorist of the earlier period, in 1966 produced two articles,[1] which while maintaining some token elements of the old style (for example, the first article began by glorifying the party and its leader Brezhnev as those who lead the nation by directing it toward its grandiose social goals),[2] nonetheless, by their very substance began to initiate the new style of analysis. For instance, we find a very serious and precise comparison of the utilization of high technology in the U.S. and the USSR.[3] Moreover, Kurakov called for the imitation of Western achievements in advancing high technology especially by creating special centers for the development of science and technology.[4] Such recommendations constituted a very far cry indeed from the times when Kurakov and his colleagues sternly maintained that the development and application of high technology in the conditions of capitalist society spell only total disaster and collapse for this type of society.

Illustrative of how seriously these two articles were taken was the fact that each of them opened the respective editions of the most prestigious Soviet journal in the field of social sciences--Voprosy Filosofii. Further, in the same year, another distinguished veteran of theoretical endeavors, P.A. Rachkov, utilized the theoretical experience of Western social theories to advance his own argument as seriously and respectfully as had Kurakov.[5] The new credence being lent

by Soviet industrial scholars to Western theories was
further enhanced by the work of a rising star in this field--
Dzh.M. Gvishiani (who also happened to be Kosygin's son-
in-law). In the standard vein, he, too, paid token homage
to the earlier traditions of Soviet industrial theory by
stating that:

> The antagonistic contradictions of the capitalist
> method of production and the contradictions
> between the basic classes of bourgeois society
> which are conditioned by them, unavoidably find
> their reflection in the growing incapability of
> the capitalist system of management to rationally
> utilize the productive forces of their societies.
>
> The socialist system removes these obstacles
> which are being created in the conditions of the
> capitalist system, by rationally solving the prob-
> lems of management. Moreover, the socialist system
> brings the forms and methods of management into
> accordance with the needs of the contemporary large
> scale system of production. The socialist relations
> of production are set on the very same base on
> which are also formulated the new, progressive
> principles of management which answer the needs of
> the rapidly developing system of production.
> V.I. Lenin discovered the principle of democratic
> centralism in the management of the national
> economy, that is, the principle of combining
> centralized leadership with the broad participa-
> tion of the workers in the organization of the
> process of production. This Leninist principle
> expresses the objective needs of the contemporary
> system of large scale social production, needs
> which could be only satisfied in the conditions
> of socialism.   6

Such praise notwithstanding, Gvishiani nevertheless concludes that Soviet society must strive to achieve a new
complex and scientific system of management[7] which had
already been achieved in the U.S. process of production.

The new factors [of the developing forces of
production--V.Z.] require new solutions to the
problems of management. The quantitative
changes in the field of information cause qualitative changes in the field of the organization
of production. So, in connection with the introduction of IBM computers into the administrative
practice of American corporations, right now,
it is possible to observe the tendency to re-
centralization the process of production there
(for example, General Motors, Standard Oil
Company of New Jersey). [8]

Still, in the same year, N.S. Bud'ko glorified the

role of IBM computers as the "thinking machines" and in so

doing, he conceptualized them as part of the forces of

production and based his theoretical speculations on a

variety of Western theories on this subject.[9] Interestingly

enough, in Bud'ko's article there was not even a trace of

a distinction made regarding the role of the computer in the

conditions of different socio-economic systems.

In this way, some examples taken from the advanced

capitalist societies and some elements of Western post-

industrial theories were introduced to the body of Soviet

industrial theory. At the outset, it was neither known nor

clearly established by Soviet scholars what the role of

differing elements of Western post-industrial theories

would be in the body of Soviet theory. Instead, only general

phenomena could be established and identified while their

particular dimensions were left to be worked out by a

trial and error method of borrowing from Western experience.[10]

The following years brought an intensive effort on

the part of those Soviet scholars who experimented with the

liberal approach to post-industrial concepts, to establish
more precise boundaries for their emerging paradigm.[11]
Hence, the year 1967 brought a collective work (which in
the specific conditions of Soviet culture always carries
with itself some added weight)--<u>Sovremennaia</u> <u>Nauchno-</u>
<u>Tekhnicheskaia</u> <u>Revoliutsia</u>[12]--which began to selectively
reconceptualize the theory of the Scientific and Technological Revolution. Although this work to some extent leaned
on the traditions of the early STR theory,[13] the enthusiasm
of the preceeding period had already entirely vanished.
The Scientific and Technological Revolution was still
vaguely conceptualized as the dialectically natural vehicle
which was supposed to transform the Soviet brand of socialism
into a communist system.

> Thus, the transformation into communism as the
> transformation into the second phase of the socio-
> economic formation presupposes the radical trans-
> formation of the technical system, technological
> methods of production, division of labor, the
> human place in the productive processes--and as
> the consequence of all that--the transformation
> of the social structure of the society. The
> sphere of production of the communist society...
> might have only a complex-automated character.
> This kind of production might be established as
> a result of a new productive revolution for which
> the precondition is surely the contemporary
> Scientific and Technological Revolution.   14

However, it should be noted that the STR was no longer
being perceived as the sole vehicle of this transformation,
but instead was seen as only the initial phase of it.
Following the completion of the period of the STR, other
future stages of this productive revolution were supposed

to follow and as a result, communism would be achieved. However, it was obvious that these future (post-present Scientific and Technological Revolution) phases of the general productive revolution were the song of the distant future, so they were not even discussed by the authors of the work in question. Of course, the time span in which the communist system was supposed to be achieved in the Soviet Union ceased to be discussed. Instead, a body of very abstract theory began to emerge, theory which was deliberately very vague on this subject.

Of course, from the point of view of the Soviet theory of Marxism-Leninism, the historical importance of the Scientific and Technological Revolution, in this way, had greatly diminished. The future, vague and unspecified productive revolution was supposed to lead to communism and the STR was only an initial stage of it. Thus, the future productive revolution was strictly connected with and determined by the character of the socialist system, and, it could only occur in the socialist system:

> The second obligatory condition [the first con-
> dition being the prior successful completion
> of the present Scientific and Technological
> Revolution--V.Z.] for the new productive revo-
> lution is the presence of the socialist
> relations of production, i.e., the new pro-
> ductive revolution can only originate in the
> socialist countries; in the countries where
> the socialist revolution has already occurred. 15

However, the present Scientific and Technological Revolution was now dwarfed by the historical prominence of the new

productive revolution which in turn was supposed to occur
in such a distant future time that Soviet theoreticians
conceptualized it in a most vague manner. Hence, now
the STR was reduced to the role of only the strictly technological precondition for the future system-transforming
productive revolution and, as such, it could clearly be
defined by the Soviet scholars as not being determined by
the character of the social system: "The Scientific and
Technological Revolution might also originate in capitalist
countries."[16]

The difference on this point between the early STR
theory and its new phase of development is crucial. During
the early, optimistic period of the development of Soviet
industrial theory, the Scientific and Technological Revolution itself was to serve as the vehicle for the transformation of the Soviet brand of socialism into a full
fledged communist society within twenty years. According
to the early theory it was possible for the STR to originate within the context of advanced capitalism, but in
that situation, as the lone motor of progress in human
society, it would find itself in antinomous conditions
and as a consequence, it would totally destroy the capitalist system during an equivalent period of time. Now,
however, the STR, i.e., post-industrial society, would be
conceptualized by Soviet scholars as one which could also
be advanced in capitalist societies without bringing about
their almost instantaneous demise. Of course, it was

clearly pointed out that in the conditions of capitalism
the Scientific and Technological Revolution would experience
a much more problematic course of development than in the
conditions of socialist society by, for example, aggravat-
ing unemployment, and intensifying the class struggle.[17]
Importantly, these problems were not now viewed as having
a fatal quality in terms of the ultimate viability of
these systems.

In this way, the path was cleared for the selective
and prudent utilization by the new Soviet theory of the
Scientific and Technological Revolution of both the practical experience of Western post-industrial societies, as
well as the experience of Western post-industrial theories.
Thus, the Sovremennaia Nauchno-Tekhnicheskaia Revoliutsia
itself admiringly pointed out the success of computerization in advanced capitalist societies.[18] In the same vein,
while discussing the advancement of automation, it drew its
examples equally from the experience of the U.S. and the
USSR.[19] Moreover, Western post-industrial theories which
were so savagely criticised during the early optimistic
period, had now begun to be analyzed and critiqued in a much
milder manner.[20]

It can hardly be argued that the publication of any
single work such as the Sovremennaia Nauchno-Tekhnicheskaia
Revoliutsia or Gvishiani's article constituted the actual
breakthrough which spawned the emergence of the entire
paradigm of the liberal wing of Soviet industrial theory.

During this period a number of works exhibiting a similar
approach had appeared. For example, in 1967, Panov drew
most of his argument supporting the advancement of computerization from Western publications on this subject.[21] In
the same year, while analyzing the interrelationship between
science and production, Volkov supported his argument by
harmoniously intertwining elements of Western and Soviet
theories from this field.[22]

In the next year, the paradigm appeared to be putting
down even deeper roots. In his effort to offer a precise
definition of the Scientific and Technological Revolution,
Meleshchenko drew heavily from both Soviet and Western
theories. However, most importantly, he used as a foundation for his synthesis both the traditional maxims derived
from the science of Marxism-Leninism as well as Kuhn's
theory of the revolutionary transformation from one paradigm
to another one.[23] On the other hand, the veteran of Soviet
industrial theory, Kurakov, opted for brutal specificity
and precision. He coldly presented data in drawing a comparison between the U.S. and the USSR which pointed out
that the Soviet economy was roughly half the size of the
U.S. economy and that the indicators of the rate of their
respective industrial growth did not differ as greatly as
they had in earlier years. Most importantly, while discussing a number of aspects of the growth of the Scientific
and Technological Revolution, he pointed to the specific
post-industrial achievements of the U.S. which, according to

him, should simply be imitated in the USSR:

> After 1965, U.S. expenditures for the education
> and preparation of the cadres [in the sphere of
> production, V.Z.] rose dramatically. The same
> growth in expenditures was also undertaken in
> the sphere of scientific research. According to
> the prognoses of some U.S. economists, these
> expenditures might reach approximately 20% of
> national income around the year 1980. Obviously,
> growth in these types of expenditures must be
> assured in our country, because in the contemporary
> epoch of the Scientific and Technological Revolu-
> tion, that country which possesses the proper
> productive cadres as well as the greater pro-
> ductive skills will dominate social production.   24

Elsewhere, while discussing the ratio between the growth of

productivity and workers' income with its relation to the

return on invested capital, he again found the example of

the most developed capitalist societies as worthy of imi-

tation by the Soviet economy:

> After the Second World War, scientific-technological
> progress was utilized for that purpose [the return
> on invested capital, V.Z.] By utilizing the newest
> aspects of the productive technology, it was
> possible there not only to reduce the lowering
> of the returns on invested capital, but also, in
> many cases, to raise the rate of return on
> investment. Therefore, during the last 10 years,
> one may note that in some Western countries the
> tempo of the growth of the productivity of labor
> was outstripped by the tempo of the growth of
> workers' pay.
>
> In light of these observations concerning
> the interrelationship between technological
> knowledge, the productivity of labor and workers'
> pay, we may conclude that there must be further
> important improvements made in the economic
> policy of the development of socialist production.
> Now, principal attention must be concentrated not
> on a simple increase in productive capital and
> its investment, but instead, on scientific-
> technological progress, on the improved utiliza-
> tion of productive resources, on the most

> effective method for creating the material-
> technological base of communism and rapid improve-
> ment in workers' social conditions.   25

Like most of the representatives of this style, Kurakov, too,

attempted to soften the impact of his work. At the end of

his work, he added, in a somewhat artificial manner, certain

statements which obviously were drawn from the experience

of the early optimistic period in the development of Soviet

industrial theory. He argued that the reason for the

scientific-technological advancement of capitalist societies

was their competitive struggle with socialist countries. In

this point, the readers were assured that despite all the

changes, the socialist system was still superior to the

capitalist one and that all was well:

> In the new conditions, the socialist system
> has been strengthened not weakened in its
> superiority over the capitalist system. Our
> prospects in this competition with capitalism
> have improved substantially.   26

However, these assurances lacked their earlier enthusiasm

and precision, and instead seem quite mechanically done and

even ritualistic.

Another writer, Petrov, went even further than Kurakov.

His discussion of the problems of the organization of

science in the epoch of the Scientific and Technological

Revolution was based almost exclusively upon Western

literature and especially upon U.S. publications which

dealt with this subject.[27] The *de rigeur* token assurances

regarding the superiority of the socialist system were

absent, and instead, Petrov found inspiration for the conclusion of his work in Plato's writings from which he quoted.[28] Still another theoretician, Shkaratan, found the example of the U.S. as the most helpful in his discussion of the dynamics of advanced industrial society:

> In all the industrially developed countries, both capitalist and socialist, the proportion of workers which are preoccupied with a predominantly physical type of labor is diminishing. Thus, in 1965, more than half (62%) of the hired labor in the U.S. were engaged in the performance of some aspect of non-physical labor. Of course, the social origins, the social connections, as well as the social situation of these people had changed. [29]

Most importantly, for him the U.S. was clearly the pathbreaker in this field for both the socialist and capitalist societies. This kind of thinking would be clearly unimaginable only a few years earlier. At that time, certain technological achievements within advanced capitalist societies could be recognized, but their conceptualization as those which were supposed to bring to their societies progressive social changes would be unthinkable. Even Shkaratan's feeble assurance that:

> In the conditions of socialist society, this process is much more complex because it is only one of many aspects of the dynamic of the transformation from the class society into the classless one. [30]

was nothing but a faint, vague and unconvincing echo from the old days of unabashed enthusiasm.

The general climate of Soviet industrial theory was
changing so much that even those, who like G.N. Volkov,
attempted to maintain the old enthusiastic style, ultimately
arrived at conclusions of a quite different nature indeed.
Volkov's massive work Sotsiologia Nauki, Markov's Nauchno
Tekhnicheskaia Revolutsia and Kamaev's Sovremannaia
Nauchno-Tekhnicheskaia Revolutsia[31] were undoubted designed
as optimistic works which, by maintaining many features
of the earlier period, were supposed to demonstrate that
all was still well. Their argument, heavily dependent
upon the works of Marx and Lenin, was to persuade readers
that the Soviet Union was a dynamically developing society
which was intrinsically far superior to its paramount com-
petitor, the U.S. However, the nature of its superiority
was now seen in terms of its social potential for further
development rather than its actual superiority in the area
of scientific and technological progress. Moreover, they
avoided any more specific discussion of the time span within
which these great progressive dynamics were to result in the
transformation of Soviet society into communism.

The most important feature of these works which placed
them in the new liberal school of Soviet theory was empirical
comparison between the U.S. and the Soviet Union. Under-
standably, they endeavored to present empirical evidence
which would cast Soviet development in the most positive
and optimistic light. Yet, they also presented data on
U.S. development which clearly illustrated the dynamic

development of the post-industrial mode of production there.
Even if the robust development of U.S. post-industrial
technology did not endanger such development in the Soviet
Union, it greatly undermined hopes for a speedy disintegration
of the capitalist system. Thus, if these works were
deliberately vague on the subject of the Soviet transformation
into a communist system, they left no doubt that they
thought that the advanced capitalist system was here to
stay. Consequently, the old argument of the early enthusiastic period in the development of Soviet industrial theory
which pointed out the phenomena which were supposed to
spell the doom of advanced capitalist society had now been
reformulated. The revised theory suggested now that the
advancement of science and technology would simply cause
problems for advanced capitalist societies rather than
leading to their collapse. For example, it was stressed in
these works that the capitalist system neglects education
in those areas which do not affect its profit making;[32] it
makes a fetish of science;[33] the achievements of technology
frequently (during the early enthusiastic period they always)
worsen the living conditions of the working masses;[34] science
under the capitalist system is being militarized;[35] and, of
course:

> The development of the Scientific and Technolo-
> gical Revolution and the growth of state-
> monopolistic interventions and regulations of
> the economy, which cause the obvious growth of
> production, unavoidably lead to the greater
> generalization of the process of production in
> the imperialist states, to the sharpening and

188

deepening of class contradictions and to serious
changes in the distribution of social and political forces.   36

All of those negative phenomena were supposed to bear
witness not so much to the speedy disintegration of the
advanced capitalist system, because it was now here to stay,
but instead, to highlight its moral turpitude and socially
abominable character--to make it appear utterly repugnant.
The moral repulsiveness of advanced capitalist societies did
not prevent Volkov from calling for Soviet imitation of the
technological and organizational achievements of advanced
capitalism. For instance, he pointed to the efficient
utilization of highly skilled manpower in U.S. corporations,
where the waste of time of such skilled employees would be
considered an unaffordable luxury. He bitterly reminded the
reader that this type of "luxury" is the common practice of
Soviet enterprises:

> Unfortunately, we quite frequently allow this
> kind of luxury to flourish. We also allow
> ourselves to indulge in the 'luxury' of the
> irrational distribution of scientific workers. 37

Volkov was able to call for the imitation of the scientific
and organizational achievements of the morally repugnant
advanced capitalist societies because he, as well as all
Soviet industrial scholars, stood very firmly on the principle that science and technology have a politically
neutral and classless character:

> Science in its very nature has an international
> and classless character. Scientific objectivity,
> scientific theory do not know national and
> political borders;... it is truly the achievement
> of all humanity. The international character of
> science reveals itself also in that, for the
> achievement of the multitude of research goals
> in the cosmos, in the oceans and in the biosphere,
> the effort of all of humanity is needed.   38

Altogether, the abandonment of precise discussion of

the timetable according to which the communist system was

supposed to be achieved in the Soviet Union, coupled with

the implicit admission that advanced capitalist systems

were here to stay despite their intrinsic moral turpitude,

as well as clear calls for the imitation of the achievements

of the sciences and the organization of production in

advanced capitalist systems and the analysis and criticism

of Western post-industrial theories which was much more

extensive when compared to the early enthusiastic period,

were the most clear and consistent characteristics of the

newly emerged liberal wing of Soviet industrial theory.

However, a definitive position on the issue of whether the

post-industrial society emerges as an historical and syste-

matic phenomenon in the advancement of humanity was never

clearly taken by Soviet scholars who, in so doing, left the

general and abstract problem of post-industrial society

unresolved. While shying away from the immediate resolu-

tion of this general issue, Soviet scholars nevertheless

did initiate a very cautious and selective examination of

some aspects of the general issue.

Zhemianov, for example, attacked those aspects of

Western post-industrial theories which argue that post-industrial society witnesses the "bourgeoisification" and "middle classization" of its working class. He argued that:

> The authors of the concept of the 'bourgeoisiza-tion' of the working class attempt to base their arguments upon concrete reality. Presently however, they also attempt to strengthen their theories by attempting to find some support in the works of Marx and Engels. However, the diligent analysis of the fundamental assumptions of these theories convinces us of their intrin-sically superficial approaches to a variety of complex and controversial phenomena, and their conscious perversion of the very essence and the very meaning of contemporary events which are occurring in the socio-political life of the developed capitalist countries. [39]

This seemingly modest statement carried within itself explosive content. However humbly, Zhemianov in effect broke away from one of the most fundamental traditions of the very science of Marxixm-Leninism itself. Marxism-Leninism incorporated Marx's critique of early, laissez-faire capitalist society as the universal means of criti-cizing every type of capitalist society which evolved later. Thus, Marxism-Leninism opted for a simplifying and even-tually simplistic vision of dynamically developing capitalist societies. Now, some of the Soviet industrial theoreti-cians like Zhemianov began to abandon this fundamental vision of capitalist systems, but in a quiet, matter-of-fact way. After the generations-long tradition of hatefully rejecting the ideas of those like Gramsci, Lukacs and other Western Marxists who viewed capitalist systems as very

complex and dynamically developing, some Soviet theoreticians began to chastise Western post-industrial theories
for their supposed lack of attention to the complexity of
advanced capitalist societies.

Although this kind of behavior exhibited tremendous
hypocrisy, there was apparently little else that could
have been done by Soviet scholars of the liberal wing of
industrial theory who were interested in experimenting with
the concept of post-industrial society. Another readjust-
ment of the fundamental doctrine of Marxism-Leninism was
outside of the question, as it would involve dangerous
tinkering with a Pandorra's box, which could cause unfore-
seeable consequences. Thus, the only possible option was
the one which was in fact pursued by the Soviet industrial
scholars, that is, the science of Marxism-Leninism would
have to be treated as an elastic bag which actually could
accommodate almost every possible theoretical stand,
regardless of whether these stands might conflict with
elements of Marxism-Leninism.

The key to maintaining the apparent integrity of
Soviet theory was indeed quite simple. The problem was
solved by the extreme tolerance practiced by Soviet
scholars in the internal relationships of their paradigm.
Thus, those who represented mutually exclusive approaches
to the same problems simply ignored each other. This
pluralism contained within the paradigm of the science of
Marxism-Leninism served the increasingly diversified needs

of Soviet society. If the maintenance of social harmony
and cooperation was still the paramount goal of Soviet
society, the increasing multitude of different political
and academic groups in a socio-economically advanced
Soviet Union required a certain degree of theoretical
pluralism.

However, the bottom line was always defined by the
need to maintain the appearance of fundamental harmony
between the variety of theoretical approaches. Thus, while
an implicit admission of the existence of post-industrial
society as well as theoretical discussion of some of its
aspects could be tolerated within the body of the Soviet
Marxist-Leninist paradigm, an open and clear admission
that the post-industrial order constituted a new stage
in the development of the capitalist formation would require
fundamental adjustments in the theory of Marxism-Leninism,
which was a political impossibility.

As a result, theorists such as Zhemianov could
acknowledge the new situation of the working classes in
post-industrial societies, all the while maintaining the
Marxist-Leninist line of criticism of the advanced capitalist society:

> The authors of the concept which we are consider-
> ing [the concept of the bourgeoisization of
> the working class in post-industrial societies,
> V.Z.] define as this process the improvement
> in the material conditions of the working
> class' socio-economic situation, which, of
> course, was caused by the successes achieved
> by this class in its class struggle, as well
> as by the satisfaction of the objective growth

of the material needs. These new material
needs stem from the complex conditions of the
reproduction of labor power in the conditions
of the contemporary Scientific and Technological Revolution and connected with it the
growth of the value of the labor force. In
the developed capitalist societies, improvement in the material situation of the workers
does not mean their 'bourgeoisization.'
Instead, it has been naturally conditioned
by the changing arrangement of class forces,
as well as by the actions of the workers
themselves. By contrast, advocates of the
'bourgeoisization' thesis viewed these new
phenomena as the basis of the transformation
of the objective situation of the working
class, which was supposed to bring it closer
to the bourgeoisie.   40

Another author who acknowledged the growing complexity
and social density of advanced capitalist society and thus
implicitly acknowledged the emergence of the post-industrial
system was Moiseenko who dealt only with one very specific
aspect of post-industrial society--the new role of the technical intelligentsia. However, the approach to this problem
exhibited in his work bore witness to the growing influence
of the new liberal wing of Soviet industrial theory. Observe
his analysis of the new role played in post-industrial
society by the technical intelligentsia:

In the contemporary socio-economic practice of
bourgeois society in the conditions of the
Scientific and Technological Revolution,
scientists and engineers are...transforming
themselves into hired workers. The border
between these workers and other groups of
the working masses becomes even more ephemeral.
Together with the broadening of their socio-
economic practice, scientists and engineers,
as the hired workers of capital, had become
more like the proletariat in terms of their
economic situation, their socio-political

interests, and their socio-economic maturity.
On the other hand, in the context of the Scientific and Technological Revolution, the role of
the intellectual factor in production has grown
in importance to the extent that workers now
must 'possess a rudimentary though systematic
mastery of a whole range of the most advanced
technological skills;' thus, bringing their
spiritual-professional development closer to the
position of the scientific-engineering intelligentsia.
                                                41

If Moiseenko found the labor force in advanced capitalist

society to be drastically different from that vision of

capitalism which had been traditionally perpetuated by

the science of Marxism-Leninism, at the same time, he

made a clear effort to reconcile the newly emerging tech-

nocratic character of the labor force in post-industrial

society with the Marxist-Leninist concept of class struggle:

The majority of scientists and engineers,
according to their objective social situation,
are the potential allies of the revolutionary
and transforming social classes. By changing
their place and role in the society, that is,
by transforming them into a hired labor force,
contemporary capitalism creates those objective
conditions which facilitate the transformation
of the scientific-engineering intelligentsia
into an active, functional branch of the
revolutionary forces.
                                                42

On the other hand, Khmylev, who of course sternly

maintained the superiority of the socialist system over the

capitalist system, nonetheless observed that advanced

capitalism was in fact dynamically developing:

In the conditions of contemporary state-monopoly
capitalism, the growth of the process of the
generalization of labor moves at a rapid pace.

> The Scientific and Technological Revolution
> is the powerful catalyst of this process.   43

Karkhin too admitted that a new form of capitalist

society had emerged, and in discussing this new form of

capitalism he moved far afield from the simplistic concep-

tual schemes of scientific Marxism-Leninism:

> The statization of science and its subordination
> to the state-monopolistic apparata of the
> capitalist countries occurred in a most pro-
> nounced way at the end of the nineteen-fifties
> and at the beginning of the nineteen-sixties,.
> when major developments in science and tech-
> nology were taking place. The managing apparata
> of the bourgeois states did everything possible
> to help the largest monopolies to make the best
> use of the objective growth of science and tech-
> nology.   44

Even if the simplistic vision of the capitalist system as

traditionally presented by Marxism-Leninism was abandoned

by Kharkin, he together with the rest of the Soviet theore-

ticians still clearly maintained the fundamental logical

premise of Leninism, that is that technology had a neutral

character with regard to social systems. Thus, post-

industrial technology was not intertwined with the advanced

capitalist system which had spawned it, but instead it had

grown somehow in an objective manner.

A particular impression was made, however, on Kharkin

by the newest capitalist methods of management. Although,

in his work, he took the position that Soviet society had

gained absolute mastery over the methods of management, he

could not hide his fascination with the newest achievements

of advanced capitalist societies:

> The new methods of the state-monopolistic
> intervention into the economy are developing
> along two lines: <u>programming</u>--the preparation
> of 'plans' at the general social level, as well
> as the preparation of programs and projects
> connected with large-scale budgeting and state
> credits, and prognostication, the analysis of
> the perspectives of the future social and pro-
> ductive transformations, as well as examina-
> tion of the potential future utilization of
> technological achievements undertaken to advance
> the interests of the large monopolies. Analogous
> works in programming and prognostication now
> form part of state policy in all capitalist
> societies although the concrete forms and methods
> differ in different quarters. 45

As was the case with other representatives of the

liberal wing, Karkhin skillfully intertwined the identifi-

cation of technological and managerial achievements in

advanced capitalism with the radical critique and the

fundamental and indignant rejection of that social system.

Basically, there was nothing substantially new about this

rejection and critique of the capitalist system when com-

pared to the earlier optimistic period. What was missing

however, was the early period's enthusiasm and standard

discussion of the time frame of capitalism's predicted

demise. Instead the old litany of social miseries alleged

to have been caused by the Scientific and Technological

Revolution in the advanced capitalist societies was now

only half-heartedly, and quite mechanically repeated. The

STR was supposed to greatly sharpen class conflict,

cause the growth of unemployment, as well as the growth of

mental fatigue among those who still would remain employed,

would provoke the growth of crime, and so forth. It was
evident that the liberal wing did not have the slightest
intention of challenging either the science of Marxism-
Leninism, or the fundamental theoretical inheritance of
the earlier enthusiastic period, or even the conservative
wing of Soviet industrial theory. Moreover, the conceptualization of the STR remained the same. Thus, every
Soviet industrial scholar, whether of the liberal or
conservative wing of the industrial theory identified the
phenomenon of the STR in strictly technological categories
with special stress upon the features of high technology.
The only difference in defining the STR now was made by
the objective growth of computerization as well as other
high technology features which were only beginning to
develop during the earlier optimistic period.

In sum, the main feature of the liberal wing of the
industrial theory was its dualistic quality. On the one
hand, the new socio-economic features of advanced capitalist society were admitted and identified, and thus the
emergence of a post-industrial capitalist order was implicitly admitted. On the other hand, instead of adjusting
fundamental Soviet theory to this new phenomenon, the
liberal wing still maintained however mechanically and
half-heartedly, the old canons of classical scientific
Marxism-Leninism. The question thus emerges: if the
implicit recognition of the emergence of post-industrial
society in advanced capitalism was not supposed to influence

basic Soviet social doctrine, then what was its role in

Soviet industrial theory? Karkhin answered this question

in the most simple and straightforward fashion:

> Earlier, we systematically analyzed the difference
> between planning and prognostication in social
> management in the conditions of socialist society.
> Capitalist programming, forecasting and other
> methods of social management are radically dif-
> ferent from socialist economic planning,
> forecasting and management, with regard to their
> social goals and their limited possibilities of
> influencing the socio-economic processes.
> However, considering what we have already said
> about the material environment of social manage-
> ment...we cannot be limited by constant and
> exclusive concentration on this fact.   46

Karkhin then proceeded to divide bourgeois managerial

technology into two aspects: first, its class content and

use which he solemnly rejected; second, however, the objec-

tive aspect which was not supposed to be rejected by

Soviet theory, but instead was supposed to be assimilated:

> The particular objective failure of programming
> and other advanced methods of centralized and
> direct intervention by the bourgeois state in order
> to influence the economic development of their
> societies must be noted. On the other hand, we
> also have to objectively notice that bourgeois
> prognosis involves the analysis of complex
> situations to achieve the best understanding of
> dynamically evolving events, as well as to
> achieve the best possible management of the
> enterprises...[thus] it is necessary to soberly
> and critically approach the achievements of
> the bourgeois economy in planning and forecasting. 47

Hence, the duality of the liberal wing of Soviet

industrial theory serves the purpose of theoretically

clearing the way for the absorption of these elements of

post-industrial technology which were considered by Soviet

scholars to be free of the class content of bourgeois

society. Considering that the technology itself was

traditionally considered by Soviet industrial theory to be

value neutral, those elements of capitalist technology

which could possibly be argued to have class content

were few and far between and were limited to a class of

managerial devices deriving from the existence of the

capitalist class. Nevertheless, even if this were a rather

academic issue from the point of view of scientific

Marxism-Leninism, there was a need to put a theoretical

"dot over the i" and the scholars of the liberal wing of

Soviet industrial theory were those who undertook this

enterprise.

When compared to the conservative wing of this theory

or its earlier variants, the liberal wing appears to have

developed a distinctively different approach. This did not,

however, indicate any intent to sow disunity in the field

of Soviet industrial theory. Instead, it points to the

inherent inconsistency of the very science of Marxism-

Leninism itself. The issue of the internal consistency

of the theory of Marxism-Leninism fell outside of the pur-

view of industrial scholarship during this period and was

consequently ignored. Thus, the reason for the lack of

antagonism between the two wings of Soviet industrial theory

becomes somewhat clearer.

Despite the fact that Soviet theory held that technology

was value-neutral and had emerged from the achievements of the whole of humanity, the issue of scientific-management posed some delicate questions. Some of the most advanced managerial methods had not only been designed in the advanced capitalist societies, but also, the main reason for many of these technological achievements was the enhancement of the social role of the capitalist class. Unquestionably, the claim that in capitalist societies the science of management in particular, and more generally, science itself, served solely the interests of the capitalists themselves, had been one of the most dogmatically repeated canons of Soviet industrial theory. Nonetheless, in Karkhin's case, the point was made that even those methods of management which were invented in capitalist societies to enhance the social role of the capitalist class also possessed some objective content. This was an extremely important point because it was suggested that the class character and the oppressive content of this technology would disappear once it had been transplanted into a non-capitalist society. Consequently, if Soviet society found the objective side of a capitalist method of management to be useful, then it could borrow it freely because after the transplant, the capitalistic and oppressive content of this technology would disappear automatically.

The inconsistent duality of the liberal wing of Soviet industrial theory was even more apparent in Gvishiani's massive Organisation and Management,[48] which could be considered to be a most appropriate symbol of the entire

school of thought. On the one hand, we see Gvishiani, the

humble borrower, who is fascinated by the achievements

of advanced capitalist societies in the field of scientific

management. This humility was underscored with a brutally

sincere assessment of Soviet achievements in the field.

Thus, in the opening of his book he stated that:

> It is a well-known fact that in the USSR scien-
> tific research on the problems of management
> was considerably curtailed at the end of the
> thirties, and that little was done in this field
> until recent times. This inevitably affected
> the scientific validity of certain organisational
> decisions and led in practice to an approach to
> problems of management that was often purely
> empirical.   49

As a result, in light of this deficiency in the develop-

ment of the Soviet theory of management, Gvishiani proposed

the utilization of the experience of the advanced capital-

ist societies in this field:

> Underestimation of foreign experience may be
> attributed in no small degree to underestimation
> of the scientific problems of management organi-
> sation in general which, at any rate until
> recently, was to be found both in specialised
> literature and in practical work.   50

Following these observations, Gvishiani set out to

systematically introduce the Western theories of management

to circles of interested students. So systematic, diligent

and comprehensive was his introduction that undoubtedly

it could have served as a useful tool for Western graduate

students in the field. Of course, this work was primarily directed to interested Soviet academic circles, as the systematic introduction to Western theories of scientific management and the detailed analysis of those theories encompassed approximately 90% of this work. Finally, in the conclusion of his work Gvishiani again pointed to the achievements of advanced capitalism's methods of management:

> Having accumulated extensive experience in
> rationalising management, American executives,
> scientists and technicians have found numerous
> efficient methods of solving various organisa-
> tional problems. All this naturally is also
> reflected in the development of the American
> theory of management.   51

Having said this, he then places "the dot over the i" by proposing a massive borrowing of the ultra-advanced, bourgeois methods of management, especially those based upon cybernetics, mathematical modelling, statistics and automation, as well as relevant theoretical underpinnings.

On the other hand, there was another, completely different line of argument in Gvishiani's work, one of supreme confidence, if not arrogance. According to that line of thought, the history of the development of Soviet scientific management was a history characterized by a steady chain of successes, which in part had been respon- sible for the great success of the Soviet social transfor- mation:

Guided by Lenin's principles of management and

developing them creatively in accordance with
changing historical conditions, the Soviet
state and the Soviet people, led by the
Communist Party, have throughout their history
been grappling with and solving the extremely
difficult problems of organising the management
of the constantly growing planned economy of our
country. This was one of the things that contributed fundamentally to the execution of such
great historic tasks as the complete elimination
of capitalist elements in both town and country,
the unprecedented rapid industrialization of the
national economy, the collectivisation of agriculture, the victory over Nazi Germany in the
Great Patriotic War, the colossal work of the
post-war restoration and development of the
national economy, and improvements in the material
standards and conditions of life of the Soviet
people.   52

Moreover, with the systematic analysis of Western

theories of scientific management there was intertwined

also a systematic criticism made from a definite position

of the alleged intrinsic and obvious superiority of some,

though unspecified theory of Soviet scientific management.

Although this alleged body of Soviet theory of scientific

management had an unspecified character, nevertheless it

gave Gvishiani a tremendously strong basis for criticising

Western theories because its greatest achievement had been

a definitive contribution to the construction of the

socialist system in the Soviet Union which according to

Gvishiani was a task that had already been accomplished

there:

Thanks to correct Marxist-Leninist guidance of
social development, thanks to the party's tremendous organisational work, the Soviet people
have made socialist society a reality and are
successfully building the material and technical
basis of communism.   53

204

Thus, the powerful criticism which was delivered by
Gvishiani's second line of thought gave, in turn, the
impression that his systematic presentation and analysis
of Western theories of scientific management served the
sole purpose of their categorical refutation and rejection. However, Gvishiani provided a definite, although
quite discretely expressed, key to the puzzle created by
his dual line of thought. That is, his severe criticism
of the capitalist methods of scientific management was not
so much a criticism of the particular methods themselves,
as it was an accusation against the capitalist superstructure: "Under conditions of capitalist domination...any
management also acts as a specific form of exploitation of
the working people."[54] However, it is very important here
to keep in our minds, that for Gvishiani, the exploitative
elements of the capitalist methods of management belong to
the social superstructure and not to the social base.
Hence, Gvishiani could conclude his work by calling first
for the rejection of the elements of the capitalist superstructure from the capitalist science of management. Thus,
Gvishiani implored Soviet industrial theoreticians to

> Study and critically use everything positive
> contained in the concepts of the bourgeois theory
> of organisation and management which, notwith-
> standing all their contradictions, to some extent
> reflect the objective requirements of modern
> large-scale social production.   [55]

Clearly here, the fundamental logical premise of
Lenin's philosophy is repeated. That is, technology, i.e.,

"large-scale social production," has an "objective" and
universal character. This "large-scale social production"
develops according to its own "objective" dynamics, which
are only utilized by the capitalist superstructure.
However, technology has basically a value-neutral character, and hence, it can be taken from the capitalist society
(where it "reflects the objective requirements of modern
large-scale social production") and transplanted to the body
of a socialist type of society where this "objective" technology will be utilized to advance the socialist transformation. Of course, the entire consistency of the views
represented by the liberal wing of Soviet industrial theory
depends upon the validity of the fundamental premise that
technology itself is value-neutral. As a result, any attempt
at a more general assessment of Soviet efforts in this
field automatically pushes us to the much broader question
of the consistency between the philosophies of Marx and
Lenin, the analysis of which remains outside of the scope of
this work. Thus, we return to discussion of the more specific aspects of the liberal wing of the Soviet industrial
theory.

If the duality of the two lines of thought was the
main characteristic of the liberal wing of Soviet industrial theory, at the same time, it embodied other, more
esoteric but still very important features. One of these
esoteric elements was the rather injudicious yet pronounced
fascination with some elements of Western social theories

contradictory to the principles of scientific Marxism-Leninism. Here, some echoes of the important Western debate over group theories of society entered into the realm of Soviet industrial theory. In some cases this amounted to a merely mechanical and unexplained borrowing of some tidbits of theoretical jargon which had been created by the group theorists. These oddities sporadically appeared within the body of Soviet industrial theory without much content or elaboration suggesting that the reader was supposed to automatically understand how to incorporate these new concepts into the rest of Soviet theory. For example, Shubin expected to see the rapid proliferation of a variety of new groups as the Soviet Union advanced in socio-economic terms. He argued further that these groups would actively support the process of the strengthening and enhancement of the democratic system:

> Experience indicates that those groups of working
> people which are most dependent upon and most
> saturated with scientific-technological progress
> are the ones which are the most active in this
> process. 56

However, much more interesting than such sporadic mentioning of the existence of social groups was an isolated but nevertheless systematic attempt to introduce group theory into the body of Soviet industrial theory. Thus, Kugel argued that the Scientific and Technological Revolution brings with itself substantial growth in the structural divisions of society. These divisions have different characters: "functional, professional, according to qualifications, and demographic."[57] Consequently, he conceptualized the social structure of an industrially advanced society in the following way:

> The social structure of the national popula-
> tion is one of the more important subjects of
> social studies. It represents the totality
> of the population of a country, which consists
> of the dynamically developing social classes
> (groups), which include in their range profes-
> sional groups of all kinds of categories, as
> well as collectives of varying degree of
> complexity and also their mutual interrelation-
> ships. In this way, social groups are the
> elements of social structure.   [58]

Even more interesting is Kugel's definition of the social group itself:

> In its very sense, a social group is a group
> of people who are in active contact with one
> another. In the more concrete and precise
> meaning, a social group is a relatively stable
> totality of people who are unified by common
> social functions, interests, and goals in their
> activities.   [59]

After such a start, Kugel' then proceeded to engage in all kinds of mental acrobatics to argue that this kind of group conceptualization of society was nothing else but the advancement of Lenin's theory of social classes. While Kugel' was apparently literate enough to be fascinated by Western group theories, he did not know that in the West group theories served as the antidote for Marxian class analysis of society.

Another bizarre twist of the liberal wing of Soviet

industrial theory was the concern voiced about the environmental damage caused by the industrially advanced societies.
At first sight, these works appear to be just another
variation in the conservative wing of Soviet industrial
theory because the approach to this subject was exceedingly
simplistic and narrowly cast. The content of these works
could be aptly summarized in one sentence: how it is that
wicked and degenerate capitalism destroys the environment
and how the glorious socialist societies protect it. Hence,
for instance, Medunin lamented the environmental pollution
of the large centers of population in the advanced capitalist societies: Paris, London, Tokyo, large American
cities. Moreover, he expressed a great deal of concern
about the dangers of nuclear testing. Next, he proceeded
to contrast Western and Soviet efforts in containing these
dangers. Here, the authorities of capitalist societies
were presented as being indifferent and negligent in
dealing with these problems. In contrast, the Soviet
Party untiringly and ceaselessly combats these problems.

Most importantly, however, Medunin presented Western
scientists as pessimistic, almost to the point of decadence
on the subject of environmental destruction:

> Some bourgeois sociologists (G. Friedman, Ch. Boduin,
> V. Ogburn and others), maintain that scientific-
> technological progress creates an artificial tech-
> nological environment from the natural environ-
> ment, and assert in a pessimistic way that man
> will never be capable of adjusting to the new
> conditions of life, and as a result, argue
> that humanity is destined for unavoidable
> annihilation.

60

By contrast, Soviet scholars were supposed to untiringly
struggle for an optimistic and humanistic reconciliation
of industrially advanced society with the natural environment.[61]

Sometime later, Fedorov and Novik viciously attacked
U.S. environmental policies, claiming that the U.S. deva-
states the global biosphere and that the Soviet Union
protects it.[62] Also, member-correspondent of the Soviet
Academy of Sciences, G.A. Aksenenok, accused the international monopolies of pursuing policies which devastated
and plundered global resources and more generally, the
world's environment. In glaring contrast, the Soviet
Union, led by its great Party, protects and judiciously
uses its own natural resources and, on a global scale,
counters the harmful influences of capitalist societies.[63]

Of course, there was nothing extraordinary in the way
in which these scholars dealt with the problem of environmental destruction, but the bizarre aspect lay in the very
selection of the problem itself. Not only was it aping
the environmental controversy which had emerged in
Western post-industrial societies, but in this case, the
Soviet Union, which to a great extent still was continuing
a primarily industrial (and, thus, much more environment-
ally damaging) development, itself had produced statistical
data clearly suggesting that in the Soviet Union, the rape
of the environment had taken on a much more brutal character than in the advanced capitalist societies. Moreover,

from a political point of view, the environmental movement
had originated as a result of grass roots pressure on
political authorities to curb the destructive actions of
the industrial sector. By contrast, in the Soviet Union
such a movement would be plainly illegal and, according
to the Soviet legal code, undoubtedly would have to be
classified as anti-social activity.

There was still another bizarre twist within the
liberal wing of Soviet industrial theory which had an
extremely elusive and subtle character; this was the
imitation of the writing style and especially the jargon
of Western social scientists. There changes occurred
very slowly and evolved over decades. However, this
borrowing accumulated over time and the style of writing
and the jargon used by the liberal wing of Soviet industrial theory greatly differed from even that of the period
immediately preceeding its development. The source of
these changes was obvious: bit by bit, Soviet industrial
scholars were picking up elements of the working style and
the elements of the terminology of Western social scientists,
and were abandoning their own traditional style of writing
and discussion.

Of course, those bizarre twists in the development
of the liberal wing of Soviet industrial theory cannot
overshadow its achievements. First of all, this was the
only body of industrial theory which although in a vague
and implicit way, still somehow addressed the collapse of

the earlier enthusiastic period of Soviet industrial theory.
Moreover, not only had it begun to redefine and reconceptualize the Soviet attitude to the emerging post-industrial
society, but it became the channel for the cautious and
selective adaptation and diffusion of Western post-industrial
theories into the body of Soviet industrial theory. In so
doing, the liberal wing of Soviet industrial theory began
to cautiously synthesize some elements of Western post-
industrial theories with Soviet views on the subject, and
as a result, Soviet industrial theory began itself to be
transformed into a post-industrial theory.

The Conservative Wing

A clear distinction must be made between the conservative line of thought which was presented as an alternative to the liberal line of thought in the works of the
liberal wing of Soviet industrial theory and the conservative wing of Soviet industrial theory itself. In the
first instance, conservatism served as a balancing mechanism which would allow the introduction of some elements
of Western post-industrial theories while maintaining a
cautious, prudent stance. In the second instance, conservatism served as the organizing principle. Upon first
impression, one might conclude that the works of the
conservative wing of Soviet industrial theory were merely
a continuation of the earlier enthusiastic period, and that

nothing had happened to warrant a change in style. Only
after careful scrutiny could one discover that the fundamental ingredient of the enthusiastic period--the
enthusiasm itself--was missing. However, every other
feature remained unchanged. Beyond predicting the achievement of communism in the Soviet Union and the total destruction of the capitalist system in a very short and
definite time-span, nothing new was said by the conservative wing of Soviet industrial theory.

In a way, the conservative wing of Soviet industrial
theory returned to the traditions of the early, Stalinist
industrial theory, when the content of the theoretical
works was very limited and extremely formalized and only
the form of those works, i.e., their particular subjects,
length, title and authorship changed. If the content of
the works of the conservative wing of Soviet industrial
theory basically did not change in comparison to the
enthusiastic period, its form changed dramatically.
Another decade brought increases in the numbers of academicians in the field resulting in increased publication.
Further, a new generation of Soviet industrial scholars
had come of age.[64] It would be more than redundant to
repeat all those theoretical claims which were already
well known from the earlier enthusiastic period. There
was nothing new in these works. If the specific time for
the achievement of communism and the collapse of capitalism
was not given, still the theoreticians of the conservative

wing sternly maintained that the Scientific and Technological Revolution would undoubtedly elevate the Soviet
system into communism and at the same time would bring the
capitalist system to its final destruction. The style of
writing itself had not changed. Soviet theoreticians
quite simply could scarcely marshall sufficient praise and
adulation in describing the glory of their social system
and their vanguard party which was wisely guiding the
society to the communist paradise as described in the
Marxist-Leninist scientific blueprint. On the other hand,
no invective was strong enough for them to describe their
moral revulsion, emotional contempt and theoretical
condemnation and rejection of the degenerate and exploi-
tatively wicked and inhumane capitalist system, which
undoubtedly was well on its way to a self-generated and
well deserved annihilation.

Why did the conservative wing of Soviet industrial
theory emerge if the liberal wing included a self-regulating
conservative line of thought? There is nothing in the
writings of the conservative school which would justify a
claim that its role was to contain the liberal wing.
First of all, the conservative wing did not show even a
trace of a theoretical assault upon the liberal wing. To
the contrary, each wing displayed utter disinterest in
its counterpart. Rather than a pluralistic clash of
different views, there existed instead a strange harmony
where a plurality of theoretical perspectives existed as

if in isolation. Thus, one might conclude that the conservative wing of Soviet industrial theory played a
larger social role than that of just another theoretical
position in the industrial field.

The scholarly activities of the conservative wing of
the industrial theory, as well as of the conservative wings
of other branches of the social sciences which were
springing up then, were designed to contain the possible
social frustration which could be spawned by the rapid
collapse of the earlier enthusiastic period. Soviet
elites gained enough experience from the tumultuous period
following the disappearance of another great social myth--
the death of Stalin himself and the eventual collapse of
the personality cult--not to take note of all those potentially dangerous phenomena which could result from widespread social frustration, ideological insecurity and
pessimism. Thus, the conservative wing of Soviet industrial theory engaged in a massive effort of persistent
(if not rhythmic) repetition that all was still well with
the Soviet system, that nothing had really changed, that
the Science of Marxism-Leninism still did not require any
modification, that even if the particular reasons for the
enthusiasm of the earlier period had somehow disappeared,
still there were general reasons for the steady flow of
general enthusiasm. In this way, they attempted to contribute to the preservation of the status quo in the
Soviet Union.

Undoubtedly this strategy would work for those less educated or more naive, and for those who were ideologically indifferent. On the other hand, its massive institutional character was perhaps intimidating enough to silence many of those who might have capitalised on the erosion of social enthusiasm in order to begin some kind of reform movement. Finally, the conservative wing left a free hand for those who were interested in a quiet, judicious and responsible modification of Soviet industrial theory which at first sight appeared so dull, simplistic and utterly repetitious, but in fact performed a very complex and sophisticated social function.

Nevertheless, from the point of view of Soviet industrial theory, the conservative wing hardly contributed to its advancement. Its one minimal contribution was, however, quite important and this was the conservative critique of Western post-industrial theories themselves. While this critique of Western post-industrial theories involved as brutal and uncompromising a refutation and rejection as had theory from the earlier enthusiastic period, the form of this critique itself undertook a meaningful transformation. Soviet industrial theory of the early enthusiastic period treated Western post-industrial theories in a chauvinistic, nonchalant and cavalier manner and readers could learn little about Western post-industrial theories from it. In contrast, the critique of the conservative wing was characterized

by a more diligent review of Western post-industrial
theories which preceded their no less categorical rejection. Although it may appear that the result was the same
in each case, the conservative wing was actually involved
in introducing, (however awkwardly) those theories to
Soviet students, and thus, performed a function somewhat
paralleling the efforts of the liberal wing of Soviet
industrial theory.

Thus, Vasil'chyk, repetitiously attacked the post-
industrial concept of the changing situation of the
working class in advanced capitalist society, by maintaining that the Scientific and Technological Revolution
would bring nothing but increased class-conflict to
capitalist societies instead of diminishing it as was
predicted by the post-industrial theories. However, in
so doing, he introduced in a quite precise way many important elements of the argument of Western post-industrial
theories and thus made them more familiar to Soviet
readers, although he still concluded that the new productive milieus of post-industrial society do not alter the
basic class relationship: "The hired labor force, which is
exploited by industrial capital in agriculture or in the
sphere of services still remains the component of the
industrial proletariat."[65]

While assessing post-industrial changes in U.S.
agriculture from a conservative standpoint, Bulochnikova
argued that the most important feature of U.S. agriculture

was the struggle of the peasant masses against exploi-

tative monopoly capitalism:

> We have to notice, that in the present conditions
> of the contemporary developed capitalist
> societies, the nationalization of land [i.e.,
> the concentration of the agricultural lands,
> V.Z.] takes on an increasingly political rather
> than economic character. Thus, the main direc-
> tion of the class struggle in the village is the
> struggle of the working masses against monopoly
> capital.   66

Despite its ideological simplicty, her article provided a

great deal of data on the process of the concentration of

capital in U.S. agriculture, the emergence of agribusiness

and the basic sociological changes that were occurring

in the U.S.

Kantor's conservative critique of the New Left is an

exquisite example of the new approach. With the standard

resort to condemnation and castigation, the struggle

against capitalism was depicted as being divided into two

streams: one correct, the other incorrect and even decadent.

> In the contemporary conditions of the struggle
> against capitalism, two distinctive tendencies
> have emerged. One is the older tendency, petit
> bourgeois and anarchistic. The other tendency
> is new and communistic which above all is directed
> toward free development of the individual in the
> conditions of universal collective social inter-
> action and not in the conditions of individualistic
> limitations.   67

There is no mystery as to which tendency symbolizes Soviet

designed development and which symbolizes the New Left.

However, what is so obvious from the point of view of Soviet theoreticians might be puzzling for many other students because, as Kantor admits, contemporary capitalist society is extremely complex and these two tendencies tend to be intertwined: "In the real process of the contemporary struggle against the state-monopolistic capitalism, these two tendencies are intertwined in a complex way and they overlap one another."[68] In this confusion, Soviet theory rises to the task of revealing the true nature of the New Left:

> The individualism of the petit-bourgeoisie and the intelligentsia is apparently changing. Today it attempts to peddle itself as an 'authentic,' 'democratic socialism' and utilizes as a supporting argument one-sided interpretations of the Scientific and Technological Revolution, to find an outlet, although a hidden one, for its narrow-minded tendency toward individualistic independence.   [69]

This style of reproach and the revelation of the true nature of the New Left theories did not differ from the earlier period, but now encompassed only the concluding parts of these works rather than their entirety. Thus, the rest of Kantor's article was actually preoccupied with presenting the views of Marcuse, Garaudy and other New Left theoreticians. As a result, elements of the actual New Left theories are presented to Soviet audiences.[70]

The new style of conservative assault upon Western post-industrial theories was exhibited in many other works of the conservative wing of Soviet industrial theory.

Among those who particularly excelled in the introduction
of that innovative style were: Kormer and Senokosov,[71]
Galkin,[72] Skvortsov,[73] Mitin[74] and Khromushkin.[75] The
emergence of the new style itself provided more evidence
of the fact that Soviet industrial theory had entered a
period of harmonious-cooperative pluralism. The existence
of an elaborate panorama of differing views and approaches,
their basic division into two wings, and the subsequent
subdivisions of these two wings into separate trends and
lines of argument had nevertheless a purely academic character. Soviet industrial theoreticians would never acknowledge the existence of analytical distinctions in their
work or the existence of two main ideal types and a further
subdivision into ideal subtypes. As was stressed earlier,
they religiously avoided any kind of ideological and
philosophical confrontations. Instead, they sought to
advance those aspects of the industrial theory which were
called for by the socio-eocnomic development of the Soviet
Union.[76] Their allegiance to the fundamental science of
Marxism-Leninism, whether seriously expressed by conserva-
tives or tokenly expressed by liberals, was unquestionable.
Eventually, pragmatism had begun to dominate the fields
of Soviet industrial theory. The Soviet Union had become
a gigantic complex society consisting of diverse groups
and interests and Soviet industrial theory had developed an
equally complex and diverse theoretical smorgasbord designed
to feed intellectually diverse social needs. The conflict

between these diverse interests was not allowed to surface
or be expressed in the industrial theory and thus it was
characterized by the bizarre coexistence of two mutually
exclusive theories whose advocates simply ignored one
another.

Individual theoreticians went about their separate
activities intent upon serving diverse social needs
as well as maintaining allegiance to the general doctrine
of Marxism-Leninism. As a result, the actual state of
Soviet industrial theory was that of extreme atomization.
Although it is possible to establish the two extreme ideal
types and then to associate most of the literature with
either of the two groups, still there exist definite grey
areas where conservative elements were as strong as liberal
elements. Moreover, even the works which clearly could be
subsumed under one or the other of the two ideal types
still exhibit some elements typical of the opposite group.
Thus, the liberal wing exhibited a definite conservative
line of thought and the conservative critique of Western
post-industrial theories greatly complemented the works of
the liberal wing.

Of course, the state of Soviet industrial theory could
hardly be seen as impressive by its Western students. It
was a puzzling enigma without a definite line of development, a theoretical amoeba which moved in many directions
at the same time. Ultimately, it was a multidimensional
response to both Soviet and Western socio-economic developments.

ENDNOTES

1. I.G. Kurakov, "Nauka i Effektivnost' Obschestvennogo Proizvodstva," Voprosy Filosofii, 5, (1966), and 10, (1966).

2. Kurakov, 5 (1966) p. 3.

3. Ibid., pp. 6-12.

4. Ibid., p. 13.

5. P.A. Rachkov, "Problemy Effektivnosti Nauki v Sovremennyi Period," Voprosy Filosofii, 5, (1966).

6. D.M. Gvishiani, "Problemy Upravlenia Sotsialisticheskoi Promyshlennostiu," Vorprosy Filosofii, 11 (1966), pp. 4-5.

7. Ibid., pp. 11-12.

8. Ibid., p. 13.

9. N.S. Bud'ko, "Iavliaiutsia li Mashinami Ustroistva, Prednaznachennyie dlia Pererabotki Informatsii?," Voprosy Filosofii, 11 (1966).

10. See: G. Danilin, "Sovremennaia Nauchno-Teknicheskaia Revoliutsia: Sushchnoist', Znachenie, Perspektivy," Mirovaia Ekonomika i Mezhdunarodnye Otnoshenia, 12, (1966).

    G. Mekhanik, "Nauchno-Tekhnicheskaia Revoliutsia i ee Vozdeistvie na Kapitalisticheskuiu Ekonomiku," Mirovaia Ekonomika i Mezhdunarodnye Otnoshenia, 12, (1966).

    M. Moshenskii, "Teoria Pribavochnoi Stoimosti i Sovremennaya Metody Kapitalisticheskoi Eksploatatsii," Mirovaia Ekonomika i Mezhdunarodnye Otnoshenia, 12, (1966).

11. See especially such prominent works as:
    A.A. Zvorykin, Nauchno-Tekhnicheskaia Revoliutsia i ee Sotsial'nye Posledstvia, (Moscow: Izdatel'stvo Znanie, 1967);

    Iu.G. Meleshchenko, Tekhnicheskii Progress i ego Zakonomernosti, (Moscow: Lenizdat, 1967);

    Ekonomicheskie Zakonomernosti Pererastania Sotsializma v Kommunizm, (Moscow: Izdatel'stvo Nauka, 1967).

12. <u>Sovremennaia Nauchno-Tekhnicheskaia Revoliutsia</u>,
    (Moscow: 1967, Izdatiel'stvo "Nauka.")

13. Ibid., especially pp. 76-81.

14. Ibid., pp. 164-165.

15. Ibid., p. 165.

16. Ibid.

17. Ibid., especially pp. 172-180.

18. Ibid., pp. 144-145.

19. Ibid., p. 109.

20. Ibid., pp. 80-81.

21. D.Iu. Panov, "O Vzaimodeistvii Cheloveka i Mashiny,"
    <u>Voprosy Filosofii</u>, 1, (1967).

22. G.N. Volkov, "Vzaimosviaz' Nauki i Proizvodstva,"
    <u>Voprosy Filosofii</u>, 2, (1967).

23. Iu.S. Meleshchenko, "Kharakter i Osobennosti Nauchno-
    Tekhnicheskoi Revoliutsii," <u>Voprosy Filosofii</u>, 7, (1968).

24. I.G. Kurakov, "Prognozirovanie Nauchno-Tekhnicheskogo
    Progressa," <u>Voprosy Filosofii</u>, 10, (1968), pp. 24-25.

25. Ibid., pp. 28-29.

26. Ibid., p. 35.

27. M.K. Petrov, "Nekotoryie Problemy Organizatsii Nauki
    v Epokhu Nauchno-Tekhnicheskoi Revoliutsii," <u>Voprosy
    Filosofii</u>, 10, (1968).

28. Ibid., p. 44.

29. O.I. Shkaratan, "Rabochii Klass Sotsialisticheskogo
    Obschestva v Epokhu Nauchno-Tekhnicheskoi Revoliutsii,"
    <u>Voprosy Filosofii</u>, 11, (1968), p. 21.

30. Ibid.

31. G.N. Volkov, <u>Sotsiologia Nauki</u>, (Moscow: 1968, Izdatiel'-
    stvo Politichieskoi Litieratury); N.V. Markov, <u>Nauchno-
    Tekhnicheskaia Revoliutsia:Analiz, Perspektivy, Posled-
    stvia</u>, (Moscow: Izdatel'stvo Politicheskoi Literatury,
    1973); Kamaev, V.D., <u>Sovremennaia Nauchno Nauchno-
    Tekhnicheskaia Revoliutsia</u>, (Moscow: Mysl', 1972).
    See also: <u>Nauchno-Teknicheskaia Revoliutsia i Sotsializm</u>.
    Moscow: Politizdat, 1973.

32. Volkov, pp. 180-185; Markov, pp. 7-108; Kamaev, pp. 6-95.

33. See especially: Volkov, p. 186 and also Markov and Kamaev.

34. Volkov, p. 195; Kamaev, pp. 158-159.

35. Volkov, pp. 199-200.

36. Ibid., p. 209.

37. Ibid., p. 219; see also Kamaev, pp. 256-257.

38. Ibid., p. 213; see also Markov and Kamaev on the advancement of the Scientific and Technological Revolution.

39. O.N. Zhemianov, "Kritika Kontsepsii 'Oburzhuazenii' Rabochego Klassa," Voprosy Filosofii, 12, (1970), p. 3.

40. Ibid., p. 6.

41. G.M. Moiseenko, "Nauchno-Tekhnicheskaia Intelligentsia v Sovremiennom Kapitalisticheskom Obschestvie," Voprosy Filosofii, 12, (1971), p. 43.

42. Ibid., p. 53.

43. P.N. Khmyliev, "Nauchno-Tekhnicheskaia Revoliutsia i Problema Prakticheskoi Napravlennosti Obschestvennykh Nauk," in Sotsializm i Nauchno-Tekhnicheskaia Revoliutsia, (Leningrad: 1971, Izdatel'stvo Leningrad-skogo Universiteta), p. 8.

44. G.I. Karkhin, Sviazi Nastoiashchego i Budushchego v Ekonomike, (Moscow: 1970, Izdatiel'stvo "ekonomika"), pp. 156-157.

45. Ibid., p. 161.

46. Ibid., p. 175.

47. Ibid.

48. Dz. Gvishiani, Organisation and Management, (Moscow: 1972, Progress Publishers).

49. Ibid., pp. 7-8.

50. Ibid., p. 28.

51. Ibid., p. 437.

52. Ibid., p. 7.

53. Ibid.

54. Ibid., p. 379.

55. Ibid., p. 442.

56. V.A. Shubin, "Razvitie Demokraticheskogo Tsentralizma v Usloviakh Nauchno-Tekhnicheskoi Revoliutsii," in Sotsializm i Nauchno-Tekhnicheskaia Revoliutsia, op. cit., p. 157.

57. S.A. Kugel', "Izmenenie Sotsial'noi Struktury Sotsialis- ticheskogo Obschestva pod Vozdeistvem Nauchno- Tekhnicheskoi Revoliutsii," Voprosy Filosofii, 3, (1969), p. 13.

58. Ibid.

59. Ibid., pp. 13-14.

60. A.E. Miedunin, "Vliianie Nauchno-Tekhnicheskoi Revoliutsii na Prirodu Zemli," Voprosy Filosofii, 3, (1969), p. 32.

61. See also on this subject: T.I. Oizerman, "Istoricheskii Materializm i Ideologia ' Tekhnologicheskovo' Pessimizma," Voprosy Filosofii, 8, (1973).

62. E.K. Fedorov & I.B. Novik, "Problemy Vzaimodeistvia Cheloveka s Prirodnoi Sredoi," Voprosy Filosofii, 12, (1972).

63. G.A. Aksenenok, "Priroda i Chelovek v Usloviakh Nauchno-Tekhnicheskogo Progressa," Voprosy Filosofii, 10, (1973); I. Laptev, Planeta Razuma, (Moscow: Molodaia Gwardia, 1973).

64. A true excellence of its own kind was achieved here especially in the following works:

    G.V. Teriaev, Vysshaia Faza Kommunizma. Obshchie Zakonomernosti Pererastania Sotsializma v Kommunizm, (Moscow: 1966, Izdatel'stvo "Mysl'").

    V. Afanasiev, Scientific Communism, (Moscow: 1967, Progress Publishers).

    KPSS vo Glavie Kul'turnoi Revoliutsii v. SSSR. Moscow: Izdatel'stvo Politicheskoi Literatury, 1972.

V.G. Afanasyev edit., Nauchnoe Upravlenie Obschestvom, (Moscow: 1967, Izdatel'stvo "mysl'"), as well as its continuation throughout years 1968-1973).

Problemy Nauchnogo Kummunizma, (Moscow: 1970, Izdatel' stvo Mysl').

K.S. Shariia, Nekotoryie Voprosy Razvitia Sotsialis-ticheskikh Obschestvennykh Otnoshenii v Piriod Stroitel'-stva Kommunizma, (Tbilisi: 1972, Izdatel'stvo "Metsnereva").

"Peredovaia," Voprosy Filosofii, 4, (1969).

C.P. Trapeznikov, "Leninizm i Sovremennaia Nauchno-Tekhnicheskaia Revoliutsia," Voprosy Filosofii, 4, (1970).

R.I. Kosolapov, "Na Puti k Besklassovomu Obschestvu," Voprosy Filosofii, 5, (1971).

"Peredovaia," Voprosy Filosofii, 10, (1971), (3-16).

"Nauchno-Tekhnicheskaia Revoliutsia i ee Sotsial'naia Problematika," Voprosy Filosofii, 12, (1971).

Redaktsionnaia, "Cheloviek-Nauka-Tekhnika," Voprosy Filosofii, 8, (1972).

V.G. Afanasyev, "Chelovek v Sistemie Upravlenia," Voprosy Filosofii, 8, (1972).

G.I. Tsarogorodtsev, "'Tikhnizatsia' Sredy i Zdorove Cheloveka," Voprosy Filosofii, 10, (1972).

V.M. Munipov, V.P. Znichenko, "Chelovecheskii Faktor v Sovremiennoi Tekhnike," Voprosy Filosofii, 11, (1972).

F.V. Konstantinov, "Nauchno-Tekhnicheskaia Revoliutsia i Problemy Nravstvennogo Progressa," Voprosy Filosofii, 8, (1973).

Borba Idei i Nauchno-Teknicheskaia Revoliutsia, (Leningrad: Leninzdat, 1973.

"Nasha Filosofia Mira--Filosofia Istoricheskogo Optimizma," Voprosy Filosofii, 11, (1973).

N.I. Makeshin, "Nauka kak Faktor Ekonomicheskogo Razvitia SSSR," Voprosy Filosofii, 12, (1973).

65. Iu. A. Vasil'chik, "Sovremennaia Nauchno-Tekhnicheskaia Revoliutsia i Promyshlennyi Proletariat," Voprosy Filosofii, 1, (1969), pp. 11-23.

66. L.A. Bulochnikova, "Nauchno-Tekhnicheskaia Revolutsia
    v Sel'skom Khoziaistve i ee Sotsial'nye Posledstvia,"
    Voprosy Filosofii, 1, (1969).

67. K.M. Kantor, "Sootnoshenie Sotsial'noi Organizatsii
    i Individia v Usloviakh Nauchno-Tekhnicheskoi Revoliut-
    sii," Voprosy Filosofii, 10, (1971), pp. 50-51.

68. Ibid., p. 51.

69. Ibid.

70. See also K.M. Kantor, "Nauchno-Tekhnicheskaia Revoliut-
    sia i Sovremennyi Rabochii Klass," Voprosy Filosofii,
    12, (1971); and Budushchee Chekovecheskogo Obshchestva,
    (Moscow: Progress, 1973).

71. V.F. Kormer, Iu.P. Senokosov, "Ot 'Tekhnologicheskovo
    Determinizma' k 'Posttekhnokraticheskomu Videniu,'"
    Voprosy Filosofii, 7, (1972).

72. A.A. Galkin, "Sotsial'naia Struktura Sovremennogo
    Kapitalisticheskogo Obschestva i Burzhuaznaia Sotsio-
    logia," Voprosy Filosofii, 8, (1972).

73. L.V. Skvortsov, "Ideologicheskie Mify Antikommunizma:
    Evoliutsia i,Novyie Tendentsii," Voprosy Filosofii,
    9, (1972).

74. M.B. Mitin, "Problemy Borby Protiv Burzhuaznoi
    Ideologii i Antikommunizma," Voprosy Filosofii,
    7, (1971).

75. G. Khromushkin, "Novye Manery Antikommunizma,"
    Politicheskoe Samoobrazovanie, 2, (1969).

76. See for instance: K. Varlamov, Leninskaia Kontseptsia
    Sotsialisticheskogo Upravlenia, (Moscow: Izdatel'stvo
    Mysl', 1973);

    Chelovek i EVM (Psikhologicheskie Problemy Avtomati-
    zatsii;

    Upravlenia, (Moscow: Ekonomika, 1973); Tekhnika

    Tekhnologia i Kadry Upravlenia Proizvodstvom,

    (Moscow: Ekonomika, 1973);

    V. Kosolapov, Chekovechestvo na Rubezhe XXI Veka,
    (Moscow: Molodaia Gvardia, 1973).

227

Georgi Smirnov, <u>Soviet Man. The Making of a Socialist</u> <u>Type of Personality</u>, Moscow: Progress Publishers. 1973.

Lebin, D.A., <u>Nauchno-Tekhnicheskaia Revoliutsia i</u> <u>Sotsialisticheskaia Integratsia</u>. Moscow: Izdatel'stvo Nauka, 1973.

Smirnov, V.S., Semibratov, V.G., Lebedev, O.T. <u>Nauchno-Teknicheskaia Revolutsia i Filosofskie Problemy</u> <u>Formirovania Inzhinernogo Myshlenia</u>. Moscow: Vyshaia Shkola, 1973.

Afanasyev, V.G., <u>Nauchno-Tekhnicheskaia Revoliutsia,</u> <u>Upravlenie, Obrazovanie</u>. Moscow: Izdatel'stvo Politi-cheskoi Literatury, 1972.

Chapter VI

Current Industrial Theory (1974-1982)

Western distaste for the Soviet industrial theory of the
Stalinist period (1937-1953) aside, the theory, nonetheless,
stood as an original theoretical creation of the Soviet
system, which, above all else, was extremely congruent with
it. Each successive period in the development of Soviet
industrial theory brought new and frequently very innovative
and original developments in the theory (as for instance,
the period of enthusiasm). Each step was marked by distinct
growth in the sophistication and complexity of the theory.
Thus, during the short transforming period (1953-1956), the
adaptation of Soviet industrial theory to its life without
Stalin began. During the period of enthusiasm (1957-1965)
that followed, Soviet industrial theory had matured and had
also decisively rejected the emerging Western post-industrial
theories.

The phase preceding the most recent stage in the development of Soviet industrial theory, the stage of partial
reconciliation with the emergence of post-industrial society
within advanced capitalism (1966-1973)--exhibited the highest
level of complexity and sophistication. At that point,
Soviet industrial theory entered a stage of quasi-pluralism
which, as was demonstrated in the preceding chapter, was
characterized by a great deal of diversity and conflict
between frequently contradictory views expressed, however,
in a non-conflictual atmosphere, that is, by simply failing
to acknowledge the existence of differing positions.

The quasi-pluralistic period of Soviet industrial theory

had waned by the early nineteen-seventies, and during the mid-nineteen-seventies a new period in the development of Soviet industrial theory had apparently emerged. There was every reason to have expected that the newest period in the development of the theory would bring further growth in terms of its originality, complexity and sophistication. However, in light of such expectations, the latest stage in the development of Soviet industrial theory could only be considered a bitter disappointment.

Although the latest stage in the development of Soviet industrial theory undoubtedly served as a continuation of the period which immediately preceeded it, this continuation was hardly progressive. That is, while the liberal wing of Soviet industrial theory which had been so prominent during the earlier period had degenerated, atrophied, and had virtually disappeared, the conservative wing had taken over and in the latest period had become the dominant component of soviet industrial theory. However, the liberal wing had not declined as the result of any sort of theoretical purge brought on by attacks from other theoretical quarters as had occurred before to other trends in Soviet theory and culture. Rather, the liberal wing of Soviet industrial theory withered away in as quiet, harmonious and unobtrusive a way as it had coexisted with its counterpart, the conservative wing during the quasi-pluralistic period. This was greatly facilitated by the very character of the liberal wing itself. As we remember from the preceeding chapter, the liberal wing

was a complex and controversial creation which, in fact, was
a mosaic of conservative and liberal trends. Hence, in
view of the fact that the Soviet industrial theory did not
undergo a purge of any type, it appears that the conservative
trend within the liberal wing of Soviet industrial theory
overtook and subsequently eliminated its liberal elements
altogether, resulting in the emergence of a new stage in
the theory.

The newest stage in the development of Soviet industrial theory primarily relied upon the conservative, repetitious argument that was taken from the earlier periods of its
development. This does not suggest, however, that the theory
was static. One could see a definite line of continuity
and progression with regard to the earlier period. Already
during the earlier period, some Soviet theoreticians of the
liberal wing, preoccupied with synthesizing some of the
theoretical achievements of Western post-industrial theories
with the achievements of Soviet industrial theory, zealously
appealed for the incorporation of the most advanced Western
methods of industrial management, based upon mathematical
modelling and statistics, into the body of Soviet industrial
theory and called as well for their further development.

During the latest period, those appeals began to be
increasingly heeded and there appeared a steady stream of
works brimming with mathematical and statistical models
designed to increase the productivity of labor and to
facilitate and improve the general flow of industrial inputs

and outputs. However, there was nothing peculiarly Soviet
about these works. They simply utilized mathematical and
statistical formulae to optimize the process of production
with no attention paid to such concepts as socialism,
cultural transformation, or the communist man, to mention
only a few. In other words, they endeavored to link the
Soviet population with the post-industrial high-technology
without any regard for the original goals of the Soviet
transformation. In fact, these works could easily have
been published in any advanced capitalist society without
raising any suspicion that they might be the product of
Soviet minds. In addition to the absence of any pretense
of ideological concern, these works moreover took the form
of work in applied areas rather than the social sciences.

To illustrate this point we will examine several works
which are most typical of this style. To begin with, we see
the example of Lakhtin's work which outlined the conditions
for optimal decision-making.[1] He set out to identify the
logical parameters of the perfect decision-making environment:

> When we are talking about perfecting methods of
> management, we recognize in this way that it might
> be more or less perfect. Therefore, we pose a
> question about the conditions in which we can
> achieve the greatest perfection, i.e., we are
> talking about optimal conditions. [2]

Consequently, Lakhtin proceeded to define his sense of these
optimal conditions in terms derived from mathematics and
natural sciences and began to examine the following question:

234

when is it worthwhile to undertake work on the improvement
of management?

> At the outset, we will consider the following
> problem: the study of the physical labor of
> a single worker who is digging a ditch. To
> discover how much energy he expends in the
> performance of this task, the worker was con-
> nected to the measuring apparatus. As long as
> the power which is needed to operate the measuring
> apparatus is incommensurably small in comparison
> with the power lost during the labor process, we
> may tentatively conclude that we achieved this
> information without any cost because the measure-
> ment still did not adversely influence the pro-
> ductivity of labor. However, if we desire to
> increase the accuracy of the measurement (i.e.,
> to increase the quantity of the information), we
> would have to increase the input of energy until
> the power needed becomes equal to the power needed
> to undertake the labor task. If the former out-
> paces the latter, then the situation which occurs
> may be described as the situation when 'the inves-
> tigator eats up the producer.'   3

Although there is nothing especially objectionable in
the logic of Lakhtin's argument, the argument itself is
totally devoid of any kind of ideological content. Most
importantly, the social content of the labor process (a
characteristic which is fundamental to Marxian philosophy)
is entirely ignored thus pushing it to the realm of the
natural sciences. Consequently, the labor process and the
reasons for its scientific analysis are seen in terms of
the utilization of thermodynamic energy. The proud
socialist worker is treated as a guinea pig, connected
to a measuring apparatus for the purpose of discovering
the best way of utilizing his labor power. This is hardly
shocking in light of Lenin's own fascination with
Taylorism. However, for Lenin,

Taylorism was a tool that could be employed in the achievement of communism, while Lakhtin is apparently completely
disinterested in combining his work with any larger kind of
theory other than the abstract logical model of management
which was based on systems theory:

> To put it simply, we will consider that the
> system consists of two elements--the one which
> manages and the one which is managed. The manag-
> ing elements produce decisions, and to substan-
> tiate them they carry out (or order) the under-
> taking of necessary research, which in turn
> spells the loss of resources utilized in the
> research effort. As a result of decision-
> making, the managed element achieves the optimal
> effects which may be measured according to con-
> crete economic rules. [4]

Still another example of such value-free professionalism may be found in Gavrilova's work.[5] She dreams of
constructing an omnipotent superbureaucracy, a superbly
self-contained body approaching managerial perfection. It
would be organized to resemble a gigantic cybernetic machine
where electronic impulses would be substituted by human
elements whose task would be so superbly codified and controlled that they would operate in a truly automated fasion:

> The functioning of managerial systems consists
> of the aggregate of concrete organizational pro-
> cedures, all of which represent the instructions
> and the rules of operation for people and groups
> working within the system. Therefore, the
> reorganization of managerial systems is under-
> taken in operating economic enterprises. Moreover,
> work on new types of managerial systems will
> result in the creation of an entire complex of
> codified organizational systems and procedures
> which will incorporate all the operations of the
> functioning system of management which are per-
> formed both by the people as well as by the
> man-machine systems. [6]

236

What is more, Gavrilova proposed that those who serve this
system of superbureaucratic management should be controlled
by a sense of "responsibility" to the set of "necessary
laws"[7] by which they would be bound. While Gavrilova's
ideas might be admired for their ingenuity, nonetheless, it
is difficult to find within her work any clues which might
connect it to that body of normative theory which proposes
the creation of communist society. If anything, Gavrilova's
ideas are more reminiscent of another body of philosophical
work--that of Jeremy Bentham.

Such ideas were further advanced in one of Afanasyev's
works.[8] Although he was well known for his hard-nosed
conservatism, in this instance, this conservativism was
very moderated. Afanasyev argues rather straightforwardly
for the implementation of the most advanced methods of
social management because of his belief in the inherent
limitations of the human mind:

> Finally, there is still another way of overcoming
> the contradiction between the continually
> increasing volume of information and man's
> limited memory and capacity for processing infor-
> mation, namely, the utilization of scientific
> and technical means and the creation of infor-
> mational systems and especially of automated
> informational systems with the help of electronic
> computers. To an increasing extent, computers
> today serve as gigantic repositories of informa-
> tion and are replacing traditional archives,
> reference manuals, and encyclopedia.
>
>   At the present time, there exist three
> types of automated systems:
> --systems for the regulation of equipment
>   and technology;
> --systems for the regulation of enterprises
>   and sectors;

--systems of scientific and technical information
which are essentially information retrieval
systems.

It is anticipated that in the future these
systems will be integrated into country-wide
information systems, required for the regulation
of productive activities. It seems to us that
ultimately this will be an integrated information
system for the regulation not only of production
but of society as a whole, including its economic,
socio-political, and spiritual processes.   9

This "professional" and value-free subfield of Soviet

industrial theory constituted virtually the only innovation

in the newest stage of its development. Instead of respond-

ing to new developments with some kind of theoretical

innovation and improvement, Soviet industrial theory began

to recycle and rejuvenate its achievements from the earlier

periods. Consequently, Soviet industrial theory stood as a

kind of smorgasbord, a mosaic of elements drawn from

earlier periods. On the other hand, the latest period of

Soviet industrial theory became a theoretical monument of

sorts embodying those achievements from the earlier periods

of its development which remained viable in the eyes of

Soviet academia. It is to a discussion of those specific

elements now preserved in the latest stage of Soviet

industrial theory that we shall now turn.

Elements of the Stalinist industrial theory rather

astonishingly are considered by contemporary Soviet

academicians as worthy of inclusion in what amounts to a

kind of institutionalized theoretical immortality. Chief

among these elements was a reinvigorated stress upon the

supreme theoretical role of the Communist party, the party's
First Secretary and the fundamental theory of Marxism-
Leninism. This is not to suggest that a rebirth of Stalinism in its totality had been seen. Stalinism, of course,
was as much a socio-economic phenomenon as it was a
theoretical position. It is to the elements of that theoretical position (which was discussed in detail in the
first chapter of this study) that we refer here.

Examples of the Soviet industrial scholars' pursuit
of Stalinist ideals in this particular field are not only
numerous, but what is more important, appear to increase
over time, suggesting that a revised perspective is still
developing. Right from the outset of the current period,
the theoretical omnipotence of Marxism-Leninism was stressed
much more strongly than in any other of the post-Stalinist
periods. Zvorykin, for example, points out that the
Marxist-Leninist theory has answers for virtually all problems of advanced industrial society:

> General problems of work changes in the USSR
> have been investigated in Marxist-Leninist social
> theory with sufficient profundity. This refers
> to the questions of overcoming essential dif-
> ferences between physical and mental work,
> industrial and agricultural labour, increased
> requirements placed on all types of labour
> activity by the scientific and technological
> revolution. [10]

Further, Kozikov maintained that the theory of Marxism-
Leninism had mastered already the way in which post-industrial
technology would be employed to further the historical

transformation of humanity:

> The problem of the correlation of the scientific-
> technological and social revolutions in a broad
> plan is the problem of the correlation of scien-
> tific technological and social progress during
> historical development. The classics of Marxism-
> Leninism have successfully solved already the
> problem of this correlation in their teachings
> on the laws of socio-economic formations. They
> showed that the transformation from one historical
> formation into another is accomplished in accor-
> dance with objective laws. One of the most
> important of those laws is the law of the com-
> pliance between productive relations and the
> character and the level of the development of
> the productive forces. The manifestations of
> this universal sociological (sic!) law in
> the historical process characterize the complex
> dialectical intercorrelation of the material-
> technological base, in which, above all,
> the scientific-technological progress is being
> manifested, with the entire system of social
> relations. [11]

On the other hand, Mcheglov found Marxism-Leninism
to be the only true philosophy located in the middle of
the ideological spectrum where it was besieged by attacks
from the right and left:

> Marxism-Leninism had to struggle with two
> sources of perversion in its efforts to
> solve the problem of the correlation between
> socialist and universally human values.
> Although, at first sight, these perversions
> appear to be diametrically opposed, never-
> theless, their roots lay in a similar method-
> ological position. These are: on the one
> hand, left-wingism which is a kind of naive
> puritanism which rejects any kind of succession
> between socialism and the previous stages
> in the development of society, and this atti-
> tude at times even reaches the sphere of material
> production. Moreover, similar zealots of
> the 'purity' of socialism deny the existence of
> any universally-human values derived from the
> culture of the past, because they claim that
> they are thoroughly reactionary and anti-socialist.

240

On the other hand, the followers of the doctrine
of ideological and political conciliation who
alienate themselves from real universal human
values, which were achieved in earlier (and
contemporary) social formations, bury in oblivion
the essence of the distinctions between the
different historical formations. This kind of
methodological defect is typical of right-wing
revisionists.   12

This steady elevation of Marxism-Leninism to the posi-

tion of absolute theoretical supremacy resulted in calls

for it to serve as the sole framework for any kind of

theoretical activity. Thus, in the case of Soviet indus-

trial theory, Gvishiani stated that:

The teachings of Marxism-Leninism on the
development of society are the basis for
understanding the essence of the socio-
economic determinism and social role of the
Scientific and Technological Revolution.   13

This is a far cry indeed from the work of theorists

in the liberal wing of Soviet industrial theory who only a

few years earlier attempted to synthesize some of the

theoretical achievements of Western post-industrial theories

with Soviet industrial theory. Now, however, the tradition

of a certain degree of pluralism, even if only a quasi-

pluralism, in Soviet industrial theory is being abandoned.

Moreover, with time, this renewed enthusiasm for Marxism-

Leninism is being strengthened and ossified. Here, theo-

reticians such as Tikhomirov,[14] Egorov,[15] Rumiantsev,[16]

Afanasyev,[17] Kronrod,[18] Fedosieyev,[19] Semenov[20] and

Shcherbitskii[21] excelled in restoring the theoretical

supremacy of Marxism-Leninism to a position more exalted

than at any time after the collapse of Stalinism in the

Soviet Union. Those Soviet industrial theoreticians who

were preoccupied with the rejuvenation and readaptation

of some elements of the Stalinist industrial theory went

so far as to even employ some of the most classical

language of the Stalinist style of argument. Observe

carefully how Paton opened his work:

> Our country, which is full of creative forces
> and energy, confidently advances in the con-
> struction of communism. Amongst all of the
> grandiose accomplishments of our nation in
> its socio-economic transformation, the role
> of Soviet science is exceptionally important. 22

Although Soviet industrial scholars of the most recent

period were closest on the ideological spectrum to the

ideals of Stalinism, they still fell short of Stalinist

achievements in their treatment of Marxism-Leninism. As

was pointed out earlier, Stalinist industrial theoreti-

cians not only staunchly and vigorously declared their

adherence to the supreme guidance of Marxism-Leninism, but

also their discussions of the particular details of this

theory, although very repetitious and ritualistic, never-

theless, were very elaborate, passionate and profuse. If

during the current period the pronouncements of faith them-

selves were no less staunch and vigorous than during the

Stalinist period, the elaboration of the details of

Marxism-Leninism was missing entirely. It appears that on

the issue of the theoretical position of Marxism-Leninism, Soviet industrial scholars of the latest period have been following the combined influence of both the Stalinist period as well as the experience of the later periods. Hence, if they declared their faith and adherence to Marxism-Leninism in almost the same way as had Stalinist theoreticians, they appeared to consider, following the example of the post-Stalinist industrial theory, more detailed discussion of Marxism-Leninism as rather inadvised because of its inherent theoretical vulnerability. Of course, during the Stalinist period, this vulnerability could be neutralized by the cult of Stalin's personality, but once Stalinism had disappeared, in the context of industrial theory, it was more prudent to discuss Marxism-Leninism in a very vague and general way.

If the return of Soviet industrial theory to the Stalinist schemes on the subject of the theoretical supremacy of Marxism-Leninism had only a relative character, then, on the subject of the party's role in Soviet industrial theory, the return to Stalinist schemes had an almost absolute character. While at the beginning of the latest period the party's unquestionable guidance over Soviet industrial theory was stressed more strongly than ever before during the post-Stalinist years, with the passage of time the party's role was restored to the position that it had held during the Stalinist period. Soviet industrial scholars ritualistically declared their party to be the supreme leader and that their works were written with total obedience to the party's guidance. Certainly, the party and the fundamental doctrine of Marxism-Leninism had always been recognized by Soviet industrial scholars as their supreme guiding light, but the way in which such a profound statement of faith was made was very much related to the degree of creative freedom and theoretical independence exhibited in their works. Hence, during the Stalinist period and during the recent period, Soviet industrial scholars outstripped each other in their efforts to stress their unquestionable allegiance to the guidance of the party and the fundamental doctrine of Marxism-Leninism.

Their theories were characterized by almost an entire lack of inventiveness and originality and were extremely conservative and repetitious. On the other hand, when as during the period of enthusiasm or as in the case of the liberal wing of Soviet industrial theory during the period of quasi-pluralism, the proclamations of allegiance to the guidance of the party and Marxism-Leninism had only a casual intent and were only infrequently invoked, Soviet industrial theoreticians exhibited substantial creativity and inventiveness. Consequently, the degree of intensity employed and the form in which Soviet industrial scholars expressed their pronouncement of faith and allegiance to the party and Marxism-Leninism were themselves very important indicators of the state of the theory itself.

Moreover, it may be argued that these indicators were also very important signals directed to the broad milieus, scholarly and otherwise, which were interested in studying and actively pursuing industrial theory. Those signals could be easily interpreted as a call for an ideological "circling of the wagons," avoidance of creative and often precarious adventures, while conservatively protecting those achievements already accomplished. Considering the fact that those signals emanated from the top of the academic hierarchy, they could hardly be ignored by the lower echelons of Soviet academicians. Such signals could facilitate the transformation of the entire paradigm of Soviet industrial theory.

Illustrative of the renewed emphasis upon the role of the party is Grinchel's work, professional and otherwise value-free in character, which nevertheless pointed out that the party was the force which outlined the horizons of further industrial development in the Soviet Union.[23] On the other hand, Sadykov's work was spawned by the party's expression of interest in the subject matter:

> The XXIV Congress of the CPSU paid great atten-
> tion to the intensification of the speed of
> scientific-technological progress, as well as
> to the broad utilization of the achievements
> of science and technology in all the spheres
> of social life.   [24]

Moreover, for him the party was above all the locus of the scientific wisdom of socialist industrial development:

> In the economic policy of our party which
> takes into consideration the specificity
> of the contemporary stage of the construction
> of communism, a great intensification of
> production is foreseen, as well as the speeded
> up development of the productive forces which
> will be based on scientific-technological
> progress.   25

Further, at the beginning of the present period, it was

stated in no uncertain terms, in a study very appropriately

entitled Partia i Sovremennaia Nauchno-Tekhnicheskaia

Revolutsia v SSSR (The Party and the Contemporary Scientific-

Technological Revolution in the USSR), that:

> Following the Leninism course and fulfilling
> V.I. Lenin's legacy, the party strives to
> achieve a close connection between science
> and production. The achievements which are
> gained in this way meaningfully increase the
> productivity of labor and the effectiveness
> of production. During the last few years,
> the party devised and introduced into practice
> a whole range of organizational devices which
> are directed at increasing the level of
> development of different branches of industry
> and speeding the solution of scientific-
> technological problems, as well as stimulating
> creative research in science and technology
> and encouraging the greatest possible growth
> in the role of science and strengthening its
> bond with production.   26

From the beginning of the recent period, industrial

theoreticians surpassed theoreticians of the Stalinist

period in terms of the importance they attached to the

role of the party. During the heyday of the Stalinist

period, every aspect of social life, including of course

the party, was dwarfed by the position of Stalin himself.

By contrast, during the recent period, while Soviet

industrial scholars have made a decisive effort to pair
the growing theoretical importance of the conservative
and dogmatic adherence to Marxism-Leninism with the growing theoretical importance of political authority, they
have not made an attempt to reinstitute any form of
personality cult. Thus, their theoretical elevation of
the position of the party may be viewed as an attempt to
fill the vacuum left by the collapse of the personality
cult.

Most apparent, however, was the return to the Stalinist
type of ritualism in the composition of the works of
Soviet industrial scholars. As was seen earlier, works
of the Stalinist period typically opened with the paying
of homage to the hierarchy of the Olympus of socialist
theory and then followed with a more moderated tribute to
the authority of the party and the fundamental theory of
Marxism-Leninism. By contrast, works produced during the
recent period sought to compensate for the absence of the
personality cult and the now reivsed hierarchy of the
socialist Olympus with intensified emphasis upon the
party's role in Soviet industrial theory. Industrial
scholars of the current period, like their predecessors
from the Stalinist period, wanted their readers to believe
that they were simply disseminators of the ideas and
theories which were derived from superior authority,
either that authority emanating from the super-human
socialist Olympus or from the no less super-human

collective authority of the party. Thus, during the
recent period, the quality and specific character of the
particular arguments of Soviet industrial scholars were
decisively overshadowed by this linkage with the party and
Marxism-Leninism, just as had been the case with Stalinist
industrial theory. This association rendered both sets
of theory extremely uninventive, ritualistic and dogmatic.

Typically, works of the recent period extend what
had been only a paragraph long homage to the party's
supreme authority during the Stalinist period to pages
long (and in some cases, chapters long) homages to this
authority. The wording of these homages took on new
vigor and imaginary achievements were presented as in fact
having been accomplished. For instance, Rubtsov boasted
that:

> After having created a developed socialist society
> under the guidance of the CPSU, the Soviet nation
> is able to proceed with the practical achievement
> of the material-technological base of communism. 27

Frequently, the homage paid to the party's supremacy was
cast in such strong language that it almost could be considered an attempt to create a cult of the party which
would be analogous to Stalin's personality cult. Observe
the opening to Fedoseyev's article:

> According to the common assessment of not only
> communists but also of all the progressive
> people of the world, the XXV Congress of the
> CPSU indeed had tremendous historical signi-
> ficance. This was one of the most important
> events of our times. 28

Afanasyev argued that it was the party's task to outline
the research horizons for Soviet industrial scholars,[29]
and for the accomplished veteran of Soviet industrial
theory, Iu.E. Volkov, the XXV Congress served spectacularly
in this capacity. He went so far as to argue that the
minutes from the Congress were themselves a pathbreaking
theoretical achievement:

> The documents from the XXV Congress of the
> CPSU which summarize the achievements of the
> development of our society during the last
> years as well as the ambitious goals of per-
> fecting our mature socialist society--the goal
> of social policy in contemporary conditions--
> are a very rich source for the scientific analysis
> of the concrete processes of communist construc-
> tion. Further, these documents and the
> theoretical concepts which are embedded in
> their foundation constitute an essential
> resource in the process of enriching and
> refining general philosophical and sociolo-
> gical concepts which are relevant to the process
> of the development of society in general and the
> development of socialism in particular. These
> concepts are: the dialectics of the objective
> and subjective elements of this development,
> the essence and the structure of political
> activity and of social management, the essence
> of socialist humanism, the structure of social
> phenomena and relations, the content of the
> concept of the 'socialist picture of life'
> and its relationship with the actual conditions
> of life, etc.   [30]

Soviet scholars stated very bluntly that the party was
not only the supreme political, social, ideological leader
as well as the sole source of theoretical illumination and
guidance, but above all, they maintained that the party
was actively creating the new Soviet consciousness and
consequently shaping the new Soviet man.[31] Thus,

individuals as well as the entire Soviet society were the
products of the party's creative activities, and as such
their attitude and relationship with the party had to be
intrinsically one of total submission and subservience,
just as had been the case decades earlier during the
Stalinist period.

What is most important, however, is the further evolution of the party's role in Soviet industrial theory.
Initially, the extreme emphasis upon the party appeared to
be something of a novelty but in the more recent years it
increasingly became its characteristic feature. Moreover,
this development was accompanied by the rejuvenation of
another feature of the Stalinist period, that is, a
partial return to a much more formalized structure for
scholarly works. The characteristic rhythm of Stalinist
works was partially restored with the inclusion of the
highly routinized and stylized tributes to the party and
to the fundamental theory of Marxism-Leninism.

While the influence of the Stalinist period on specific
issues could clearly be established, the influence of the
first post-Stalinist period--the period of transforming
industrial theory--had a much more subtle and tentative
character. We are able to clearly identify only one such
area in which this influence may be seen. This was the
issue of the role of the party's First Secretary. In all
other areas, the confidence and optimism of the present
recent contrast with the insecurity expressed in the works

of the transforming period.

During the transforming period as well as throughout
the other post-Stalinist periods there was a definite
atmosphere of ambivalence surrounding the role of the
party's First Secretary. While the role of the party
itself was growing, there was a clear effort to curb the
importance of the party's First Secretary. The reasons
for this were twofold: first of all, if most of the elements of the personality cult were being dismantled, then,
of course, the importance of the office of the party's
First Secretary which was one of the main attributes of
the cult had to diminish visibly at least in part to
prevent that office from ever becoming a kind of spring-
board for the reemergence of the personality cult.
However, although the general framework for the new,
post-Stalinist role of the party's First Secretary had
been established, nevertheless, the particular details had
not yet been ironed out which resulted in a certain tentativeness in their work concerning this issue.

This trend has been drastically reversed during the
recent period with the growth in the theoretical importance
attached to the position of the party's First Secretary.
Eventually, more theoretical importance was attached to it
than had been the custom during any of the post-Stalinist
periods. Yet, the weight attached to the role during this
period paled in comparison with the Stalinist period.
Nevertheless, it has become the custom of Soviet industrial

scholars in the recent period to stress the importance of
the party's First Secretary's guidance much more strongly
than ever before during the post-Stalinist period. If
during the post-Stalinist period the name of the party's
First Secretary rarely appeared on the pages of the works
on industrial theory, in the present period it has become
quite routine to pay theoretical homage to his authority
and illuminating guidance. The homage paid to the First
Secretary increasingly has been treated as a customary
part of the more and more obligatory homage to the
supreme role of the party itself. During the Brezhnev era,
the industrial scholars sought to imprint in the minds of
their readers the message that Brezhnev was to be viewed
as the main spokesman for the supreme body of the party.
Most commonly this message was presented in the following
way:

> The communist party of the Soviet Union creatively
> develops Marxist-Leninist theory, and while doing
> so it is guided by the Leninist requirements of
> class-consistency, partyness and because of that,
> it uses a strictly scientific, concrete-historical
> and multi-dimensional, as well as complex approach
> to social phenomena and processes. Consequently,
> the party bases its activity on the methodology
> of dialectical materialism. The party considers
> as one of its important ideological-theoretical
> tasks the deep generalization and comprehension of
> the world revolutionary process, as well as the
> international practice of the construction of
> socialism and communism, scientific inquiry into
> the dialectic of social development (in particular,
> scientific inquiry into the laws of the developed
> socialist society). As a result, the party wants
> to master all of these tasks to achieve the his-
> torical goal which faces the international working
> class--the construction of communism. The content,
> the forms and methods of the ideological-
> theoretical activity of the CPSU on the

contemporary stage of the development of Soviet
society in the conditions of mature socialism
were analyzed and substantiated in a multidimensional way in the conclusions of the XXIV
Congress of the CPSU, in the lectures and pre-
sentations of comrade L.I. Brezhnev and in
other party documents...   32

This characterization of Brezhnev as the leading pur-
veyor of wisdom concerning development became the standard
means for opening and concluding works on industrial theory
during the recent period.[33] However, as was the case with
the transforming theory which waivered in its treatment of
Stalin, Soviet scholars lately neglected to specify their
precise understanding of the theoretical role to be played
by the First Secretary. Viewed as perhaps the most important living bearer of the torch of wisdom, nevertheless,
it was clear that the Secretary could not begin to claim
the status accorded Marx, Engels or Lenin. The closest
Brezhnev could come to the Olympic trio, was to have his
opinions included in discussions of their teachings.

All in all, despite the strengthening of the First
Secretary's position within the industrial theory, Brezhnev
nevertheless was treated by Soviet industrial scholars of
the recent period in a manner resembling the treatment
accorded to Stalin by the theorists of the transforming
period. That is, Stalin's place within the transforming
industrial theory was located somewhere between the peak
of the socialist Olympus and the party leadership.

Considering the ambiguity involved in defining Stalin's role, we can understand why the scholars of the transforming period exhibited such a great degree of ambivalence and tentativeness on that subject. Similarly, while Brezhnev's authority as the party's First Secretary was recognized by the industrial scholars of the recent period as surpassing that of other prominent party leaders, that authority did not even begin to approximate the authority of the figures of the socialist Olympus.

In the contemporary period, this approach was the result of a much more independent and calculated choice. While the work of the theorists of the transforming period was deeply influenced by their genuine insecurity and relatively much weaker institutional position vis-à-vis the political elites and their lack of previous experience in influencing policy formulation there, the position of the theorists of the recent period has been much stronger politically; the tradition of industrial scholars having a certain input into policy formulation had already been well established. Their input would undoubtedly be welcomed if they were to contribute a theoretical explanation of the relationship of the First Secretary to the Olympic figures and the party's elites themselves and integrate this effort with the rest of the body of Marxism-Leninism. Of course, while undertaking such an endeavor, they would not encounter any difficulties in integrating any kind of new theoretical discoveries with the science of Marxism-

Leninism, because this particular brand of science itself
was aptly designed to be an elastic bag which could be
stretched in every possible direction as long as a consensus prevented any kind of inner dispute between the ill
fitting elements. It was quite irrelevant, indeed, whether
and how the different elements of Marxism-Leninism agreed
with one another as long as the theory's supremacy was not
questioned in any kind of open or overt manner. Consequently, new elements could be added to Marxism-Leninism
regardless of how they might contradict other aspects of
the theory, as long as they conformed to the need to pay
homage to the general concept of Marxism-Leninism, to the
Olympic authorities and to the party.

It has been argued on numerous occasions in earlier
chapters of this work, that throughout the period examined,
the science of Marxism-Leninism could be viewed as a kind
of a happily growing, omnivorous amoeba which was capable
of ingesting and integrating within itself virtually
every kind of needed theoretical adaptation. The issue of
internal consistency remained almost totally irrelevant
as long as there existed a standing commitment to the idea
of the correctness of the general and very abstractly
defined whole.

However, just the opposite was the case when the
expulsion of any element of the theory of Marxism-Leninism
was involved. Above all, such occurrences were extremely
rare, but when they did in fact take place, they were

engendered by truly earth shattering events. Following
Stalin's demise, the element of the personality cult was
expunged from the theory of Marxism-Leninism. However,
this alteration in the theory, certainly quite modest
given the dimension of the social upheaval that ensued,
was accompanied by countless assurances that the rest of
the body of Marxism-Leninism which had been developed
during the Stalinist period was still sound. Such assurances were necessary in order to demonstrate that the
traditional tolerance of contradictory elements, the very
essence holding the theoretical amalgam together, would
continue to be maintained.

However, this essential consensus would be potentially
undermined if Soviet industrial scholars were to clearly
explain the theoretical position of the party's First
Secretary within their theory because such a clarification
would involve an inherent reshuffling of the other elements
of Marxism-Leninism. Only during the Stalinist period was
the position of the party's First Secretary, that is,
Stalin himself, clearly specified. In fact, the entire
body of the theory of Marxism-Leninism had been constructed
around this central and pivotal point and served as a
complement to it. The scholars of the transforming period,
in their vague and tentative manner, became proficient at
the art of preserving the integrity of Marxism-Leninism
while drastically reducing Stalin to the ranks of those
merely "important" mortals. The party's First Secretary

was treated as the most important leader who was located, in terms of that importance, somewhere between the party elite and the Olympic figures but without specifying how close the First Secretary approached either group.

However, there was now a decisive need to strengthen the theoretical justification for the authority of the First Secretary, but without becoming overly specific, because that would necessitate another reshuffling and rearranging of the elements of Marxism-Leninism. Hence, it was much more judicious for the Soviet industrial theoreticians of the recent period who enjoyed a relatively strong social position, to imitate on this point the tentative style of the industrial scholars of the transforming period whose social position was much weaker.

If the theoretical treatment of Marxism-Leninism, the party and the First Secretary could be considered a decisive step backward, still there emerged another element of Soviet industrial theory in its newest stage which perhaps outweighed all the other elements put together. This was the rejuvenation and reapplication of the theoretical enthusiasm which was so dominant during the late nineteen-fifties and the early nineteen-sixties.

Upon first consideration, this idea would seem to be absurd. The enthusiasm of the earlier period was not only spawned by political and cultural factors which stemmed from the post-Stalinist thaw, but most of all by the favorable indicators of economic growth which coincided with

the initiation of the program of broad economic reforms
which were supposed to lead the nation to even greater
prosperity in the near future. Moreover, all those hopes
were greatly enhanced by rapid advancements in the area of
high-technology which then seemed to promise a _panaceum_
for all the socio-economic problems of the Soviet brand of
socialism. In contrast to the earlier period, there were
no material justifications for the reappearance of
unbounded enthusiasm within Soviet industrial theory. The
consensus among economic experts is that the Soviet economy
has encountered substantial difficulties in recent years
and in certain sectors registers very low growth rates
and in some cases even stagnation. Although the strict
management over and discipline demanded of the Soviet
population enabled the regime to successfully avoid undue
political stress resulting from economic disappointments,
it is nonetheless ludicrous for theorists, given the present
material conditions characterizing the population, to
expound upon the glorious level of abundance soon, to be
achieved. Nor is it reasonable to claim mastery over the
dilemmas of the historical development of society through
the soon-to-be created communist society.

Such restraint, however, has not characterized recent
work in the area, which, in turn, became reminiscent of
works produced twenty-five years earlier. For example,
Grinchel' characterizes the development of the Soviet
economy during the nineteen-sixties in the following way:

> As a result of the broad utilization of the
> achievements of science and technology in our
> national economy, a substantial increase in
> national income is occurring.   35

Sadykov, on the other hand, pointed to a specific

achievement, one of Lenin's favorite indicators of indus-

trial transformation--electrification--and found that the

Soviet Union had made stunning progress in this field

during the nineteen-sixties:

> Of course, the more energy there is in a
> given country per capita, the more powerful
> is the productive potential of the people
> there. In the year 1960, 1365 kht-hours of
> electric energy was the average for every
> citizen of the USSR. It meant that every
> man in our society had 5 electric helpers.
> In the year 1972, those indicators substan-
> tially increased. In the USSR 858 billions
> kht-hours of electric energy were produced,
> that is, for every inhabitant of our country,
> there were about 3,613 kht-hours of electricity
> or to use different words, 15 electric helpers
> were working for every member of our society. 36

Sadykov's apparent goal was to present a picture of Soviet

economic development during the nineteen-sixties which

would demonstrate that the dreams of the original enthu-

siastic period had been fulfilled. Sadykov's argument

sought to prove that Soviet society as a whole had pro-

gressed tremendously in the economic area rather than

arguing that the lives of individuals had changed

noticeably. Consequently, the point was stressed that the

whole community had elevated itself to a higher level of

development.

The assessment of the nineteen-sixties as a time of
great economic triumph became the standard characterization
of the recent experience with economic development efforts
in the industrial theory of the recent period. Considering the steadily growing professionalism of Soviet
industrial theoreticians, hard statistical evidence was
more and more frequently favored in the validation of
arguments. Thus, Glagolev in pointing to the tremendous
economic achievements of Soviet society zeroed in on the
success of the nineteen-sixties:

> In the year 1972, the industrial output of
> our country was 105 times greater when com-
> pared to pre-revolutionary Russia. Only during
> the previous five years (1966-1970), the out-
> put of industrial production has increased 1.5
> times. The branches of production which assure
> technological progress in the national economy
> as well as increases in the effectiveness of
> social production developed rapidly.   [37]

On the other hand, Afanasyev found that during the
nineteen-sixties the Soviet Union had tremendously aug-
mented the production process:

> The augmentation of production assumes, above
> all, the general introduction of modern machinery
> and equipment, the latest materials and fuels,
> highly effective technological processes (physico-
> chemical, electro-physical, electronic, etc.)
> and the general modernization of existing equip-
> ment. Suffice it to say that in the ten years
> between 1957 and 1966 the Soviet Union produced
> 29,000 new types of machines and equipment and
> more than 10,000 new types of instruments. In
> 1970 alone nearly 3,000 models of new machines,
> equipment, apparati and about 1,000 new types of
> instruments were designed. About, 1,500 new
> types of articles with improved working and

technico-economic characteristics were put into
mass production.   38

Moreover, the nineteen-sixties were for Afanasyev not
only the period of rapid growth in the Soviet Union but
also they had produced an economic boom all throughout
Eastern Europe, fulfilling the predictions of the industrial
theoreticians of the original enthusiastic period who saw
the nineteen-sixties as the period in which giant strides
were taken toward the achievement of the mature socialist
system all throughout the countries of People's Democracy.

> In the period from 1958 to 1968, for instance,
> the net proportion of increase in industrial out-
> put achieved through raising labour productivity
> was more than 70 percent in the USSR, 65 percent
> in Poland, 80 percent in Czechoslovakia, 80 per-
> cent in the GDR, 75 percent in Rumania, and only
> 55 percent in Bulgaria.   39

After finally reaching the conclusion that the period
of the nineteen-fifties had seen enormous progress toward
achieving an advanced socialist system, brightening the
mood of the latest Soviet industrial theory and renewing
its positive and optimistic dimension, Soviet industrial
theoreticians began to argue that the economic development
of their society during the nineteen-seventies was a continuation of this colossal success. Thus, Skhukhadrin
argued that during the first half of the nineteen-seventies
the party was engaged in guiding the economic development
of the Soviet Union in the direction of a society characterized by material abundance:

> One of the conditions for the rapid fulfillment
> of the task of technologically transforming our
> national economy is the speedy renewal and trans-
> formation of aging technology. According to the
> directives of the XXIVth Congress of the CPSU
> concerning the five-year-plan for the development
> of the national economy of the USSR during the
> years 1971-1975, it was envisioned that the share
> of new productive funds would constitute 46% of
> industry and 60% of agriculture. During the first
> three years of this five-year-plan, much was
> accomplished in the direction of meeting this
> goal. Thus, in the year 1973 alone, 3,700 new
> techniques of industrial production were mastered
> and employed in mass-production. During the same
> period, 1,500 aging machines, tools and apparata
> were removed from the sphere of production.
> During the past year, about 4,000 elements of new
> technology as well as 3.7 million innovations,
> facilitating and rationalizing production were
> introduced into the national economy.   40

The simple and logical consequence of maintaining that

current Soviet development had fulfilled the theoretical

prophecies of the original enthusiastic period was to

conclude that Soviet society had entered the stage of

advanced socialism during the nineteen-seventies. Thus,

the only new theoretical achievement of current industrial

theory was the claim that the Soviet Union was already

an advanced socialist society. Such assurances were pro-

vided in virtually every work on industrial theory pro-

duced during this period. Moreover, since according to the

Soviet industrial scholars of the present period, the

advanced socialist system had already been achieved, the

other simple and logical conclusion to be drawn was that

Soviet society was in the midst of the transformation to

a communist society. To be sure, the Soviet industrial

scholars of the present period, like their counterparts
from the enthusiastic period, envisioned communist society
in quite the same way as Marx had some time ago. For
example, this is how Afanasyev conceives of the quintes-
sential communist society:

> The aim of communist society is the fully and
> harmoniously developed individual. To achieve
> this great goal the amount of time man spends
> in work must be cut to the minimum and his free
> or leisure time increased to the maximum. Both
> his working and leisure time must consist of
> activities that help to endow him with the highest
> qualities of the working man, the active partici-
> pant in public life, a person with fully developed
> intellectual and physical powers. And not only
> must we help to form these qualities, we must
> also see to it that they are used to the best
> possible effect.   41

Given this conceptualization, one probably would expect
to find Soviet scholars maintaining that the period of
advanced socialism would endure for some time into the
future, thus placing the time of the advent of communism
in the distant future. However, this was not the case.
Instead, Soviet industrial scholars clearly present the
contemporary historical epoch as the actual period of the
transformation from an advanced socialist system into communism. This is not to suggest that the Soviet industrial
scholars claim that this is the case in some kind of a
scholastic, abstract and formalistic way just to satisfy
their sense of dialectical historicism. Indeed, instead
of providing vague or abstract "evidence" supporting this
claim, Soviet scholars point to evidence from the current

Soviet social context which, in theory, demonstrates that
communism is now within easy reach. For example, automation, which twenty years earlier had caused so much optimism
amongst the Soviet industrial scholars, now is supposed to
bring Soviet society into the final stage of human development.

Zvorykin discusses the example of the advanced industries
and in so doing utters the immortal words: "Man is practically freed from physical work." Now, "His task is to
watch automated processes with the help of control instruments and to interfere only when there occur deviations
from the normal flow of the process." However, despite such
stunning successes, the labor of the advanced socialist
system still poses some problems: "But in these conditions
motor tension connected with physical labour is replaced
by sensory tension." However, even the problem of the
fatigue caused by mental labor will be soon solved by
Soviet scholars and thus the society will be able to step
right into its fully automated and communistic future:

> Over a longer term the supervisory functions
> will be handed over to automatic devices which
> in case of breakdowns in production will imme-
> diately switch on additional installations or
> take other measures. [42]

For the Soviet industrial theoreticians of the present
period, automation has become as important a condition of
the communist transformation as it had been for their
colleagues twenty-five years earlier. Automation was a sure

264

bet, because Marx himself saw in it the potential for a
futuristic technology. Belov underscores this point
although he does so in such a way as to avoid the dangers
inherent in a more extensive analysis of Marx's philosophy: "K. Marx foresaw that the development of the working
machines would bring about the creation of an automated
system which would steer the character of production into
the future."[43]

Altogether, Soviet scholars present a picture which
would suggest that total unanimity of thought existed
between Marx and Lenin on the issue of advanced technology,
a picture that has been painted by industrial scholars in
the Soviet Union from the very beginning. However, if
during the earlier periods those rosy and highly enthusiastic characterizations of advanced technology as the
agent which was supposed to transform the Soviet system
into communism were nothing else but theoretical speculations about the future, because the Soviet Union was
largely a quite underdeveloped society, in the present
period, these works departed from past practice, declaring
essentially that the future is now. That is, the basic
conclusion stemming from these works would suggest that
Soviet society was at the last stage of the communist transformation. The advancement of high technology which had
so greatly aroused Soviet industrial scholars twenty-five
years earlier now was considered almost complete. That
is, the scheme which was outlined by the theory of the

Scientific and Technological Revolution had been fulfilled in reality.

The question arises as to which theory of the Scientific and Technological Revolution has actually been fulfilled, because the content of this theory has undergone numerous transformations during its development. The Soviet industrial theoreticians in the recent period, in fact, have resurrected the theory of the Scientific and Technological Revolution from its initial stage, that is from the enthusiastic period of the late nineteen-fifties and the early nineteen-sixties. This is nothing less than stunning in light of the fact that the early STR theory represented the continuation of the basic industrial orientation borrowed from Lenin's philosophical system which interpreted the advancement of the emerging high technology as the newest stage in industrial development, and served as a categorical and contemptuous rejection of the concept of post-industrial society.

In so doing, the present theory cuts itself off almost entirely from the traditions of the mature theory of the Scientific and Technological Revolution as exhibited during the period of quasi-pluralism. In accordance with past practice, none of the industrial theoreticians ever bother to explain or even suggest why such a dramatic turnabout has been undertaken. Instead, all of a sudden, the STR theory began to be treated as if it had always existed in its original, early form.

Of course, the absence of any explanation as to what had happened to the mature STR theory from the preceding period has not spoiled the jubilation felt by the present industrial theoreticians as they verged on the achievement of the goals outlined by the early STR theory. Observe, for example, Gatovski's argument:

> The Scientific-technological progress under the conditions of socialism is the planned realization of the goals of increased well-being and prosperity in the realm of the national economy, as well as the development of all parts of the society. Those goals are being achieved through the qualitative renovation of the process of production and the creation of and mastery over new skills. Of course, scientific-technological progress includes the corresponding fields of science and education: in maintenance, in the sphere of production and in the absorption of new technology, i.e., its utilization both in the productive sphere as well as the non-productive sphere where it satisfies essential needs. The planned management of scientific-technological progress goes beyond the national boundaries of the individual economies of the socialist countries and thus even more influences the sphere of their international relations, that is the sphere of the international socialist division of labor. 44

Moreover, not only had the Scientific and Technological Revolution triumphed, but above all, according to the consensus of Soviet scholars, the Soviet Union had already reached the level of mature socialism.

> The developed socialist society assures the universal and harmonious evolution of the economic, socio-political and cultural conditions of life, i.e., it means that the developed socialist system creates the objective circumstances for the rapid construction of communism. 45

Even those few examples should enable us to understand why the mature STR theory of the quasi-pluralistic period was so easily, if not eagerly, catapulted into oblivion during the recent eclectic period. Although, the mature STR theory could be viewed as a state-of-the-art product of Soviet industrial scholarship, it nevertheless was a desperate if not humiliating theoretical scramble which attempted to build something on the ruins and ashes of the collapsing enthusiasm of both Soviet theory and Soviet society. Moreover, the mature STR theory had to resort to a search for theoretical aid and inspiration in the body of Western post-industrial theories and to synthesize some of those views with the original achievements of Soviet industrial theory. The enthusiasm and the optimism of the earlier period had dissipated and the achievement of a communist system in the Soviet Union was viewed as quite remote. On the other hand, the other theoretical branch of the quasi-pluralistic period--the conservative wing of Soviet industrial theory--with grim determination attempted to maintain continuity in theoretical development. There, too, the enthusiasm and optimism about the future of the social system had vanished almost entirely and the achievement of the communist system in the Soviet Union was discussed in very vague and unspecified terms. During the recent period, the continuity of the original enthusiastic period was restored, hence, the ideas from the quasi-pluralistic period could be forgotten now as an unneeded and sorrowful reminder of difficult times.

Although the enthusiasm marking the recent period is based on virtually the same theoretical premises and the same logic of argument as during the late nineteen-fifties and the early nineteen-sixties, it has a somewhat different character. While the earlier wave of enthusiasm stemmed from the sure triumph that was to be achieved in the not so distant future, now the enthusiasm grew from the knowledge that the triumphant transformation to the communist society was almost completed. The earlier somewhat expectant, euphoric joy reflected confidence in Soviet society's mastery of historical development, while later the joy expressed stemmed from the satisfaction with a fait accompli.

The belief that communism was at hand grew in strength and self-assurance with the passage of time. That is, the latest work in the field demonstrates an even greater conviction in this regard than do works from the early years of the recent period. For example, we may observe the following statement:

> The advantages of the socialist system in the utilization of the achievements of the Scientific and Technological Revolution reveal themselves with particular force in contemporary conditions, when the developed socialist society and an adequate material-technological base have already been constructed in the USSR. The developed socialist society is essentially different from the socialist society of its first historical phase. During the first phase of socialist society, the socialist industrialization of the country was accomplished as well as the

collectivization of the agricultural sector.
Moreover, before the present period, the material-
technological base of socialism had already been
created, that is, the productive apparatus of all
of the branches of the national economy which
create the technological base of the socialist
society, grew tremendously and matured in the
accomplishment of complex mechanization and
automation, electrification, chemization and
other trends inhering in scientific-technological progress.   46

Of course, such tremendous advancement in the social

base of society had in no way deterred the tremendous

advancement of the social superstructure. Thus, according

to Kosolapov, the communistic sense of freedom already

has begun to emerge in the Soviet Union:

The developed socialist society which really
exists already in the Soviet Union and is being
rapidly constructed in other countries of the
world's socialist unity, shows that in reality,
only in this part of the world, the jump from
the kingdom of necessity to the kingdom of freedom which was foreseen by Marx and Engels is
being accomplished.   47

Analyzing the creation of the new superstructure,

Pyotr Fedosyev points out that the Scientific and Tech-

nological Revolution gradually contributes to the wither-

ing away of the state apparatus, because it increasingly

draws the growing masses of the population into the

sphere of social management and thus it gradually gives

it a communistic character:

In the Soviet Union the professionalization
of the executive bodies of management is
combined with the enhancement of the role
of the representative bodies--the Soviets

at all levels and the social and political mass
organizations: party, trade union and youth
organizations, production conferences, and so on.
In the socialist countries systematic work is
conducted to develop the activity and effective-
ness of all democratic bodies in every possible
way, to ensure their control over the activity
of the executive organs of government and to
draw, on an increasingly larger scale, the
masses into the administration of state affairs.
This is facilitated by raising the general and
the political education of the population,
their cultural and professional level, by their
growing social consciousness and maturity.   48

Such a radical transformation of the social super-

structure of the Soviet Union is possible mainly because

the Scientific and Technological Revolution within the

context of mature socialism is allegedly already producing

a different kind of human being gifted with the kind of

personality and attitude of labor unprecedented in the

history of human development.   Guseinov and Rossman comment

in this regard:

Scientific-technological progress is changing
the content and character of labor and transforms
its functions while imbuing it with an intellectual, creative, aesthetic and emotional content;
thus, consequently, it is being purged of its
deficiencies. The labor process is transformed
into a source of delight, creativity and joy-
ousness and serves as well as the source for
the development of individual personality, and
thus gradually becomes the essential requisite
for a human being. Therefore, it is necessary
especially to stress here that presently as well
as in the future, the labor process requires
great involvement of both the emotions and the
will as well as a great sacrifice of mental and
physical energy, and persistence in the achievement of planned goals.   49

Finally, the historical role of the Scientific and Techno-

logical Revolution could be firmly established. Tsagolov's

work, representative of a host of theorists who had arrived
at the identical conclusion, argues:

> The Scientific and Technological Revolution is
> the catalyst of the process of the transformation
> from the lower phase of the communist system to
> the higher one...It is not only necessary that
> this be accomplished, but most of all, it is
> possible to achieve this end on the basis of the
> economy of the developed socialist society.   50

We may recall that the early STR theory did not consider
the emergence of the new high-technology and the consequent
emergence of the post-industrial type of relations of
production to be a qualitative change leading to the emergence of a new type of society--the post-industrial
society--but merely as the quantitative continuation of
industrial growth. As a result, the early STR theory
maintained that the simple quantitative industrial growth
in the conditions of the Soviet brand of socialism would
naturally and unavoidably transform the society into a
communist one, relatively in no time at all (that is
approximately 25 years). This simple logic led Soviet
industrial scholars to a categorical and contemptuous
rejection of Western post-industrial theories which suggested that advanced industrial societies were being
transformed into a qualitatively new entity--the post-
industrial society. This simple early STR theory was
partially forgotten and overshadowed by the mature STR
theory which emerged during the subsequent quasi-
pluralistic period and which began to flirt with the notion

of socialist post-industrial society. However, the Soviet
industrial theory of the latest period forcefully and
totally rejected such notions and returned to the schemes
of the early STR theory.

The explanation for such a dramatic and unexpected
turnabout is actually quite simple. While during the
quasi-pluralistic period, the Soviet industrial scholars
who by then were quite well situated politically and
bureaucratically were allowed to experiment quite freely
in face of the apparent social confusion and insecurity,
a decade later this confusion and insecurity about the
further socio-economic development of the Soviet system
disappeared and it became quite obvious in which direction
the society was developing. By the mid-nineteen-seventies
even the most superficial analysis of the indicators of
the character of economic growth would clearly suggest
that while in Western post-industrial societies the growth
of the service sector outpaced growth in the productive
sector, in the Soviet Union, the reverse was true. Thus,
during the nineteen-seventies the Soviet Union became more
industrialized than it had been during the nineteen-fifties
because the service sector had actually shrunk in comparison to the productive sector. The Soviet Union thus
appeared to be experiencing development other than the
post-industrial variant.

Hence, if in those conditions continuation of the
experiments with the mature STR theory would be highly

unwise, if not entirely anti-social, the Soviet industrial
scholars had to quietly return to the only solid scheme
which securely fit the new times, that is, the philosophy
of the early STR theory, which was linked with a renewed
total, categorical and contemptuous renunciation of
Western post-industrial theories. This critique and
rejection of Western post-industrial theories bore a
slavish resemblance to the same critique and rejection of
twenty-five years earlier.

With but a change in the date of publication one could
easily mistake works of the enthusiastic period refuting
Western post-industrial theories for works of the present
period on the same subject. However, it should be noted
that repetitiveness and total lack of creativity has
not prevented the Soviet industrial theoreticians of the
present period from exhibiting great quantitative strength
in this particular subfield.[51] Unfortunately, in this
case quantity has not been translated into quality.

ENDNOTES

1. G.A. Lakhtin, "Ob Usloviakh Optimal'nosti Reshenia,"
    in V.G. Afanasyev's Nauchnoe Upravlenie Obschestvom,
    (Moscow: 1974, Mysl').

2. Ibid., p. 290.

3. Ibid., p. 292.

4. Ibid., p. 293.

5. I.A. Gavrilova, "Organizatsionnye Sistemy i Protsedury
    kak Osnova Sistem Upravlenia Proizvodstvom," in
    V.G. Afanasyev's Nauchnoe Upravlenie Obschestvom, Op.
    Cit..

6. Ibid., pp. 301-302.

7. Ibid., p. 318.

8. V. Afanasyev, Social Information and the Regulation
    of Social Development, (Moscow: 1978, Progress Pub-
    lishers).

9. Ibid., p. 356.

10. A.A. Zvorykin, Automation and Some Socio-Psychological
    Problems of Work, (Moscow: 1974, Soviet Sociological
    Association), pp. 3-4.

11. Nauchno-Tekhnicheskaia Revoliutsia i Osobennosti
    Sotsial'nogo Razvitia v Sovremennuiu Epokhu, (Moscow:
    1974, Izdatel'stvo Moskovskogo Universiteta), p. 141.

12. M.P. Mchedlov, "Obshchechelovecheskoe i Sotsialis-
    ticheskoe," Voprosy Filosofii, 5, (1976), pp. 53-54.

13. D.M. Gvishiani, "Vzaimodeistvie Nauchno-Tekhnicheskoi
    Revolutsii i Sotsial'nogo Progressa," Voprosy
    Filosofii, 11, (1976), p. 18.

14. Iu. A. Tikhomirov, "Sotsial'noe Upravlenie v Razvitom
    Sotsialisticheskom Obshchestve," Voprosy Filosofii,
    1, (1977).

15. A.G. Egorov, "KPSS--Partia Nauchnogo Kommunizma,
    Tvoricheskogo Marxizma-Leninizma," Part I Voprosy
    Filosofii, 3, (1978); Part II Voprosy Filosofii,
    4, (1978).

16. A.M. Rumiantsev, "V.I. Lenin i Nekotorye Voprosy Politicheskoi Ekonomii Sotsializma," <u>Voprosy Filosofii</u>, 4, (1978).

17. V.G. Afanasyev, "Dialektika Sotsializma: Upravlenie i Planirovanie," <u>Voprosy Filosofii</u>, 6, (1978).

18. Ia. A. Kronrod, "Aktual'nye Problema Issledovania Ekonomicheskogo Bazisa," <u>Voprosy Filosofii</u>, 12, (1979).

19. P.N. Fedoseyev, "Teoreticheskie Problemy Sotsial'no-Ekonomicheskogo Razvitia Sovetskogo Obschestva na Sovremennom Etape," <u>Voprosy Filosofii</u>, 2, (1980).

20. V.S. Semenov, "Uchenie o Razvitom Sotsializmie i ego Pererastanii v Kommunizm," <u>Voprosy Filosofii</u>, 7, (1980).

21. V.V. Shcherbitskii, "Nauchno-Tekhnicheskaia Revoliutsia i Upravlenie Obshchestvennym Protsessam," <u>Voprosy Filosofii</u>, 10, (1980).

22. B.E. Paton, "Nauka--Tekhnika--Proizvodstvo," <u>Voprosy Filosofii</u>, 10, (1980).

23. B.M. Grinchel', <u>Izmenenie Effektivnostii Nauchno-Tekhnicheskogo Progressa</u>, (Moscow: 1974, Ekonomika), p. 5.

24. K.S. Sadykov, <u>Nauchno-Tekhnicheskaia Revoliutsia i Lichnost' v Period Razvitogo Sotsializma</u>, (Tashkent: 1974, Uzbekistan), p. 3.

25. Ibid., p. 28.

26. <u>Partia i Sovremennaia Nauchno-Tekhnicheskaia Revoliutsia v SSSR</u>, (Moscow: 1974, Politizdat), p. 4.

27. I.E. Rubtsov, <u>Nauchno-Tekhnicheskii Progress v Usloviakh Razvitogo Sotsialisticheskogo Obshchestva</u>, (Moscow: 1975, Mysl'), p. 6.

28. P.N. Fedoseyev, "XXV S'ezd KPSS i Zadachi Obshchestvennykh Nauk," <u>Voprosy Filosofii</u>, 5, (1976), p. 3.

29. V.G. Afanasyev, "XXV S'ezd KPSS o Dal'neishim Sovershenstvovanii Upravlenia," <u>Voprosy Filosofii</u>, 6, (1976).

30. Iu. E. Volkov, "XXV S'ezd KPSS i Teoreticheskie Problemy Sotsial'noi Politiki," <u>Voprosy Filosofii</u>, 7, (1976), p. 3.

276

31. Especially: V.S. Markov, "Obraz Zhizni i Formirovanie
     Cheloveka," Voprosy Filosofii, 7, (1976); V.S. Semianov,
     "Nauchno-Tekhnicheskaia Revoliutsia i Problema
     Tselostnogo i Svobodnogo Razvitia Chekoveka," Voprosy
     Filosofii, 7, (1978); S.F. Medunov, "Aktual'nye
     Problemy Kommunisticheskogo Vospitania Trudiashchikh-
     sia," Voprosy Filosofii, 7, (1979); P.N. Fedoseyev,
     "Teoreticheskie Problemy Sotsial'no-Ekonomicheskogo
     Razvitia Sovetskogo Obshchestva no Sovremennom Etape,"
     Voprosy Filosofii,2, (1980); Iu.A. Krasin, "uchastie
     Trudiashchikhsia v Upravlenii i Professionalizm,"
     Voprosy Filosofii, 4, (1982). KPSS o Formirovanii
     Novogo Cheloveka. Moscow: Izdatel'stvo Politicheskoi
     Literarury, 1976.

32. M.T. Iovchik, "Dialekticheskii Kharakter Razvitia
     Obshchestvennogo Soznaia i Dukhovoi Zhizni Sotsializma
     v Nashe Vremia," Voprosy Filosofii, 5, (1975), p. 77.

33. See especially: F.M. Rudich, "Vozrastanie Roli
     Trudiashchikhsia v Upravlenii Sotsialisticheskim
     Proizvodstvom," Voprosy Filosofii, 7, (1975); N.N.
     Rutkevich, "Sotsialisticheskii Obraz Zhiznii i ego
     Razvitie," Voprosy Filosofii, 11, (1975); I.M. Makarov,
     "O Protsesse Prevrashchenia Nauki v Neposredstvennuiu
     Proizvodstvennuiu Silu," Voprosy Filosofii, 2, (1976);
     V.G. Afanasyev, "XXV S'iezd KPSS...," D.M. Gvishiani,
     "Vzaimodeistvie...," Op. cit.; P.N. Fedoseyev,
     "Teoreticheskie Problemy...," op.cit.; V.S. Semenov,
     "Uchenie o Razvitom..." op. cit.; V.M. Grigorov,
     Eksperty v Sisteme Upravlenia Obshchestvennym
     Proizvodstvom, (Moscow: Izdatel'stvo Mysl', 1976);
     and Nauchno-Tekhnicheskaia Revoliutsia: Obshcheteore-
     ticheskie Problemy, (Moscow: Izdatel'stvo Nauka, 1976).

34. For instance: Formirovanie Dukhovnogo Mira Cheloveka
     i NTR, (Moscow: 1977, Izdatel'stvo Moskovskogo Uni-
     versiteta); and P.N. Fedoseyev, "Teoreticheskiie...,"
     op. cit..

35. B.M. Grinchiel', op. cit., p. 3.

36. K.S. Sadykov, op. cit., p. 30.

37. V.F. Glagolev, G.S. Gudozhnik, I.A. Kozikov,
     Sovremennaia Nauchno-Tekhnicheskaia Revoliutsia,
     (Moscow: 1974, Vysshaia Shkola), pp. 198-199.

38   V.G. Afanasyev, The Scientific and Technological
     Revolution--Its Impact on Management and Education,
     (Moscow: 1975, Progress Publishers), p. 98.

39. Ibid., p. 94.

40. Partia i Sovremennaia Nauchno-Tekhnicheskaia Revoliu-
    tsia v SSSR, op. cit., p. 20.

41. V.G. Afanasyev, The Scientific and Technological
    Revolution..., op. cit., p. 10.

42. A.A. Zvorykin, op. cit., p. 7.

43. L.M. Belov, Nauchno-Tekhnicheskaia Revoliutsia i
    Razvitie Lichnosti, (Leningrad: 1974, Znanie), p. 7.

44. L.M. Gatovskii, Nauchno-Tekhnicheskii Progress i
    Ekonomika Razvitogo Sotsializma, (Moscow: 1974, Nauka),
    pp. 7-8.

45. I.E. Rubtsov, Nauchno-Tekhnicheskii..., op. cit.,
    p. 22.

46. Soedinenie Dostizhenii Nauchno-Tekhnicheskoi Revol-
    iutsii s Preimushchestvami Stosializma, (Moscow: 1977,
    Izdatel'stvo Moskovskogo Universiteta), p. 29.

47. R.I. Kosolapov, Sotsializm: k Voprosam Teorii,
    (Moscow: 1979, Mysl'), p. 12.

48. Pyotr Fedoseyev, "Social Significance of the Scien-
    tific and Technological Revolution," in Scientific-
    Technological Revolution: Social Aspects, (Beverly
    Hills, CA: 1977, Sage), pp. 103-104.

49. Formirovanie Dukhovnogo Mira Cheloveka i NTR. Moscow:
    Izdatel'stvo Moskovskogo Universiteta, 1977, p. 22;
    See also: P.A. Rodionov, Kollektivnost'--Vysshyi
    Printsip Partiinogo Rukovodstva. Moscow: Izdatel'stvo
    Politicheskoi Literatury, 1974.

50. Nauchno-Tekhnicheskaia Revoliutsia i Sistema Ekonomi-
    cheskikh Otnoshenii Razvitogo Sotsializma, (Moscow:
    1979, Izdatel'stvo Moskovskogo Universiteta), p. 12.

51. See especially: S.P. Novoselov, Obostrenie Ekono-
    micheskikh i Sotsial'no-Politicheskikh Protivorechii
    Katpitalizma, (Moscow: 1977, Izdatel'stvo Mysl');
    V.I. Gromeka, Nauchno-Tekhnicheskaia Revoliutsia i
    Sovremennyi Kapitalizm, (Moscow: 1976, Izdatel'stvo
    Politichieskoi Litieratury); S.I. Popov, "Sotsial'nyi
    Pessimizm v Sistemie Sovremennoi Burzhuazyinoi Ideologii,"
    Voprosy Filosofii, 9, (1980); A.G. Mileikovskii,
    "Kritika Burzhuaznykh Kontseptsii Gosudarstvennogo-
    Monopoliticheskogo Kapitalizma," Voprosy Filosofii,
    4, (1980); E.V. Demenchonok, Iu. N. Semenov,
    "Kritika Sovremennykh Burzhuaznykh Kontseptsii
    Obshcheistvennogo Progressa," Voprosy Filosofii, 12

(1979); A.G. Shchelkin, "Neupravlemaia Slozhnost':
Genezis Tekhnokraticheskogo Konservatizma," Voprosy
Filosofii, 5, (1979); E.V. Demenchonok, "Ot 'Indus-
trializma' k 'Postindustrializmu': Evoliutsia Tekh-
nokraticheskikh Kontseptsii," Voprosy Filosofii,
1, (1979); G.M. Tavrizian, "Burzhuaznaia Filosofia
Tekhniki i Sotsial'nye Teorii," Voprosy Filosofii,
6, (1978); A.G. Mileikovskii, "Ideologicheskoe Pervoo-
ruzhenie Burzhuaznoi Politekonomii v Usloviakh NTR,"
Voprosy Filosofii, 11, (1976); A.V. Gulyga, "Posle
Krakha Ekstremistskikh Illiuzii," Voprosy Filosofii,
4, (1976). Right-Wing Revisionism Today. Moscow:
Progress Publishers, 1976. Ideologicheskie Problemy
Nauchno-Tekhnicheskoi Revoliutsii. Moscow: Nauka, 1974.

Conclusion

As has been pointed out in the Introduction to this
study, the foundations of Soviet industrial theory are
fraught with controversy. This controversy derives from
the fundamental differences between Marx's and Lenin's
philosophical systems. The scope of those differences
may best be understood by examining the similarities
existing between these two philosophies.

Briefly, Lenin was heavily influenced by Marx's understanding of the historical dynamics of human development,
as well as by the tool of Marx's analysis--the logic of
dialectical materialism. As a result, his understanding of
the historical formations of human society, as well as his
critique of the capitalist system appeared to be heavily
indebted to Marx's philosophy. Moreover, Lenin's understanding of the ultimate goal of the development of
humanity--the communist system--seemed also to be identical
with Marx's concept.

The principal conflict between the two bodies of
thought is to be found in their respective visions of
that period between the collapse of the capitalist system
and the achievement of the ultimate goal of humanity--the
communist system. Essentially, they differed dramatically
on the subject of socialism. Marx, for example, believed
that socialism would emerge within the most advanced
capitalist societies. By contrast, Lenin argued that

socialism could be created within less developed contexts.
The socialist revolution a la Marx was supposed to have a
spontaneous, mass and participatory character, which would
inevitably occur when the proletariat became a social class
for itself, that is, when it had gained full class consciousness. Although Lenin viewed the socialist revolution
as having a mass character, it was not supposed to be
participatory or spontaneous, but instead, would have a
distinctively elitist character. The socialist revolution
a la Lenin was supposed to occur when the proletariat was
still devoid of class consciousness (i.e., when it was
still the class in itself). The proletariat was supposed to
be led in Lenin's type of socialist revolution by a
professional elite of superrevolutionaries, who, in turn,
would possess a fully developed class consciousness. After
the successful completion of Lenin's scenario of socialist
revolution, the vanguard party would transform itself into
the political elite of the new society and would rule the
masses for the ultimate good of those masses.

The Leninist philosophy which still professes its
adherence to Marx's dialectical-materialist logic of thought
in no way underestimates the importance of the sphere of
production for their brand of socialist society. However,
with regard to this point the apparent departure by
Leninism from Marx's philosophy had perhaps the sharpest
and most pronounced character. Lenin and his followers
admired the industrial system of production of the most

advanced capitalist societies, the very system which was so abhorred by Marx. The industrial system of the most advanced capitalist societies in Marx's scenario for socialist revolution was supposed to be totally annihilated, while on its ashes the victorious proletariat was supposed to create some new unalienating system of production. In Lenin's philosophy, the industrial system created by the most advanced capitalist societies was supposed to be reconstructed in the newly created socialist society. Thus, the success seen in borrowing and utilizing the advanced capitalist system of production by Lenin's type of socialist society would determine its success in achieving communism.

Soon after the creation of the Soviet republic, Lenin's theory on the character of the social base of the socialist society ceased to have a purely speculative character and actually, after being adapted by the Stalinists, guided the Soviet transformation. Considering Stalin's very strong belief that his interpretation of Lenin's philosophy clarified and resolved all questions concerning the fundamental theory of Soviet industrial transformation, the activities of the Stalinist industrial scholars were limited strictly to applying this fundamental theory to the very practical problems of Soviet industrial transformation. Consequently, the work of the Stalinist industrial scholars is strictly supportive of Stalin's interpretation of Lenin's industrial theory.

However, during the short transforming period after
Stalin's death (1953-1956) the Soviet industrial scholars
began the process of freeing themselves from the limitations imposed upon them by the presence of Stalin. What
were only hesitant steps in that direction during this
transforming period turned into an avalanche of bold
creativity and enthusiasm during the following period
(1956-1965). Although during that period the Soviet
scholars completely freed themselves from the burden of
Stalin's authority and, most of all, purged the most
obvious remnants of the Stalinist period--the personality
cult--from the body of Marxism-Leninism, there was ultimately an ironic shadow cast over their exuberant theoretical
efforts. That is, their theory proved to be nothing but
a faithful continuation of the Stalinist version of Lenin's
industrial theory. Hence, the fount of theoretical
enthusiasm lay in the apparent initial success of the
Stalinist program for developing the heavy industrial sector in the Soviet Union. According to both Lenin and
Stalin, this was the crucial and the most difficult step
along the way to communism. Above all, the successful
construction of this sector was supposed to serve as the
panaceum for all the problems of socialist society.

Thus, according to the Leninist-Stalinist theory, the
immediate consequence of the successful development of
heavy industry within the Soviet brand of socialist society
would inevitably lead to the unleashing of new productive

potential on an unprecendented scale. As a result, this
new capacity was supposed to facilitate the emergence
of the advanced socialist society in the Soviet Union,
i.e., the society of material abundance. The combined
influence of this material abundance with the political
and cultural advantages of the Soviet superstructure was
supposed to create a new type of human being in Soviet
society--the communist man. Hence, the state apparatus
could begin to wither away and the communist society would
emerge.

In light of the apparent success of the industrialization program in their country, the Soviet industrial
theoreticians, staunch adherents of Leninist-Stalinist
logic, arrived at the conclusion that communism would emerge
in the Soviet Union by the beginning of the nineteen-
eighties. Most importantly, however, they interpreted
the newly emerging advanced technology as the inevitable
sign of the oncoming productive explosion in their society.
Moreover, they interpreted the pains of the post-industrial
transformation of the advanced capitalist societies as the
sure sign of their rapid and inevitable demise. Thus,
during the period of enthusiasm, the Soviet industrial
scholars, armed with an unshakeable belief in the logic
of their fundamental theory of Marxism-Leninism, were
capable of putting the proverbial "dot over the i"
regarding the future development of both the socialist and
capitalist societies. What remained was simply the inevitable

fulfillment of this theory.

However, despite their confident and enthusiastic expectations about the future, the eagerly awaited vital productive explosion failed to develop. To adjust to this new situation, Soviet industrial theory entered still another phase of its development--the quasi-pluralistic theory (1966-1973). At that point, the efforts of Soviet theoreticians were directed to many different areas which also included the serious examination of the dynamics of capitalist post-industrial society as well as the study of post-industrial theories. The new quasi-pluralistic theory, it could be argued, would serve the already diversified and complex Soviet society, addressing and satisfying a multitude of needs, while the unwritten but well observed law prevented the variety of its branches from combating one another.

A stunning turnaround occurred in the middle of the nineteen-seventies when Soviet industrial theory shifted one more time. As was argued in an earlier chapter of this study, the latest period in the development of Soviet industrial theory is characterized by a return to the style and logic of argument as had been presented during the enthusiastic period, as well as a recycling and reuse of some other theoretical achievements of an even earlier past. Quietly and without any explanation Soviet indus-trial theory abandoned its experimentation with the concept of post-industrial society and returned to the simple, Leninist-Stalinist industrial schemes.

Most importantly, the Soviet industrial scholars of
the latest period have embarked upon an entirely new
venture, arguing that all of the predictions of the
enthusiastic period have actually been fulfilled and, as
a result, Soviet society may now be seen as having
triumphantly accomplished the creation of the late
socialist society. As a result of these developments,
the achievement of communist society, according to the
Soviet industrial scholars of the recent period, should be
accomplished in the near future.

It is evident, of course, that contemporary Soviet
society is much closer to the Spartan model of consumption than to anything that was envisioned by Marx (and
as a matter of fact also by Lenin and Stalin) as the late
socialist society of material abundance and explosive
productive development. Why then would contemporary
Soviet industrial scholars make such apparently preposterous claims? To answer this question we must turn to
Soviet statistics which clearly indicate that during the
last twenty years, the society actually reversed the trend
toward post-industrial development, i.e., the service
sector actually shrank in comparison to the productive
sector from the nineteen-fifties to the nineteen-eighties.
To put it differently, the service sector grew only
slightly from the nineteen-fifties with the bulk of economic growth concentrated in the productive sector.

However, industrial growth has its own natural limits
and while by the early nineteen-seventies, the dimensions
of industrial production rendered the Soviets one of the
world leaders in this type of production, the need for
further rapid increase in industrial output diminished
and from then until now the Soviet economy has registered
a decreasing rate of industrial growth.

Presently, it appears that the Soviet socio-economic
system is entering a period of permanent industrial self-
sustainability, where the major sectors of Soviet society
are in a state of harmonious equilibrium. Thus, the
burgeoning industrial sector well satisfies the needs
of the state-military apparatus which, in turn, through
an elaborate system of checks and balances, seems to
permanently contain the consumer needs of the population
so that the service sector as well as consumer goods production may be kept permanently at the level of a rudimentary industrial society. Currently, the Soviet Union
stands as a formidable, complex and self-sustainable
society. However, regardless of how desirable the condition of self-sustainability may be, the system has an
inherently static character. How then may this inherently
static character of Soviet society (which otherwise
undoubtedly is seen as highly beneficial by the Soviet
elites) be reconciled with the inherently dynamic (i.e.,
communism oriented) philosophy of Marxism-Leninism?

It is probable that the most likely sword to cut this

Gordian knot will be supplied by the Soviet industrial
scholars and their colleagues from the related academic
disciplines. That is, having observed the dynamics of
the development of Soviet industrial theory throughout
the last four decades, it would appear reasonable to
conclude that this theory is now on the verge of entering
the final phase of its development. We predict here,
that in this final phase, Soviet industrial theory will
begin to proclaim and then justify theoretically the an-
nouncement that the Soviet Union is actually a communist
society which has fulfilled and satisfied all of Marx's
dreams and predictions about the future of humanity.

In so doing, the Soviet industrial theoreticians would
play a much more important role than ever before. Theirs
will be the task of demonstrating that Soviet society has
actually become the communist society. Considering that
the Soviet Union achieved the inherently static state of
self-sustainability some time ago, and that the near future
is not likely to bring any meaningful socio-economic
changes, arguments concerning the achievement of communism
will be hard pressed for support in terms of empirical
evidence. Thus, Soviet industrial scholars will be
called upon to marshall their considerable theoretical
skills to persuade humanity that the Soviet Union has achieved
communism. In view of the fact that by the early nineteen-
eighties, Soviet industrial scholars were repeating with
a growing degree of confidence that their society had

arrived at the stage of late socialism, one could reasonably expect works to appear within several years that would present a detailed argument as to why Soviet society has advanced to communism. Soviet theoreticians might argue, for example, that material consumption and services in the Soviet Union had reached the highest possible level in non-exploitative conditions. The degree of misery and insecurity suffered within certain social milieus of capitalist society will be emphasized, contrasting those ignominous "achievements" with the exceedingly egalitarian distribution of the social pie in the Soviet Union. Moreover, they would probably argue that those individuals or social groups desirous of a higher level of material consumption than that currently available in the Soviet Union are the victims of false consciousness or in some cases are outwardly the degenerated petit-bourgeoisie.

However, there remains the task of proving that certain other elements of communist society predicted by Marx (and repeated by Lenin and Stalin) were actually realized in that allegedly communist society. Thus, the argument about the withering away of the state apparatus would conceivably suggest that it only appears that the Soviet Union maintains a strong internal apparatus, while in reality these people are performing all of these functions in a highly voluntaristic and free-spirited way and are being rewarded according to their needs. However, that segment of the state apparatus which tends to external

matters will have to be preserved to protect society from
the imperialist threat, and so on and so forth. Finally,
industrial scholars will be able to concentrate on the
unquestionable central domain of the industrial theory,
that is the argument which will depict the truly communistic character of the labor process and labor relations
in the Soviet Union.

Bibliography

Primary Books

Althusser, Luis. Lenin and Philosophy. London: NLB, 1971.

Afanasyev, V.G. Scientific Communism. Moscow: Progress
Publishers, 1967.

_____. Nauchno-Tekhnicheskaia Revoliutsia, Upravlenie,
Obrazovanie. Moscow: Izdatel'stvo Politicheskoi
Literatury, 1972.

_____. The Scientific and Technological Revolution--Its
Impact on Management and Education. Moscow: Progress
Publishers, 1975.

_____. Social Information and the Regulation of Social
Development. Moscow: Progress Publishers, 1978.

Belov, L.M. Nauchno-Tekhnicheskaia Revoliutsia i Razvitie
Lichnosti. Leningrad: Znanie, 1974.

Borba Idei i Nauchno-Tekhnicheskaia Revoliutsia. Leningrad:
Leninzdat, 1973.

Brzost, W. Importowany Postep Techniczny a Rozwoj Gos-
podarczy Polski. Warsaw: PWN, 1979.

Budushchee Chelovecheskogo Obshchestva. Moscow: Progress, 1973.

Bushuev, V.M. Khimicheskaya Industriya v Svete Reshenii
XXIV S'ezda KPSS. Moscow: Khimiya, 1974.

Chelovek-Nauka-Tekhnika. Moscow: Politizdat, 1973.

Chelovek i EVM (Psikhologicheskie Problemy Avtomatizatsii
Upravlenia). Moscow: Ekonomika, 1973.

Claudin-Urondo, Carmen. Lenin and the Cultural Revolution.
Sussex, Britain: The Harvester Press, 1977.

Dronov, F.A.; Shatokhinaia, M.N. Ekonomika Osvoenia Novoi
Produktsii. Minsk, 1970.

Ekonomicheskie Problemy Nauchno-Tekhnicheskogo Progressa v
Sel'skom Khoziaistve. Moscow: Ekonomika, 1975.

Ekonomicheskie Zakonomernosti Pererastania Sotsializma v
Kommunizm. Moscow: Nauka, 1967.

Eksperty v Sisteme Upravlenia Obshchestvennym Proizvodstvom.
Moscow: Mysl', 1976.

Faktory Ekonomicheskogo Rosta SSSR. Edited by A.I. Notkin.
Moscow: Ekonomika, 1970.

Formirovanie Dukhovnogo Mira Cheloveka i NTR. Moscow:
Izdatel'stvo Moskovskogo Universiteta, 1977.

Fundamentals of Dialectical Materialism. Moscow: Progress
Publishers, 1967.

Fundamentals of Marxism-Leninism. Moscow: Foreign Languages
Publishing House, 1961.

Gatovskii, L.M. Nauchno-Tekhnicheskii Progress i Ekonomika
Razvitogo Sotsializma. Moscow: Nauka, L974.

Glagolev, V.F.; Gudozhnik, G.S.; Kozikov, I.A. Sovremennaia
Nauchno-Tekhnicheskaia Revoliutsia. Moscow: Vysshaia
Shkola, 1974.

Goroditskii, M.L. Litsenzii vo Vneshnei Targovle SSSR.
Moscow: Mezhdunarodnye Otnoshenia, 1972.

Grinchel', K.S. Izmenenie Effektivnostii Nauchno-Tekhnicheskogo Progressa. Moscow: Ekonomika, 1974.

Gromeka, V.I. Nauchno-Tekhnicheskaia Revoliutsia i Sovremennyi Kapitalizm. Moscow: Izdatel'stvo Politicheskoi
Literatury, 1976.

Gvishiani, Dzh. Organisation and Management. Moscow:
Progress Publishers, 1972.

Ideologicheskie Problemy Nauchno-Tekhnicheskoi Revoliutsii.
Moscow: Nauka, 1974.

Industry and Labour in the USSR. Edited by Gennadii V.
Osipov. London: Tavistock Publications, 1966.

Kamaev, V.D. Sovremennaia Nauchno-Tekhnicheskaia Revoliutsia.
Moscow: Mysl', 1972.

Karkhin, G.I. Sviazi Nastoiashchego i Budushchego v Ekonomike.
Moscow: Ekonomika, 1970.

Karpov, M.M. Osnovnye Zakonomernosti Razvitia Estestvoznania.
Rostov: Izdatel'stvo Rostovkogo Universiteta, 1963.

Kelle, V.; Kovalson, M. Historical Materialism. Moscow:
Progress Publishers, 1973.

292

Khozin, G. The Biosphere and Politics. Moscow: Progress
    Publishers, 1976.

Khramoi, A.V. Avtomatika i Telemekhanika v Narodnom
    Khoziaistve SSSR. Moscow: Gosplanizdat, 1948.

Kirilin, V.A. Energetika Budushchego. Moscow, 1974.

Kosolapov, V. Chelovechestvo na Rubezhe XXI Veka. Moscow:
    Molodaia Gvardia, 1973.

Kosolapov, R.I. Sotsializm k Voprosom Teorii. Moscow: Mysl',
    1979.

Kostandov, L.A. Khimicheskaia Promyshlennost' k XXV S'ezdu
    KPSS. Moscow: Khimia, 1976.

KPSS o Formirovanii Novogo Cheloveka. Moscow: Izdatel'stvo
    Politicheskoi Literatury, 1976.

KPSS vo Glave Kul'turnoi Revoliutsii v SSSR. Moscow:
    Izdatel'stvo Politicheskoi Literatury, 1972.

Kudrashov, A.P. Sovremennaia Nauchno-Tekhnicheskaia
    Revoliutsia i ee Osobennost. Moscow: Mysl', 1965.

Kulikov, A.G. Ekonomicheskie Problemy Uskorenia Tekhniches-
    kogo Progressa v Promyshlennosti. Moscow, 1964.

Kurakov, I.G. Science, Technology and Communism. London:
    Pergamon Press, 1966.

Kuznetsov, Boris. Kommunizm i Teknika Budushchego. Moscow:
    Izdatel'stvo Adademii Nauk SSSR, 1940.

Laptev, I. Planeta Razuma. Moscow: Molodaia Gvardia, 1973.

Lebin, D.A. Nauchno-Tekhnicheskai Revoliutsia i Sotsialisti-
    cheskaia Integratsia. Moscow: Nauka, 1973.

Lenin, V.I. Sochinenia. Moscow-Leningrad: 1926-37.

Lubsanov, D. Iz Opyta Konkretno-Sotsiologicheskikh Issledovanii.
    Ulan-Ude, 1968.

Lukacs, Gyorgy. Lenin. London: New Left Books, 1970.

Man-Science-Technology. Moscow-Prague: Academia Prague, 1973.

Man, Society and the Environment. Moscow: Progress Publishers,
    1975.

Markov, N.V. Nauchno-Tekhnicheskaia Revoliutsia: Analiz,
    Perspektivy, Posledstvia. Moscow: Izdatel'stvo

Politicheskoi Literatury, 1973.

Markus, Boris, L'vovich. Trud v Sotsialisticheskom Obshchestve. Moscow: Gosudarstvennoe Izdatel'stvo Politicheskoi Literatury, 1939.

Marx, Karl. Capital. Chicago: Charles H. Kerr & Co, 1932.

_____. Notes on Machines. Buffalo: Lockwood Library, Sublation offprint no. 1.

_____. Grundrisse. New York: Random House, 1973.

_____. Economic and Philosophic Manuscripts. New York: International Publishers, 1976.

_____. A Contribution to the Critique of Political Economy. Chicago: Charles H. Kerr & Co, 1904.

Marx, Karl.; Engels, F. The German Ideology. New York: Internationa Publishers, 1976.

_____. The Holy Family. Moscow: Foreign Languages Publishing, 1956.

Medvedev, N.A. Nauchno-Tekhnicheskii Progress i Sotsial'-no-E konomicheskie Izmeneniia na Sele. Moscow: Ekonomika, 1974

Meleshchenko, Iu. G. Tekhnicheskii Progress i ego Zakon-omernosti. Moscow: Leninzdat, 1967.

Nauchno-Tekhnicheskaia Revoliutsia i Osobennosti Sotsial' nogo Razvitia Sovremennuiu Kpokhu. Moscow: Izdatel'-stvo Moskovskogo Universiteta, 1974.

Nauchno-Tekhnicheskaia Revoliutsia i Sistema Ekonomicheskikh Otnoshenii Razvitogo Sotsializma. Moscow: Izdatel'stvo Moskovskogo Universiteta, 1979.

Nauchno-Tekhnicheskaia Revoliutsia i Sotsializm. Moscow: Mauka, 1976.

Nauchno-Tekhnicheskii Progress i Khoziaistvennaia Reforma. Moscow: Institut Ekonomiki, 1969.

Nauchnoie Upravlenie Obschestvom. Edited by Afanasyev, V.G. Moscow: Mysl', 1967-1974. Volumes (Vypusk) 1-8.

Novoselov, S.P. Obostrenie Ekonomicheskikh i Sotsial'no-Politicheskikh Protivorechii Kapitalizma. Moscow: Mysl', 1977.

294

Obshchestvo i Okruzhaiushcha Sreda. Podkhod Sovetskikh
     Uchenykh. Moscow: Progress, 1976.

Osipov, G.V. Tekhnika i Obshchestvennyi Progress. Moscow:
     Izdatel'stvo Akademii Nauk SSSR, 1959.

Osnovnye Napravlenia Nauchno-Tekhnicheskogo Progressa.
     Edited by A.S. Tolkachev and I.M. Denisenko. Moscow:
     1971.

Osnovy Marksistskoi Filosofii. Moscow: Gospolitizdat, 1958.

Osnovy Marksizma-Leninizma. Moscow: Gospolitizdat, 1958.

Oznobin, N.M.; Pavlov, A.S. Kompleksnoe Planirovanie
     Nauchno-Tekhnicheskogo Progressa. Moscow, 1975.

Pannekoek, Anton. Lenin as Philosopher. London: Merlin
     Press, 1975.

Partia i Sovremennaia Nauchno-Tekhnicheskaia Revoliutsia v
     SSSR. Moscow: Politizdat, 1974.

Pribadzhakov, Nikolai. Razvitoto Sotsialistichesko
     Obshchestvo. Sofia: Nauka i Izkustvo, 1972.

Problemy Metodologii Sotsial'nogo Issledovania. Edited by
     B.A. Shtoff. Leningrad, 1970.

Problemy Nauchnogo Kommunizma. Moscow: Mysl', 1970. Vypusk
     4 and Moscow: Mysl', 1972, Vypusk 6.

Rachkov, P.A. Nauka i Obshchestvennyi Progress. Moscow:
     Izdatel'stvo Moskovskogo Universtiteta, 1963.

Right-Wing Revisionism Today. Moscow: Progress Publishers,
     1976.

Rodionov, P.A. Kollektivnost'--Vysshyi Printsip Partiinogo
     Rukovodstva. Moscow: Izdatel'stvo Politicheskoi
     Literatury, 1974.

Rubinstein, Modest, I. O Material'no-Tekhnicheskoi Baze
     Perekhoda ot Sotsializma k Kommunizmu. Moscow:
     Politizdat, 1940.

Rubtsov, I.E. Nauchno-Tekhnicheskii Progress v Usloviakh
     Razvitogo Sotsialisticheskogo Obshchestva. Moscow:
     Mysl', 1975.

Sadykov, K.S. Nauchno-Tekhnicheskaia Revoliutsia i Lichnost'
     v Period Razvitogo Sotsializma. Tashkent: Uzbekistan,
     1974.

Science and Morality. Moscow: Progress Publishers, 1975.

Scientific-Technological Revolution: Social Aspects.
    Beverly Hills, CA: Sage, 1977.

Shariia, K.S. Nekotorye Voprosy Razvitia Sotislisticheskikh
    Obshchestvennykh Otnoshenii v Period Stroitel'stva Kom-
    munizma. Tbilisi: Metsnereva, 1972.

Sheinin, Y. Science Policy: Problems and Trends. Moscow:
    Progress Publishers, 1978.

Shukhadrin, S.V. Osnovy Istorii Tekhniki. Moscow: Izdatel'-
    stvo Akademii Nauk SSSR, 1961.

Sluzhashchii Sovetskogo Gosudarstvennogo Apparata. Edited
    by Iu.A. Tikhomirov. Moscow, 1970.

Smirnov, Georgi. Soviet Man. The Making of a Socialist
    Type of Personality. Moscow: Progress Publishers, 1973.

Smirnov, V.S.; Semibratov, V.G.; Lebedev, O.T. Nauchno-
    Tekhnicheskaia Revoliutsia i Filosofskie Problemy
    Formirovania Inzhinernogo Myshlenia. Moscow: Vyshaia
    Shkola, 1973.

Soedinenie Dostizhenii Nauchno-Tekhnicheskoi Revoliutsii s
    Preimushchestvami Sotsializma. Moscow: Izdatel'stvo
    Moskovskogo Universiteta, 1977.

Sokolovskii, A.A.; Unanyants, T.P. Kratkii Spravochnik po
    Mineral'nym Udobreniam. Moscow: Khimia, 1977.

Sorevnovanie Dvukh Sistem, Sbornik. Moscow, 1963.

Sotsializm i Nauchno-Tekhnicheskaia Revoliutsia. Leningrad:
    Izdatel'stvo Leningradskogo Universiteta, 1971.

Sotsial'no-Ekonomicheskie Problemy Tekhnicheskogo Progressa.
    Moscow: Izdatel'stvo Akademii Nauk SSSR, 1961.

Sotsiologicheskie Problemy Nauki. Moscow: Nauka, 1974.

Sovremennaia Nauchno-Tekhnicheskaia Revoliutsia. Moscow:
    Nauka, 1967.

Stalin, I.V. Lenninism. New York: International Publishers,
    1928.

_____. O Tekhnike: Podbor Vazhneishikh Vyderzhek. Moscow:
    1931.

Stepanov, I. Elektrifikatsia R.S.F.S.R. v Sviazi s Perekhodom

296

Strumlin, S.G. Na Putiakh Postroenia Kommunizma. Moscow:
    Gospolitizdat, 1959.

_____. Problemy Sotsializma i Kommunizma. Moscow:
    Ekonomizdat, 1961.

Tekhnika, Tekhnologia i Kadry Upravlenia Proizvodstvom.
    Moscow: Ekonomika, 1973.

Teriaev, G.V. Vyshaia Faza Kommunizma. Obshchye
    Zakonomernosti Pererastania Sotsializma v Kommunizm.
    Moscow: Mysl', 1966.

The Essential Stalin: Major Theoretical Writings, 1905-52.
    Edited by Bruce Franklin. Garden City, NY: Anchor
    Books, 1972.

The Scientific and Technological Revolution: Social Effects
    and Prospects. Moscow: Progress Publishers, 1972.

Trotsky, Leon. Lenin. New York: G.P. Putnam, 1971.

Ulam, Adam. Stalin. New York: The Viking Press, 1973.

Usachev, I.G. Sovetskii Soiuz i Problema Razoruzhenia.
    Moscow: Mezhdunarodnye Otnoshenia, 1976.

Varlamov, K. Leninskaia Kontsieptsia Sotsialisticheskogo
    Upravlenia. Moscow: Mysl', 1973.

Vilenskii, M.A. Nauchno-Tekhnicheskii Progress i Effektiv-
    nost' Obshchestvennogo Proizvodstva. Moscow, 1962.

Vlasov, V.A. Sovetskii Gosudarstvennyi Apparat (Osnovnye
    Printsipy Organizatsii i Deiatelnosti). Moscow, 1951.

Volkov, Sotsiologia Nauki. Moscow: Izdatel'stvo
    Politicheskoi Literatury, 1968.

Volnets-Russet, E.Ya. Planirovanie i Raschet Effektivnosti
    Priobretenia Litsenzii. Moscow: Ekonomika, 1973.

Voprosy Teorii Sotsialisticheskogo Obshchestva. Moscow:
    Izdatel'stvo VPSh i AON pri TsK KPSS, 1960.

Zacher, Lech. Sterowanie Procesami Rewolucji Naukowo-
    Technicznej. Wroclaw: Ossolineum, 1978.

Zhimerin, D.G. Energetika: Nastoiashchee i Budushchee.
    Moscow, 1978.

Zvorykin, A.A. Automation and Some Socio-Psychological
    Problems of Work. Moscow: Soviet Sociological

Association, 1974.

_____. Nauchno-Tekhnicheskaia Revoliutsia i ee
Sotsial'nye Posledstvia. Moscow: Znanie, 1967.

Secondary Books

Ananichev, K. Environment: International Aspects. Moscow:
     Progress Publishers, 1976.

Azrael, Jeremy, R. Managerial Power and Soviet Politics.
     Cambridge: Harvard University Press, 1966.

Bailes, Kendall, E. Technology and Society under Lenin and
     Stalin. Princeton: Princeton University Press, 1978.

Becker, James, F. Marxian Political Economy. London:
     Cambridge University Press, 1977.

Bender, Frederic, L. The Betrayal of Marx. New York:
     Harper & Row, 1975.

Berliner, J.S. The Innovation Decision in Soviet Industry.
     Cambridge, Mass.: MIT Press, 1976.

Bernal, J.D. Marx and Science. New York: International
     Publishers, 1952.

Blackwell, William. The Beginning of Russian Industrializa-
     tion. Princeton: Princeton University Press, 1968.

Campbell, Robert, W. Soviet Energy Technologies. Blooming-
     ton: Indiana University Press, 1980.

Change in Communist Systems. Edited by Chalmers Johnson.
     Stanford, CA: Stanford University Press, 1970.

Economic Development in the Soviet Union and Eastern Europe.
     Edited by Z.M. Fallenbuchl. New York: Praeger, 1975.

Erlich, Alexander. The Soviet Industrial Debate (1924-1928).
     Cambridge, Mass.: Harvard University Press, 1960.

Graham, Loren, R. Science and Philosophy in the Soviet Union.
     New York: Vintage Books, 1974.

Gregory, P.R.; Stuart, R.C. Soviet Economic Structure and

Hammond, T.T. <u>Lenin on Trade Unions</u>. Connecticut: Greenwood
    Press, 1974.

Hanson, Philip. <u>Trade and Technology in Soviet-Western
    Relations</u>. New York: Columbia University Press, 1981.

Hegedus, Andras. <u>The Structure of Socialist Society</u>. New
    York: St. Martin's Press, 1977.

_____. <u>Socialism and Bureaucracy</u>. New York: St. Martin's
    Press, 1976.

Hegedus, Andras.; Heller, Agnes.; Markus, Maria.; Vajda,
    Mihaly. <u>The Humanisation of Socialism</u>. New York:
    St. Martin's Press, 1976.

Hoffmann, Erik, P.; Laird, Robbin, F. <u>The Politics of Economic
    Modernization in the Soviet Union</u>. Ithaca, NY: Cornell
    University Press, 1982.

_____. <u>"The Scientific-Technological Revolution" and Soviet
    Foreign Policy</u>. New York: Pergamon Press, 1982.

Hough, Jerry, F. <u>The Soviet Prefects: The Local Party Organs
    in Industrial Decision-Making</u>. Cambridge, Mass.:
    Harvard University Press, 1969.

Jakubovski, Franz. <u>Ideology and Superstructure in Historical
    Materialism</u>. New York: St. Martin's Press, 1976.

Johnson, Ron.; Gummett, Philip. <u>Directing Technology
    Policies for Promotion and Control</u>. New York: St. Martin's
    Press, 1979.

Kay, Geoffrey. <u>The Economic Theory of the Working Class</u>.
    New York: St. Martin's Press, 1979.

Kolakowski, Leszek. <u>Marxism and Beyond</u>. London: Pall Mall
    Press, 1968.

Korsch, Karol. <u>Marxism and Philosophy</u>. London: NLB, 1970.

Lane, David.; O'Dell, Felicity. <u>The Soviet Industrial
    Worker</u>. New York: St. Martin's Press, 1978.

Lane, David. <u>The Socialist Industrial State</u>. Boulder:
    Westview Press, 1976.

Laue, Theodore, H., von. <u>Why Lenin? Why Stalin?</u> Philadelphia:
    J.B. Lippincott Co, 1971.

Lee, R.W. <u>Soviet Perceptions of Western Technology</u>. Betheseda,
    Maryland: Mathtech Inc., 1978.

McLellan, David. <u>Marx's Grundrisse</u>. London: Macmillan and Co LTD, 1971.

Medvedev, Zhores. <u>The Rise and Fall of T.D. Lysenko</u>. New York, 1971.

Offe, Claus. <u>Industry and Inequality</u>. The Achievement <u>Principle in Work and Social Status</u>. New York: St. Martin's Press, 1976.

Ollman, Bertell. <u>Alienation</u>. Cambridge: At the University Press, 1971.

O'Rourke, James, J. <u>The Problem of Freedom in Marxist Thought</u>. Dordrecht, Holland: D. Reidel Publishing Co, 1974.

Pike, M. <u>Automation, Its Purpose and Future</u>. London, 1956.

Rakovski, Marc. <u>Towards An East European Marxism</u>. New York: St. Martin's Press, 1978.

Raptis, Michel. <u>Socialism, Democracy and Self-Management</u>. New York: St. Martin's Press, 1980.

Richta, Radovan. <u>Civilization at the Crossroads</u>. Prague: International Arts and Science Press Inc., 1969.

Scott, John. <u>Corporations, Classes and Capitalism</u>. New York: St, Martin's Press, 1980.

Selucky, Radoslav. <u>Economic Reforms in Eastern Europe</u>. New York: Praeger, 1972.

_____. <u>Marxism, Socialism, Freedom</u>. New York: St. Martin's Press, 1979.

Shapiro, L. Redding. Edited by. <u>Lenin</u>. New York: Praeger, 1967.

Showstack Sassoon, Anne. <u>Gramsci's Politics</u>. New York: St. Martin's Press, 1980.

<u>Soviet Science and Technology</u>. Edited by J.R. Thomas and U. Kruse Vaucienne. Washington DC: George Washington University, 1977.

Sutton, A.C. <u>Western Technology and Soviet Economic Development</u>. 3 vols covering 1917-1965. Stanford, CA: Hoover Institution, 1969, 1971 and 1973.

<u>Technology and Communist Culture</u>. Edited by Frederic J. Fleron, Jr. New York: Praeger Publishers, 1977.

The Technological Level of Soviet Industry. Edited by R. Amann; J.M. Cooper and R.W. Davies. New Haven: Yale University Press, 1977.

Treml, V.G. The Structure of Soviet Economy. New York: Praeger, 1972.

Wilczynski, J. Technology in Comecon. London: Macmillan, 1974.

White, Paul, M. Soviet Urban and Regional Planning. A Bibliography with Abstracts. New York: St. Martin's Press, 1980.

SELECTED ARTICLES

Primary articles:

Abalkin, L. "The Economy of Developed Socialism." Social
Sciences, n.3 (1981), 54-66.

Afanasyev, V.G. "Nauchnoe Rukovodstvo Stosialnymi Prot-
sessami." Kommunist n.12 (1965), 58-73.

Afanasyev, V.G. "Stroitelstvo Kommunizma--Nauchno Uprav-
liaemyi Protsess." Kommunist n.14 (1967).

Afanasyev, V.G. "XXV S'ezd KPSS o Dal'neishim Sovershenstvovanii Upravlenia." Voprosy Filosofii n.6 (1976),
3-15.

_____ "Dialektika Sotsializma: Upravlenie i
Planirovanie." Voprosy Filosofii n.6 (1978), 15-27.

_____ "Chelovek v Sisteme Upravlenia." Voprosy
Filosofii n.8 (1972), 41-52.

Akhudnov, V. "Sovetskii Khoziaistvennik." Kommunist n.17
(1965).

Aksenenok, G.A. "Priroda i Chelovek v Usloviakh Nuachno-
Tekhnicheskogo Progressa." Voprosy Filosofii n.10
(1973), 54-63.

Belozertsev, V.I.; Fomina, V.A. "Kommunisticheskoie
Razdelenie Truda ne Iskliuchaet Vsestoronnego Razvitia
Chekoveka." Voprosy Filosofii n.9 (1963), 35-39.

Bobneva, M.I. "Tekhnika i Chelovek." Voprosy Filosofii n.10
(1961), 70-81.

Bud'ko, N.S. "Iavliaiutsia li Mashinami Ustroistva,
Prednaznachennye dlia Pererabotki Informatsii?"
Voprosy Filosofii n.11 (1966), 75-80.

Bulochnikova, L.A. "Nauchno-Tekhnicheskaia Revoliutsia v
Sel'skom Khoziaistve i ee Sotsial'nye Posledstvia."
Voprosy Filosofii n.1 (1969), 24-34.

Danilevskii, V. "Na Poroge Novoi Nauchno-Tekhnicheskoi
Revoliutsii." Neva n.4 (1956).

Danilin, G. "Sovremennaia Nauchno-Tekhnicheskaia Revoliutsia:
Sushchnost', Znachenie, Perspektivy." Mirovaia
Ekonomika i Mezhdunarodnye Otnoshenia n.12 (1966),
52-64.

Demenchonok, E.V.; Semenov, Iu.N. "Kritika Sovremennykh Burzhuaznykh Kontseptsii Obshchestvennogo Progressa." Voprosy Filosofii n.12 (1979), 101-113.

Dudinskii, I.V. "Industrializatsia--Osnovnoe Zveno Stroi-tel'stva Fundamenta Sotsializma v Evropeiskikh Stranakh Narodnoi Demokratii." Voprosy Filosofii n.5 (1952), 132-148.

Dvorkin, I.N. "O Reformistskikh Teoriakh 'Vtoroi Promysh-lennoi Revoliutsii.'" Voprosy Filosofii n.12 (1958), 39-53.

Egorov, A.G. "KPSS--Partia Nauchnogo Kommunizma, Tvoriches-kogo Marxizma-Leninizma." Voprosy Filosofii n.3 (1978), 3-17.

_____. "KPSS--Partia Nauchnogo Kommunizma, Tvorich-eskogo Marxizma-Leninizma." Voprosy Filosofii n.4 (1978) 3-24.

El'meev, V.Ia. "Vozrastanie Roli Umstvennogo Truda v Razvitii Proizvoditel'nykh Sil Sotsializma," Voprosy Filosofii n.8, (1959), 33-44.

Fedorov, E.K.; Novik, I.B. "Problemy Vzaimodeistvia Chelo-veka s Prirodnoi Sredoi." Voprosy Filosofii n.12 (1972), 46-58.

Fedoseev, P.N. "Dialektika Pererastania Sotsializma v Kommunizm." Voprosy Filosofii n.10 (1961), 28-42.

_____. "XXV S'ezd KPSS i Zadachi Obshchestvennykh Nauk." Voprosy Filosofii n 5 (1976), 3-15.

_____. "Teoreticheskie Problemy Sotsial'no-Ekonomicheskogo Razvitia Sovetskogo Obshchestva na Sovremennom Etape." Voprosy Filosofii, n.2 (1980), 3-15.

_____. "The Working Class and Scientific and Tech-nological Progress." Social Sciences n.3 (1981), 23-35.

Fomin, E.A. "Nekotorye Voprosy Issledovania Organizatsii." Chelovek i Obshchestvo n.2 (1967).

Gak, G.M. "Obshchestvennye i Lichnye Interesy i Ikh Sochetanie pri Sotsializme." Voprosy Filosofii n.4 (1955).

Galkin, A.A. "Sotsial'naia Struktura Sovremennogo Kapi-talisticheskogo Obshchestva i Burzhuaznaia Sotsiologia." Voprosy Filosofii n.8 (1972), 63-73.

Gapochka, P.N. "Leninskii Podkhod KPSS k Resheniu Glavnoi
Problemy Stroitel'stva Kommunizma." Voprosy Filosofii
n.4 (1964), 16-26.

Glezerman, G. "Istoricheskii Materializm i Problemy
Sotsialnykh Issledovanii." Kommunist n.4 (1970).

Glezerman, G., Kelle, V., Pilipenko, N. "Istoricheskii
Materializm--Teoria i Metod Nauchnogo Poznania i
Revoliutsionnogo Deistviia." Kommunist n.4 (1971).

Gulyga, A.V. "Posle Krakha Ekstremistskikh Illuzii."
Voprosy Filosofii n.4 (1976), 134-138.

Gvishiani, D.M. "Problemy Upravlenia Sotsialisticheskoi
Promyshlennostiu." Voprosy Filosofii n.11 (1966),
3-13.

_____. "O Sovremennykh Burzhuaznykh Tedriakh
Upravlenie" Kommunist n.12 (1970).

_____. "Vzaimodeistvie Nauchno-Tekhnicheskoi
Revoliutsii i Sotsialnogo Progressa." Voprosy Filosofii
n.11 (1976), 16-30.

Iovchik, M.T. "Dialekticheskii Khrakter Razvitia Obshchestvennogo Soznania i Dukhovnoi Zhiznii Sotsializma
v Nashe Vremia." Voprosy Filosofii n.5 (1975), 77-94.

Iurovitskii, O.G. "Obshchestvennoe Proizvodstvo i Lichnye
Potrebnosti." Voprosy Filosofii n.11 (1959), 27-40.

Kachalina, L. "Problemy Nauchnoi Organizatsii Upravlen-
cheskogo Truda." Kommunist n.15 (1964).

Kantor, K.M. "Sootnoshenie Sotsial'noi Organizatsii i
Individia v Usloviakh Nauchno-Tekhnicheskoi Revoliutsii."
Voprosy Filosofii n.10 (1971).

_____. "Nauchno-Tekhnicheskaia Revoliutsia i
Sovremennyi Rabochii Klass." Voprosy Filosofii
n.12 (1971).

Khrapchenko, M. "The Ways of Mutual Enrichment of Social
Cultures." Social Sciences n.3 (1981), 36-53.

Khromushkin, G. "Novye Manery Antikommunizma." Politicheskoe
Samoobrazovanie n.2 (1969), 48-55.

Konnik, I.I. "O Protivorechiakh Sviazanykh s Deistvem
Ekonomicheskikh Zakonov." Voprosy Filosofii n.1 (1957),
174-181.

304

Konstantinov, F.V. "Glavnyi Dvigatel' Razvitia Proizvoditel'-
nykh Sil." Voprosy Filosofii n.1 (1953), 29-46.

_____. "Nauchno-Tekhnicheskaia Revoliutsia i
Problemy Nravstvennogo Progress." Voprosy Filosofii
n.8 (1973).

Kormer, V.F., Senokosov, Iu.P. "Ot 'Tekhnologicheskogo
Determinizma' k 'Posttekhnokraticheskomu Videniu.'"
Voprosy Filosofii n.7 (1972).

Kosolapov, R.I. "Na Puti k Besklassovomu Obshchestvu."
Voprosy Filosofii n.5, (1971).

Koval'chyk, A.S. "O Kharaktere Perekhoda k Vysshei Faze
Kommunizma." Voprosy Filosofii n.11 (1961), 16-28.

Kovalev, A.M., Kovalenko, V.I. "On the Question of the
Interrelations Between Scientific-Technological Revolution and Social Revolution." Vestnik Moskovskogo Universiteta n.2 (1971).

Kozlova, G.P., Fainburg, Z.I. "Izmenenie Kharaktera Truda
i Vsestoronenie Razvitie Cheloveka." Voprosy Filosofii
n.3 (1963), 55-62.

Krasin, Iu. A. "Uchastie Trudiashchikhsia v Upravlenii i
Professionalizm." Voprosy Filosofii n.4 (1982).

_____. "The Dialectics of Socialism and World
Progress." Social Sciences n.3 (1981), 81-94.

Kronrod, Ia.A. "Aktual'nye Problema Issledovania Ekonomicheskogo Bazisa." Voprosy Filosofii n.1 (1979), 18-30.

Kudravtsev, I.S., Fedorova, A.T. "O Likvidatsii Sush-
chestsestvennogo Razlichia Mezhdu Fizicheskom i
Umstvennom Trudom." Voprosy Filosofii n.1 (1953).

Kugel', S.A. "Izmenenie Sotsial'noi Struktury Sotsialisticheskogo Obshchestva pod Vozdeistvem Nauchno-
Tekhnicheskoi Revoliutsii." Voprosy Filosofii n.3
(1969).

Kukin, D.M. "Vdokhnovliaiushches Znania Borby za Kommunizm."
Voprosy Filosofii n.8 (1961), 28-39.

Kurakov I.G. "Nekotorye Voprosy Razvitia Tekhniki pri
Sotsializme." Voprosy Filosofii n.1 (1956), 14-29.

_____. "Razvitie Tekhniki na Baze Sotsializma."
Voprosy Filosofii n.1 (1959), 15-31.

_____. "Rol' Nauki v Sozdanii Material'no-
Tekhnicheskoi Bazy Kommunizma." Voprosy Filosofii
n.6 (1961), 18-32.

Kurakov, I.G. "Nauka i Effektivnost' Obshchestvennogo Proizvodstva." Voprosy Filosofii n.5 (1966).

_____. "Nauka i Effektivnost' Obshchestvennogo Proizvodstva." Voprosy Filosofii n. 10 (1966).

_____. "Prognozirovanie Nauchno-Tekhnicheskogo Progressa." Voprosy Filosofii n.10 (1968).

Leont'ev, L.A. "O Nekotorykh Osobennostiakh Sozdania Material'no-Tekhnicheskoi Bazy Kommunizma." Voprosy Filosofii n.6 (1962), 3-16.

Leontiev, A.N., Panov, D.Iu. "Psikhologia Cheloveka i Tekhnicheskii Progress." Voprosy Filosofii n.8 (1962) 50-65.

Lisitsin, V., Popov, G. "Razvivat Leninskuiu Nauku Upravleniia Sotsialisticheskoi Ekonomiki." Kommunist n.1 (1970).

Makarov, I.M. "O Protsesse Prevrashchenia Nauki v Neposredstvennuiu Proizvodstvennuiu Silu." Voprosy Filosofii n.12 (1976), 27-36.

Makeshin, N.I. "Nauki kak Faktor Ekonomicheskogo Razvitia SSSR." Voprosy Filosofii n.12 (1973).

Manevich, E.L. "Rasperedelenie po Trudu i Printsip Material'noi Zainteresovannosti v Period Perekhoda ot Sotsializma k Kommunizmu." Voprosy Filosofii n.2 (   ), 15-25.

_____. "O Likvidatsii Razlichii Mezhdu Umstvennym i Fizicheskim Trudom v Period Razvernutogo Stroitel'stva Kommunizma." Voprosy Filosofii n.9 (1961), 15-28.

Marakhov, V.G. "Nauka i Proizvodstvo." Voprosy Filosofii n.10 (1963), 3-12.

Markov, V.S. "Obraz Zhizni i Formirovanie Cheloveka." Voprosy Filosofii n.7 (1976), 16-25.

Maslin, A.N. "Printsip Material'noi Zainteresovannosti pri Sotsializme." Voprosy Filosofii n.4 (1954), 3-13.

Mchedlov, M.P. "Obshchechelovecheskoe i Sotsialisticheskoe." Voprosy Filosofii n.5 (1976), 52-64.

Medunin, A.E., "Vliianie Nauchno-Teknicheskoi Revoliutsii na Prirodu Zemli." Voprosy Filosofii n.3 (1969).

Medunov, S.F. "Aktual'nye Problemy Kommunisticheskogo Vospitania Trudiashchikhsia." Voprosy Filosofii n.7 (1979), 3-18.

Meleshchenko, Iu.S. "Tekhnika i Zakonomernostii ee Razvitia."
Voprosy Filosofii n.10 (1965), 3-13.

_____. "Kharakter i Osobennosti Nauchno-
Tekhnicheskoi Revoliutsii." Voprosy Filosofii n.7
(1968).

Mendel'son, A.S. "O Proizvoditel'nykh Silakh." Voprosy
Filosofii n.1 (1959), 157-166.

Mileikovskii, A.G. "Ideologicheskoe Pervooruzhenie Burzhuaznoi Politekonomii v Usloviakh NTR." Voprosy Filosofii
n.11 (1976), 86-96.

_____. "Kritika Burzhuaznykh Kontsieptsii
Gosudarstvennogo-Monopolisticheskogo Katpitalizma."
Voprosy Filosofii n.4 (1980), 142-151.

Mitin, M.B. "Problemy Borby Protiv Burzhuaznoi Ideologii
i Antikommunizma." Voprosy Filosofii n.7 (1971).

Moiseenko, G.M. "Nauchno-Tekhnicheskaia Intelligentsia
v Sovremennom Kapitalisticheskom Obshchestve." Voprosy
Filosofii n.12 (1971).

Munipov, V.M., Znichenko, V.P. "Chelovecheskii Faktor v
Sovremennoi Tekhnike." Voprosy Filosofii n.11 (1972).

"Nauchno-Tekhnicheskaia Revoliutsia i ee Sotsial'naia
Problematika." Voprosy Filosofii n.12 (1971).

Naidenov, V.S. "Sotsial'no-Ekonomicheskie Posledstvia
Tekhnicheskogo Progressa pri Sotsializme." Voprosy
Filosofii n.8 (1960), 14-24.

"Nasha Filosofia Mira--Filosofia Istoricheskogo Optimizma."
Voprosy Filosofii n.11 (1973).

"Nasushchnye Zadachi Ekonomicheskoi Nauki." Kommunist
n.11 (1971).

Naumova, N.F. "Dva Mira--Dva Otnoshenia k Trudu."
Voprosy Filosofii n.1 (1963), 15-23.

Nikolaev, V.V. "O Glavnykh Etapakh Razvitia Sovetskogo
Sotsialisticheskogo Gosudarstva." Voprosy Filosofii
n.4 (1957), 10-26.

_____. "Protiv Revizionistskikh Iskozhenii Marxists-
kogo-Leninskogo Uchenia o Gosudarstve." Voprosy
Filosofii n.11 (1958), 3-17.

_____. "O Razvitii Sotsialisticheskoi Gosudarst-
vennosti v Kommunisticheskoe Obshchestvennoe Samouprav-
lenie." Voprosy Filosofii n.12 (1960), 25-37.

Novoselov, N.S. "Razdelenie Truda pri Kommunizme ne
    Iskliuchaet Vozmozhnosti Peremeny Truda i Vsestoronnego
    Rzvitia Lichnostii." Voprosy Filosofii n.3 (1963),
    49-55.

Oizerman, T.I. "Istoricheskii Materializm i Ideologia
    'Tekhnologicheskogo' Pessimizma." Voprosy Filosofii
    n.8 (1973).

Oshanin, D.A., Panov, D.Iu. "Chelovek v Avtomaticheskikh
    Sistemakh Upravlenia." Voprosy Filosofii n.5 (1961),
    47-57.

Ostrovitianov, K.V. "Ispol'zovanie Ekonomicheskikh
    Zakonov Sotsializma v Praktike Kommunisticheskogo
    Stroitel'stva." Voprosy Filosofii n.4 (1955), 3-16.

Panov, D.Iu. "O Vzaimodeistvii Cheloveka i Mashiny."
    Voprosy Filosofii n.1 (1967).

Paton, B.E. "Nauka--Tekhnika--Proizvodstvo." Voprosy Filo-
    sofii n.10 (1980), 22-31.

Petrov, M.K. "Nekotorye Problemy Organizatsii Nauki v
    Epokhu Nauchno-Tekhnicheskoi Revoliutsii." Voprosy
    Filosofii n.10 (1968).

Popov, S.I. "Sotsial'nyi Pessimizm v Sisteme Sovremennoi
    Burzhuaznoi Ideologii." Voprosy Filosofii n.9 (1980),
    64-72.

Rachkov, P.A. "Problemy Effektivnosti Nauki v Sovremennyi
    Period." Voprosy Filosofii n.5 (1966).

Redaktsionnaia. "Chelovek-Nauka-Tekhnika." Voprosy
    Filosofii n.8 (1972).

Rudich, F.M. "Vozrastanie Roli Trudiashchikhsia v
    Upravlenii Stosialisticheskim Proizvodstvom." Voprosy
    Filosofii n.7 (1975), 3-12.

Rumiantsev, A.M. "Predmet Politicheskoi Ekonomii i Kharakter
    Zakonov Ekonomicheskogo Razvitia Obshchestva." Voprosy
    Filosofii n.2 (1955), 88-104.

_____. "Ekonomicheskaia Nauka i Upravlenie
    Narodnym Khoziaistvom." Kommunist n.1 (1966).

_____. "V.I. Lenin i Nekotorye Voprosy Politiches-
    koi Ekonomii Sotsializma." Voprosy Filosofii n.4
    (1978), 25-32.

Rutkevich, N.N. "Sotsialisticheskii Obraz Zhiznii i ego
    Razvitie." Voprosy Filosofii n.11 (1975), 46-58.

Sadykov, F.B. "Pod'em Kul'turno-Tekhnicheskogo Urovnia
   Trudiashchikhsia pri Sotsializme," Voprosy Filosofii
   n.2 (1956) 35-48.

Semianov, V.S. "Nauchno-Tekhnicheskaia Revoliutsia i
   Problema Tselostnogo i Svobodnogo Razvitia Cheloveka."
   Voprosy Filosofii n.7 (1978), 82-90.

_____. "Uchenie o Razvitom Sotsializme i ego
   Pererastanii v Kommunizm." Voprosy Filosofii n.7 (1980),
   3-18.

Shchelkin, A.G. "Neupravlemaia Slozhnost': Genezis
   Tekhnokraticheskogo Konservatizma." Voprosy Filosofii
   n.5 (1979), 96-105.

Shcherbitskii, V.V. "Nauchno-Tekhnicheskaia Revoliutsia
   i Upravlenie Obshchestvennym Protsessam." Voprosy
   Filosofii n.10 (1980), 3-21.

Shemenev, G.I. "Inzhinerno-Tekhnicheskaia Intelligentsia
   v Period Razvernutogo Stroitel'stva Kommunizma."
   Voprosy Filosofii n.8 (1960), 25-34.

Shemshev, G.I. "Sviaz Nauki s Proizvodstvom i Vsestoronnee
   Razvitie Lichnosti." Voprosy Filosofii n.9 (1963),
   29-35.

Shershunov, A.D., Shcheglov, A.V. "O Svoeobrazii Protivorechii Stroitel'stva Sotsializma v SSSR." Voprosy
   Filosofii n.12 (1958), 39-53.

Shkaratan, O.I. "Rabochii Klass Sotsialisticheskogo Obshchestva v Epokhu Nauchno-Tekhnicheskoi Revoliutsii."
   Voprosy Filosofii n.11 (1968).

Skvortsov, L.V. "Ideologicheskie Mify Antikommunizma:
   Evoliutsia i Novye Tendentsii." Voprosy Filosofii
   n.9 (1972).

Smirnov, G.L. "Razdelenie Truda i Obmen Deiatel'nost'ii
   v Sisteme Proizvodstvennykh Otnoshenii." Voprosy
   Filosofii n.5 (1958), 27-40.

Sobolev, A.I. "Velikaia Sozidatel'naia Rol' Sovetskogo
   Gosudarstva." Voprosy Filosofii n.5 (1954), 28-42.

_____. "O Zakonomernostiakh Perekhoda ot Kapitalizma
   k Sotsializmu v Evropeiskikh Stranakh Narodnoi
   Demokratsi." Voprosy Filosofii n.1 (1956), 30-46.

Stepanian, Ts.A. "Oktiabrskaia Revoliutsia i Stanovlenie
   Kommunisticheskoi Formatsii." Voprosy Filosofii n.10
   (1958), 19-36.

Stepanian, Ts.A., Osnovnye Zakonomernostii Stroitel'stva Kommunizma." Voprosy Filosofii n.12 (1961), 3-11.

Strumlin, S.G. "Kommunizm i Razdelenie Truda." Voprosy Filosofii n.3 (1963), 37-49.

Sukhomlinskii, V.A. "Trud--Osnova Vsestoronnego Razvitia Chekoveka." Voprosy Filosofii n.4 (1963), 54-63.

Suslov, M. "Obshchestvennye Nauki--Boevoe Oruzhie Partii v Stroitel'stve Kommunizma." Kommunist n.1 (1972).

Sviridov, N. "Partiinaia Zabota o Vospitanii Nauchno-Tekhnicheskoi Intelligentsii." Kommunist n.18 (1968).

Tavrizian, G.M. "Burzhuaznaia Filosofia Tekhniki i Sotsial'-nye Teorii." Voprosy Filosofii n.6 (1978), 147-159.

Tchagin, B.A., Kharchev, A.G. "O Kategoriakh 'Proizvoditel'-nye Sily' i 'Proizvodstvennye Otnoshenia.'" Voprosy Filosofii n.2 (1958), 9-20.

Tikhomirov, Iu.A. "Sotsial'noe Upravlenie v Razvitom Sotsialisticheskom Obshchestve." Voprosy Filosofii n.1 (1977), 26-35.

Toshchenko, J. "Social Infrastructure as a Concept," Social Sciences n.3 (1981), 67-80.

Trapeznikov S.P. "Leninizm i Sovremennaia Nauchno-Tekhnicheskaia Revoliutsia." Voprosy Filosofii n.4 (1970).

Troshin, D.M. "Ob Osobennostiakh Razvitia Nauki." Voprosy Filosofii n.6 (1953), 46-62.

Tsarogorodtsev, G.I. "'Tekhnizatsia' Sredy i Zdorove Cheloveka." Voprosy Filosofii n.10 (1972).

Ukraintsev, B.S. "Novyi Tip Obshchestvennogo Progressa." Voprosy Filosofii n.1 (1962), 13-24.

Vasil'chik, Iu.A. "Sovremennaia Nauchno-Teknicheskaia Revoliutsia i Promyshlennyi Proletariat." Voprosy Filosofii.

Velikhov, E. "Science and Social Progress." Social Science n.3 (1981), 13-22.

Vladimirov, B., Nakoriakov, V. "Blizhe k Liudiam, k Proizvodstvu." Kommunist n.13 (1965).

Volkov, G.N. "Avtomatizatsia--Novyi Istoricheskii Etap v Razvitii Tekhniki." Voprosy Filosofii n.6 (1964), 15-26.

310

Volkov, G.N. "Vzaimozviaz' Nauki i Proizvodstva." <u>Voprosy</u> <u>Filosofii</u> n.2 (1967).

Volkov. Iu.E. "XXV S'ezd KPSS i Teoreticheskie Problemy Sotsial'noi Politiki." <u>Voprosy</u> <u>Filosofii</u> n.7 (1976), 3-15.

Zamoshkin, Iu.A., Motroshilova, N.V. "Is Marcuse's 'Critical Theory of Society" Cirtical?" <u>The</u> <u>Soviet</u> <u>Review</u> n.1 (1970)

Zauzolkov, F.N. "Ob Opyt'e USSR po Sblizheniu Umstvennogo i Fizicheskogo Truda." <u>Voprosy</u> <u>Filosofii</u> n.5 (1956), 32-45.

Zhemianov, O.N. "Kritika Kontsieptsii 'Oburzhuazenii' Rabochego Klassa." <u>Voprosy</u> <u>Filosofii</u> n.12 (1970).

Zvorikin, A.A. "O Nekotorykh Voprosakh Istorii Tekhniki." <u>Voprosy</u> <u>Filosofii</u> n.6 (1953), 32-45.

Secondary articles:

Fleron, Frederic, J. Jr., Fleron, Lou Jean. "Administra-
    tive Theory as Repressive Political Theory: The
    Communist Experience." Telos n.12 (1972), 63-92.

Fleron, Frederic, J. Jr. "The Western Connection: Tech-
    nical Rationality and Soviet Politics." Soviet Union
    n.1 (1977), 58-84.

Heller, Agnes. "The Two Myths of Technology." The New
    Hungarian Quarterly n.30 (1968).

Hoffmann, Erik, P. "Soviet Views of 'The Scientific-
    Technological Revolution.'" World Politics n.4 (1978),
    615-644.

_____. "The 'Scientific Management' of Soviet
    Society." Problems of Communism. May-June (1977),
    59-67.

Huszar, Istvan. "The Sceintific and Technological Revolu-
    tion." A paper given at the International Symposium on
    the Sceintific and Technological Revolution and Social
    Progress held between November 26 and 30, 1973, in
    Moscow.

Kelley, Donald R. "Environmental Policy-Making in the USSR:
    the Role of Industrial and Environmental Interest
    Groups." Soviet Studies n.4 (1976), 570-589.

Leiss, William. "The Social Consequences of Technological
    Progress: Critical Comments on Recent Theories."
    Canadian Public Administration n.3 (1970).

Miller, Robert, F. "The Scientific-Technological Revolution
    and the Soviet Administrative Debate." in The Dynamics
    of Soviet Politics. Edited by Paul Cocks, Robert V.
    Daniels, Nancy Whittier Heer. Cambridge, Mass.: Harvard
    University Press, 1976.

_____. "The New Science of Administration in the
    USSR." Administrative Science Quarterly n.18 (1971).